D1451440

IMAGE COMICS, INC.

Robert Kirkman - chief operating officer
Erik Larsen - chief financial officer
Todd McFarlane - president
Marc Silvestri - chief executive officer
Jim Valentino - vice president

Eric Stephenson - publisher
Todd Martinez - sales & licensing coordinator
Sarah deLaine - pr & marketing coordinator
Branwyn Bigglestone - accounts manager
Emily Miller - administrative assistant
Jamie Parreno - marketing assistant
Kevin Yuen - digital rights coordinator
Tyler Shainline - production manager
Drew Gill - art director
Jonathan Chan - senior production artist
Monica Garcia - production artist
Vincent Kukua - production artist
Jana Cook - production artist

www.imagecomics.com

A HUNGER FOR POWER

Editorial

SERVED UP ON A PLATE

Nabe sits at the center of Mitteleuropa – both geographically and politically. It is the birthplace of modern democracy and as such its neutral status has been vital to maintaining stability and harmony across the continent for the past century.

This noble position has become considerably weakened since last week's devastating bomb attack on the Axis summit, hosted here in Nabe, left leaders from six of the eight states of Mitteleuropa dead and His Majesty the Kaiser

with emergency control over most of the subcontinent.

No group has yet claimed responsibility for the massacre, though sources close to the Kaiser have implied that His Majesty believes the culprits to be aligned with (and perhaps funded by) those members of Nabe's own government who favor closer ties with the New Alliance in the west. Indeed Ambassador Vasilyeva, advisor to His Majesty, is reported to have accused Nabe's Prime Minister of as much during an emergency cabinet session held yesterday.

Perhaps we should forgive Ambassador Vasilyeva's bluntness; exiled from Ursa during the revolution she seems to have refreshingly little time for the niceties of international relations. Indeed, the Am-

bassador has consistently demonstrated the kind of straight-talking that has to date been absent from this crisis, and may represent our best hope for reaching a diplomatic solution.

Nevertheless His Majesty has in the past openly expressed his desire to consolidate the military and industrial might of the Axis states under the flag of a single nation. His supporters assert that the Kaiser is merely responding to the potential threat posed by a growing power base in the west. Yet there is a difference; the allies' strength has been forged through consensus and cooperation, not autocracy and bullying.

Since the Kaiser centralized control of the Axis states Nabe has come under increasing pressure to fall in line with the rest of Mitteleuropa, accept His Majesty's policy of unifica-

tion, and effectively surrender its autonomy – and its neutrality.

There are cynics amongst us who might find these deaths more than a little suspicious, since they have primarily served to accelerate the Kaiser's unification efforts, and have effectively silenced any criticism from within the Axis itself. Indeed it could be argued that His Majesty has been the sole beneficiary (and lone survivor) of the massacre. Furthermore that the bombing took place here within Nabe should not be ignored. This fact has given the Kaiser the pretext needed to close Nabe's borders and blockade our trade routes, all to weed out a terrorist threat that many believe is the work of fiction.

To date the Allies have remained frustratingly diffident, tolerating (if not endorsing) His Majesty's saber-rattling – despite its member states all having ratified the Baal treaty protecting Nabe's neutral status, if necessary with military action.

Though no sane person would welcome confrontation between the world's two great powers, the danger in hesitating to act is all too apparent. Presently the forces of the Axis coalition are weak, dispersed across its vast territory, and even the threat of military action would likely be enough to drive the Kaiser from Nabe's borders. Unless the opponents of the Kaiser act now - and decisively - the opportunity for reaching a swift resolution to this crisis will have passed.

If His Majesty's plans are allowed to gather momentum the two sides will soon be more equally matched and the prospect of all-out war almost inevitable.

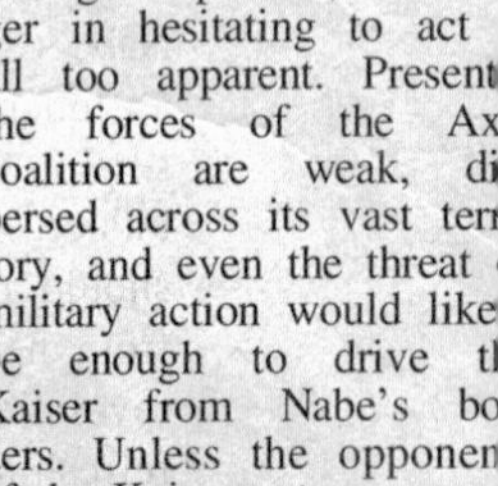

As the crow flies...

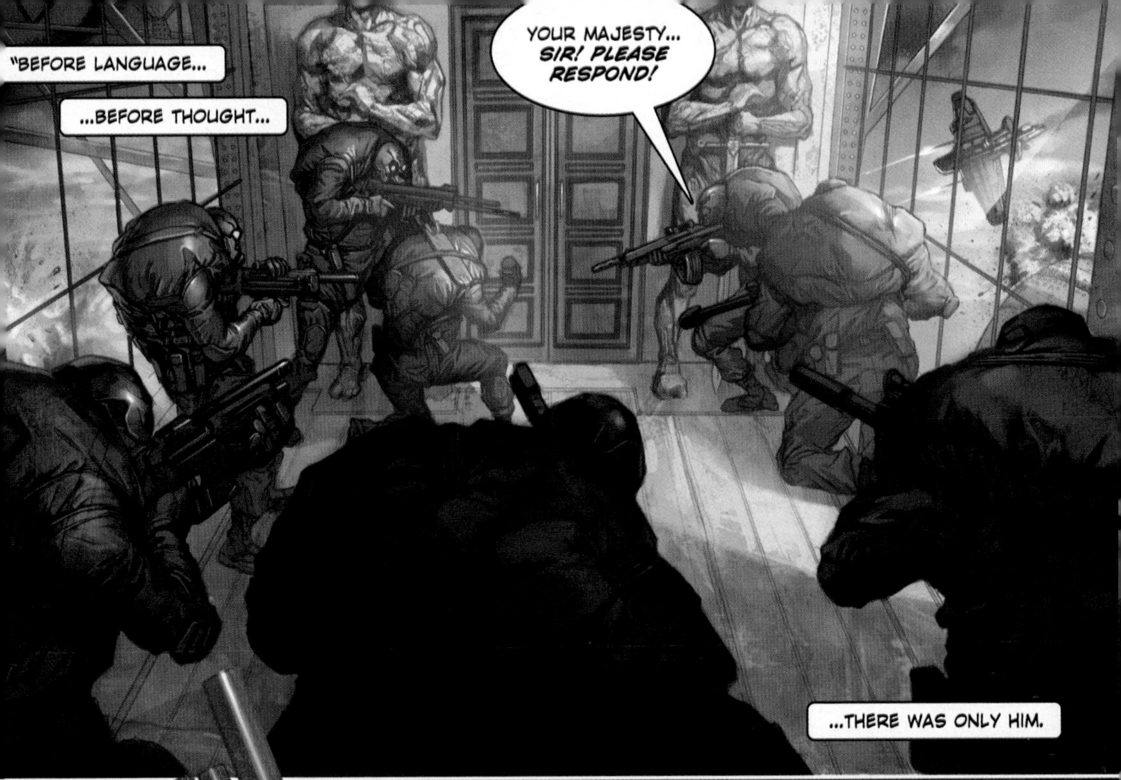
"BEFORE LANGUAGE...
...BEFORE THOUGHT...
YOUR MAJESTY... SIR! PLEASE RESPOND!
...THERE WAS ONLY HIM.

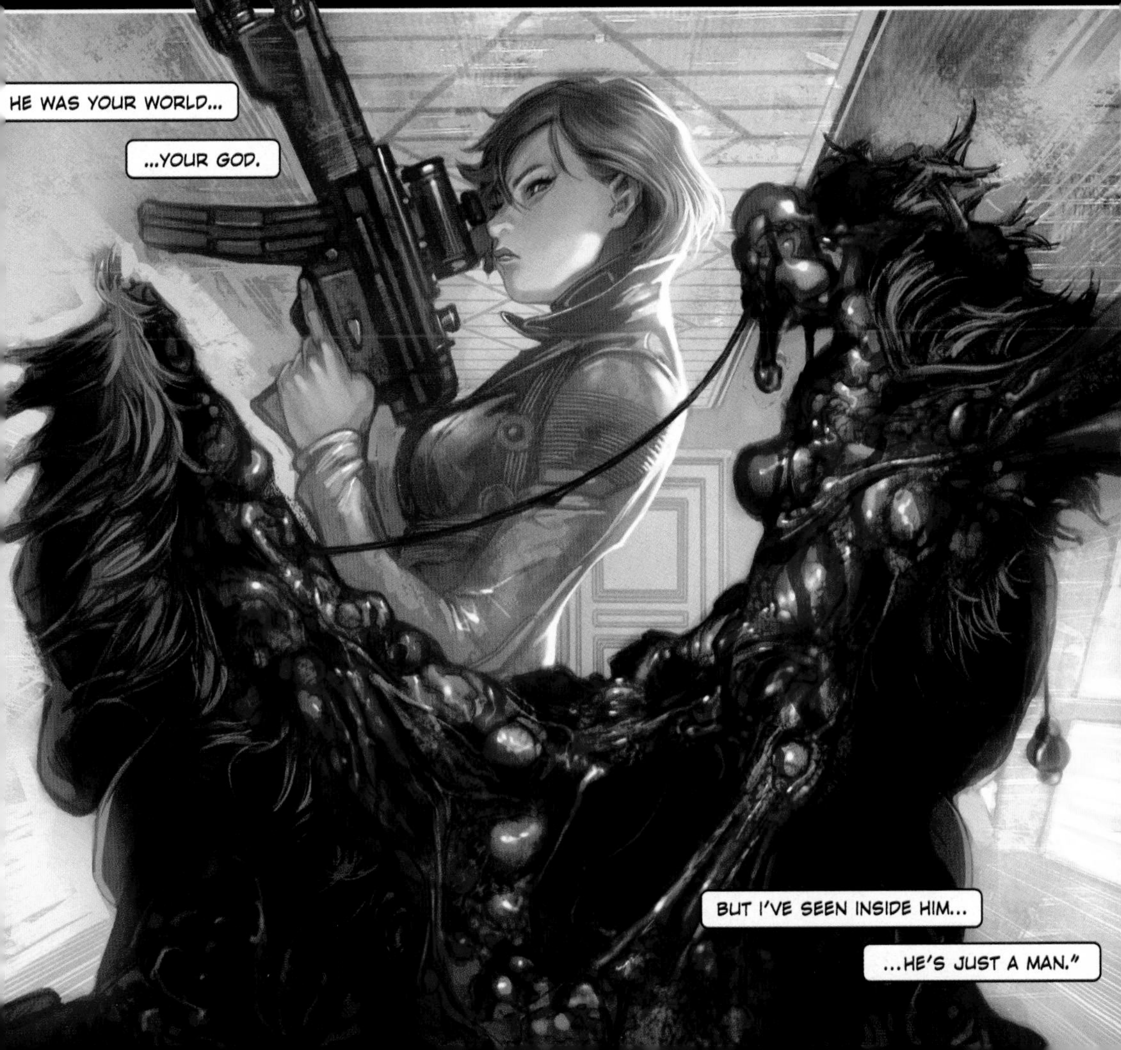
HE WAS YOUR WORLD...
...YOUR GOD.
BUT I'VE SEEN INSIDE HIM...
...HE'S JUST A MAN."

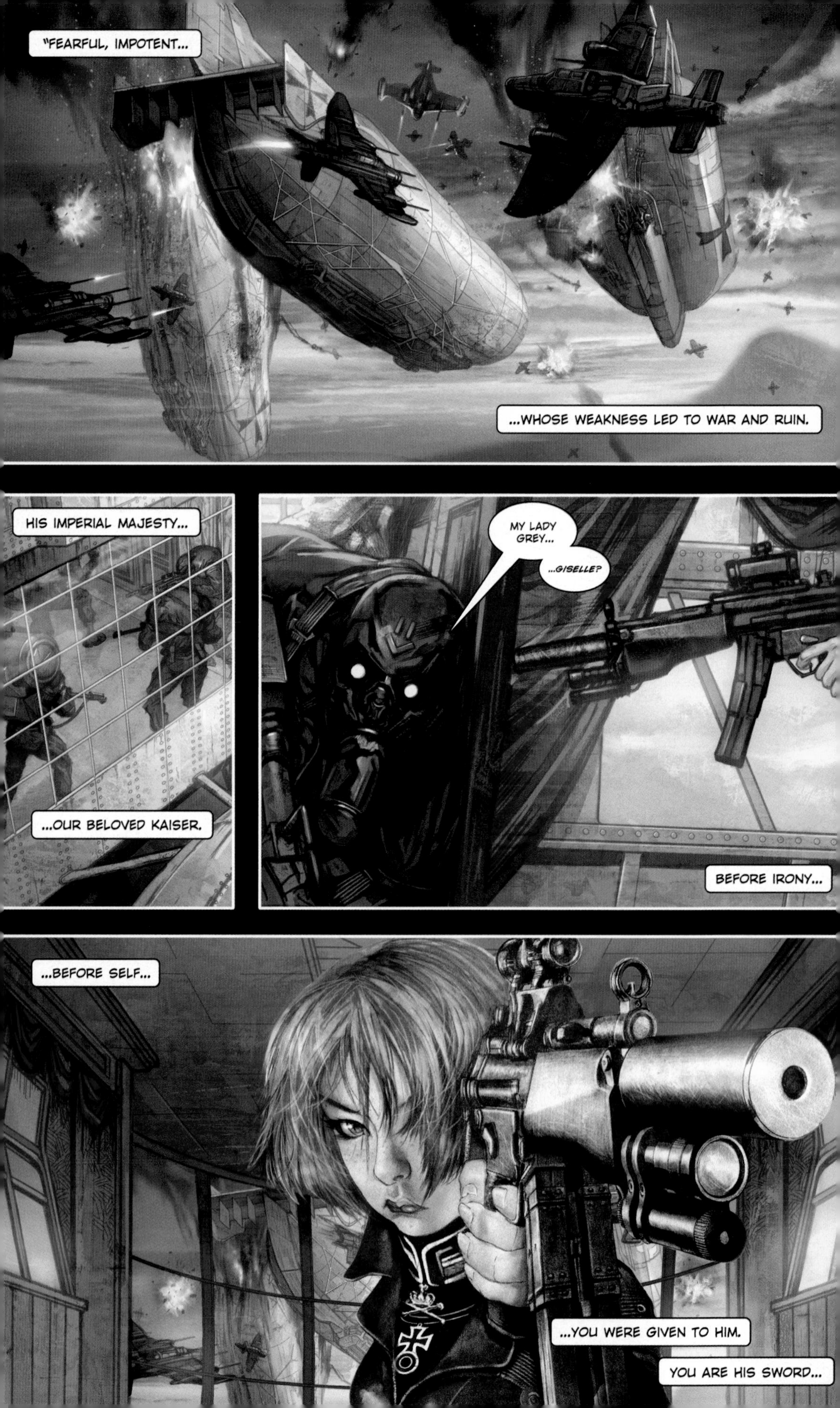
"FEARFUL, IMPOTENT...
...WHOSE WEAKNESS LED TO WAR AND RUIN.
HIS IMPERIAL MAJESTY...
...OUR BELOVED KAISER.
MY LADY GREY...
...GISELLE?
BEFORE IRONY...
...BEFORE SELF...
...YOU WERE GIVEN TO HIM.
YOU ARE HIS SWORD...

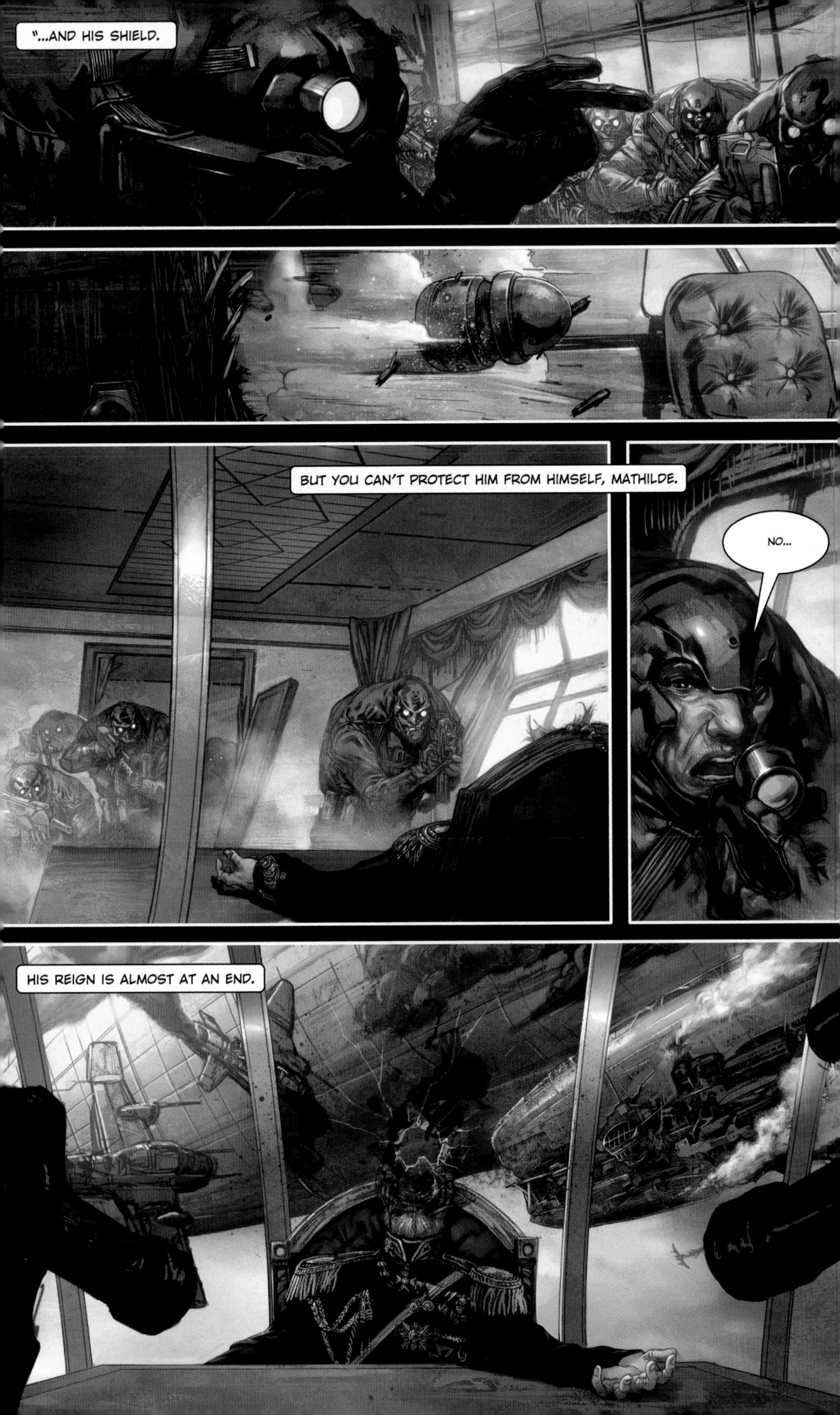
"...AND HIS SHIELD.
BUT YOU CAN'T PROTECT HIM FROM HIMSELF, MATHILDE.
NO...
HIS REIGN IS ALMOST AT AN END.

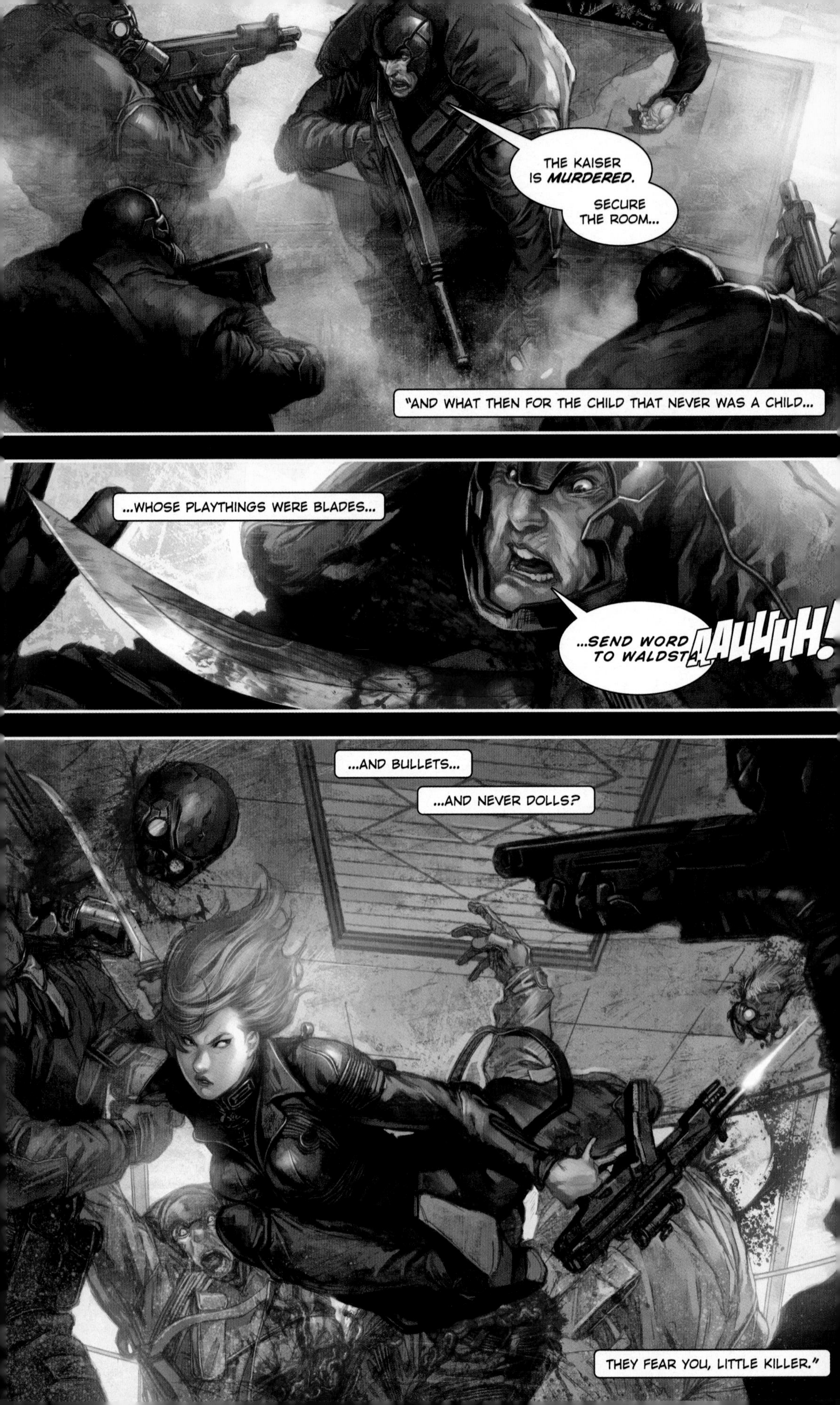
THE KAISER IS ***MURDERED.***
SECURE THE ROOM...
"AND WHAT THEN FOR THE CHILD THAT NEVER WAS A CHILD...
...WHOSE PLAYTHINGS WERE BLADES...
...SEND WORD TO WALDST-
AAUUHH!
...AND BULLETS...
...AND NEVER DOLLS?
THEY FEAR YOU, LITTLE KILLER."

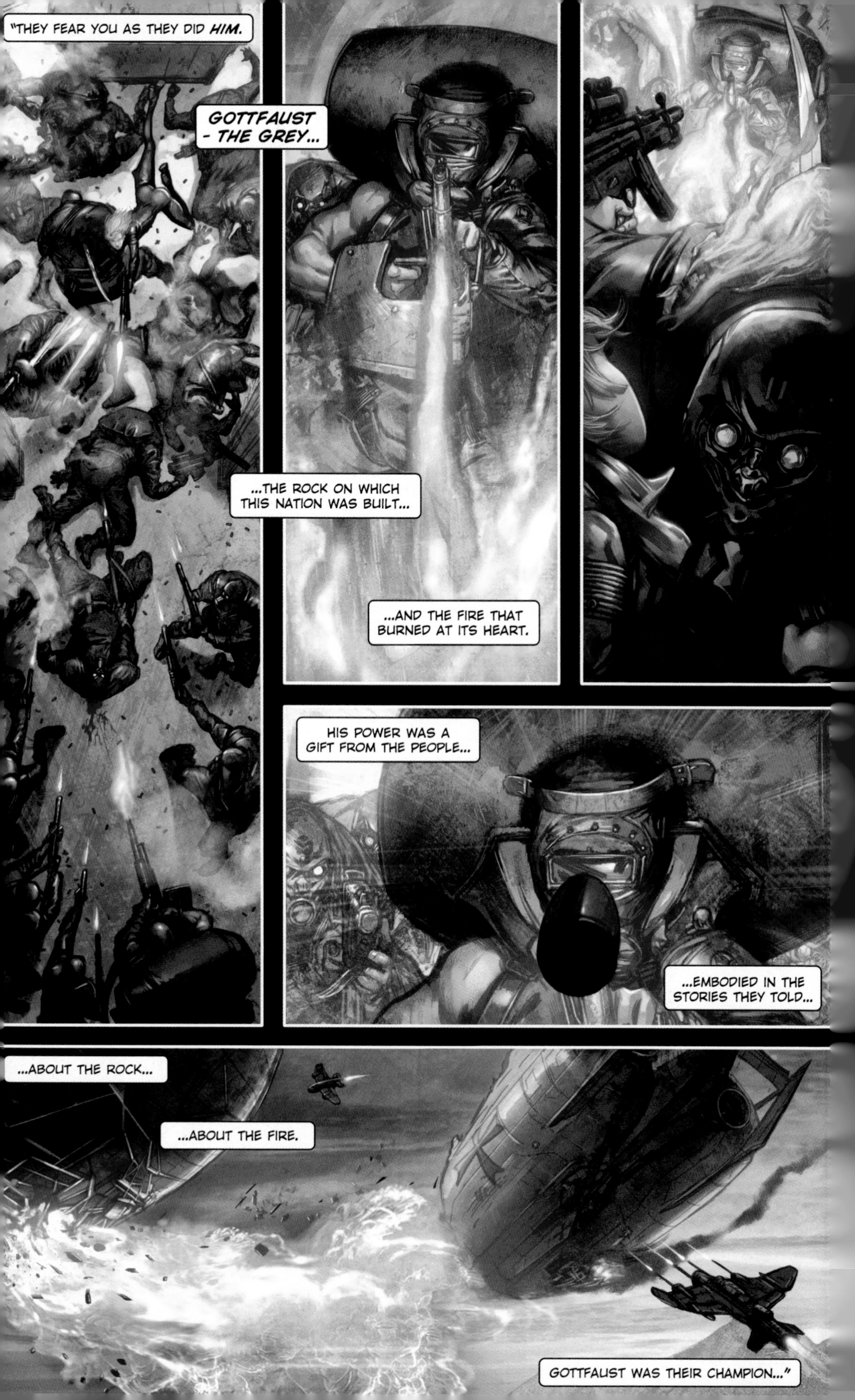
"THEY FEAR YOU AS THEY DID *HIM*.
GOTTFAUST - THE GREY...
...THE ROCK ON WHICH THIS NATION WAS BUILT...
...AND THE FIRE THAT BURNED AT ITS HEART.
HIS POWER WAS A GIFT FROM THE PEOPLE...
...EMBODIED IN THE STORIES THEY TOLD...
...ABOUT THE ROCK...
...ABOUT THE FIRE.
GOTTFAUST WAS THEIR CHAMPION..."

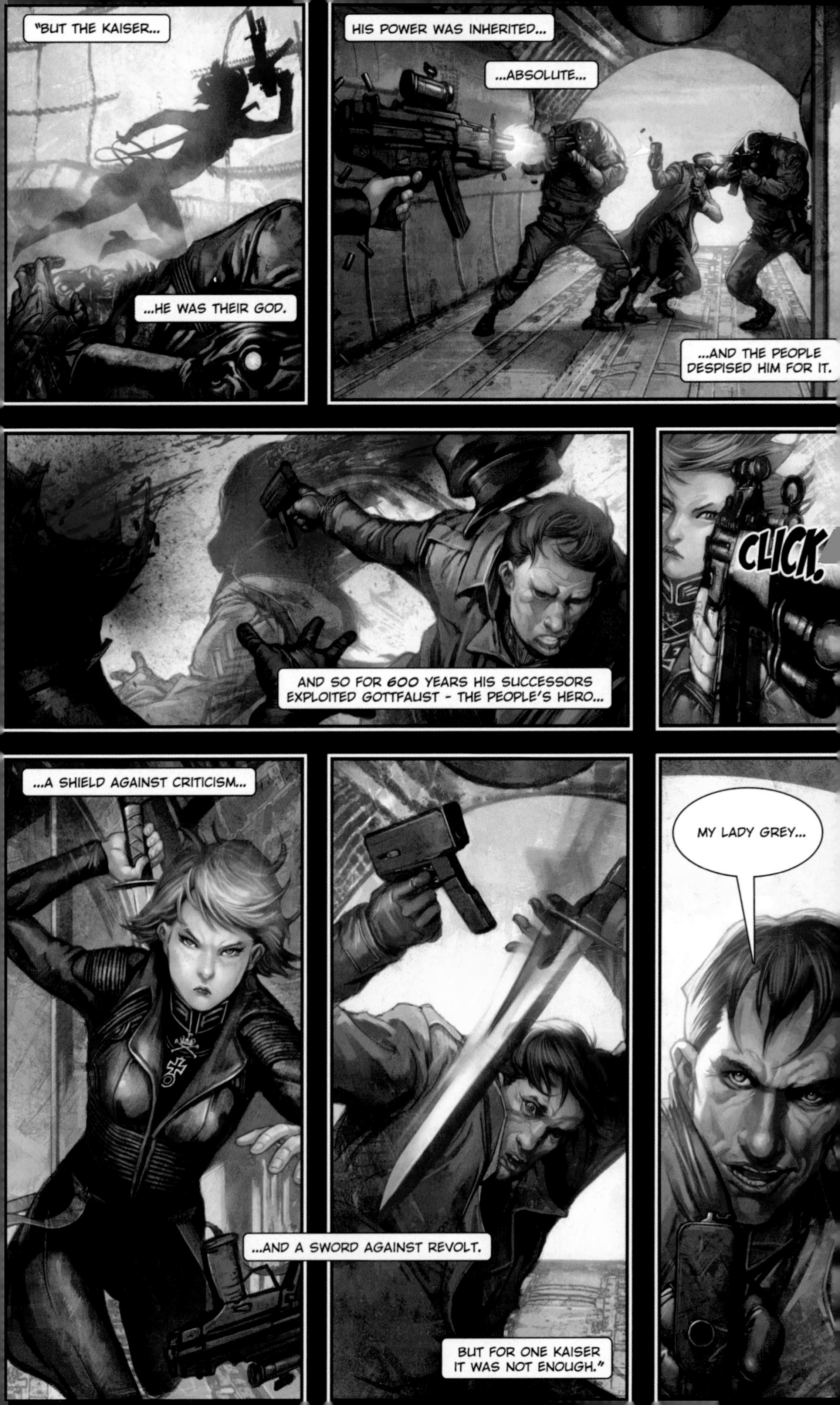
"BUT THE KAISER...
...HE WAS THEIR GOD.
HIS POWER WAS INHERITED...
...ABSOLUTE...
...AND THE PEOPLE DESPISED HIM FOR IT.
AND SO FOR 600 YEARS HIS SUCCESSORS EXPLOITED GOTTFAUST - THE PEOPLE'S HERO...
CLICK.
...A SHIELD AGAINST CRITICISM...
...AND A SWORD AGAINST REVOLT.
BUT FOR ONE KAISER IT WAS NOT ENOUGH."
MY LADY GREY...

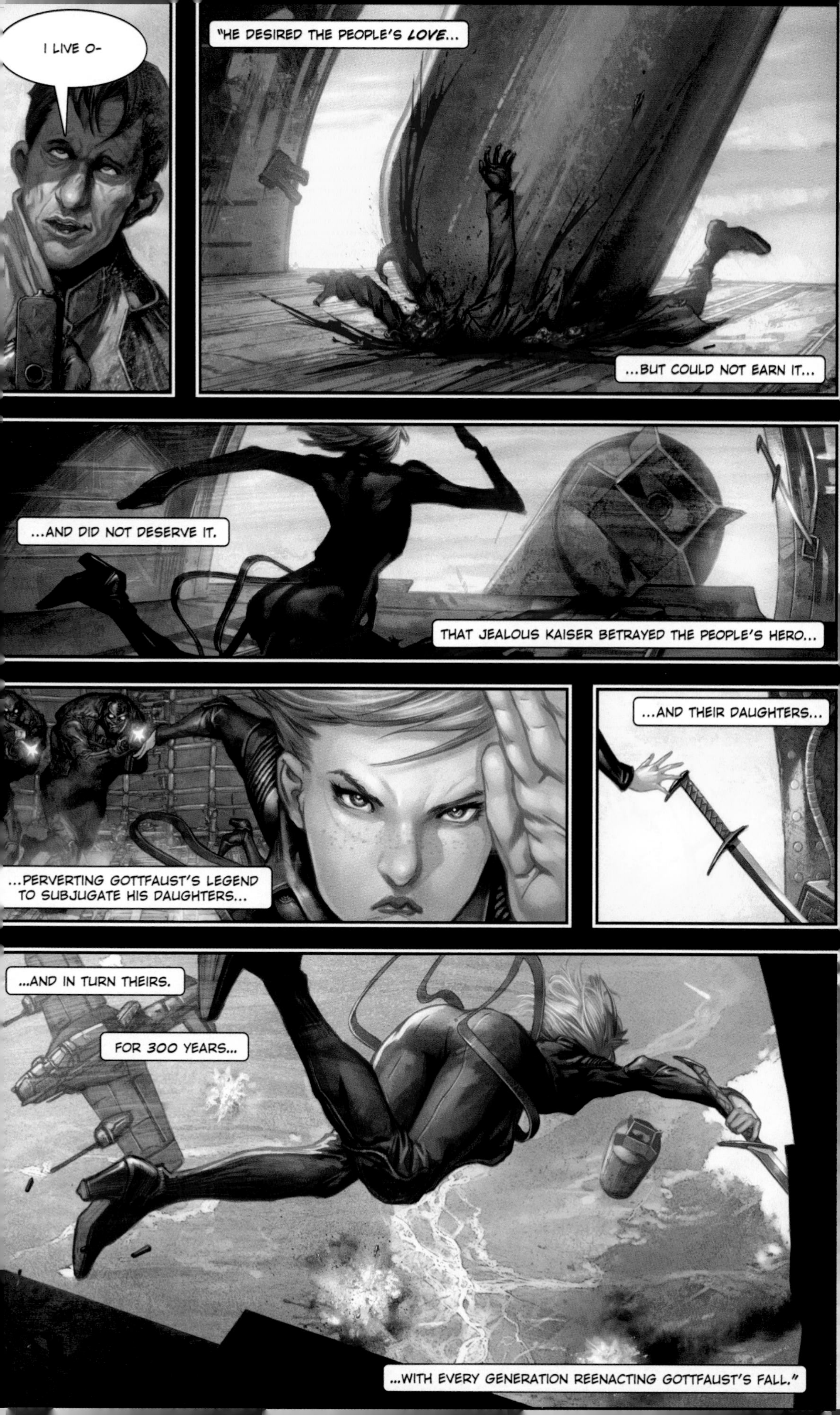
I LIVE O-
"HE DESIRED THE PEOPLE'S *LOVE*...
...BUT COULD NOT EARN IT...
...AND DID NOT DESERVE IT.
THAT JEALOUS KAISER BETRAYED THE PEOPLE'S HERO...
...PERVERTING GOTTFAUST'S LEGEND TO SUBJUGATE HIS DAUGHTERS...
...AND THEIR DAUGHTERS...
...AND IN TURN THEIRS.
FOR 300 YEARS...
...WITH EVERY GENERATION REENACTING GOTTFAUST'S FALL."

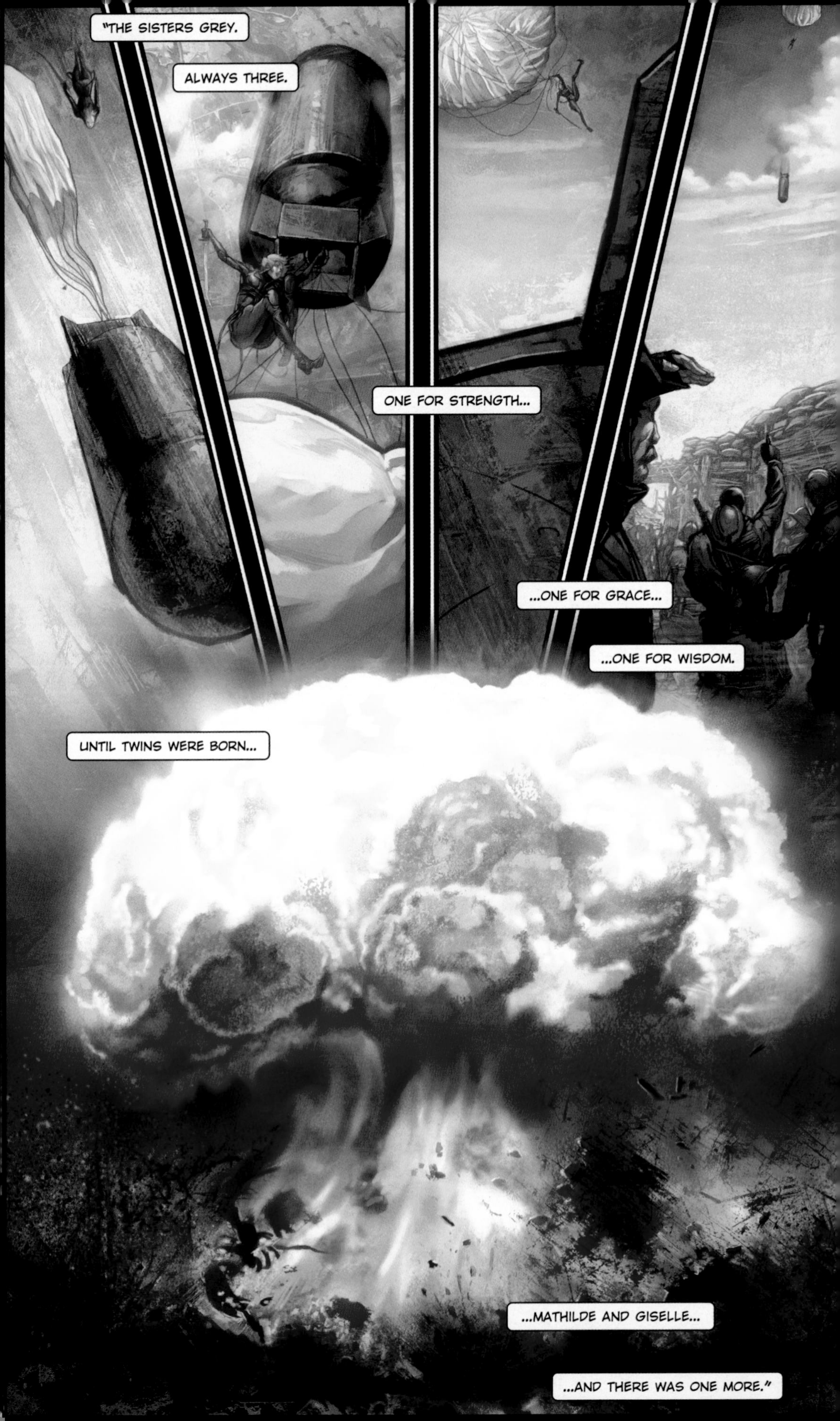
"THE SISTERS GREY.
ALWAYS THREE.
ONE FOR STRENGTH...
...ONE FOR GRACE...
...ONE FOR WISDOM.
UNTIL TWINS WERE BORN...
...MATHILDE AND GISELLE...
...AND THERE WAS ONE MORE."

"A FOURTH SISTER.

FOR REVOLUTION...

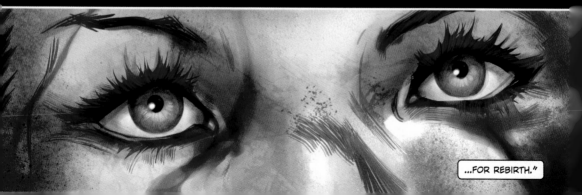

...FOR REBIRTH."

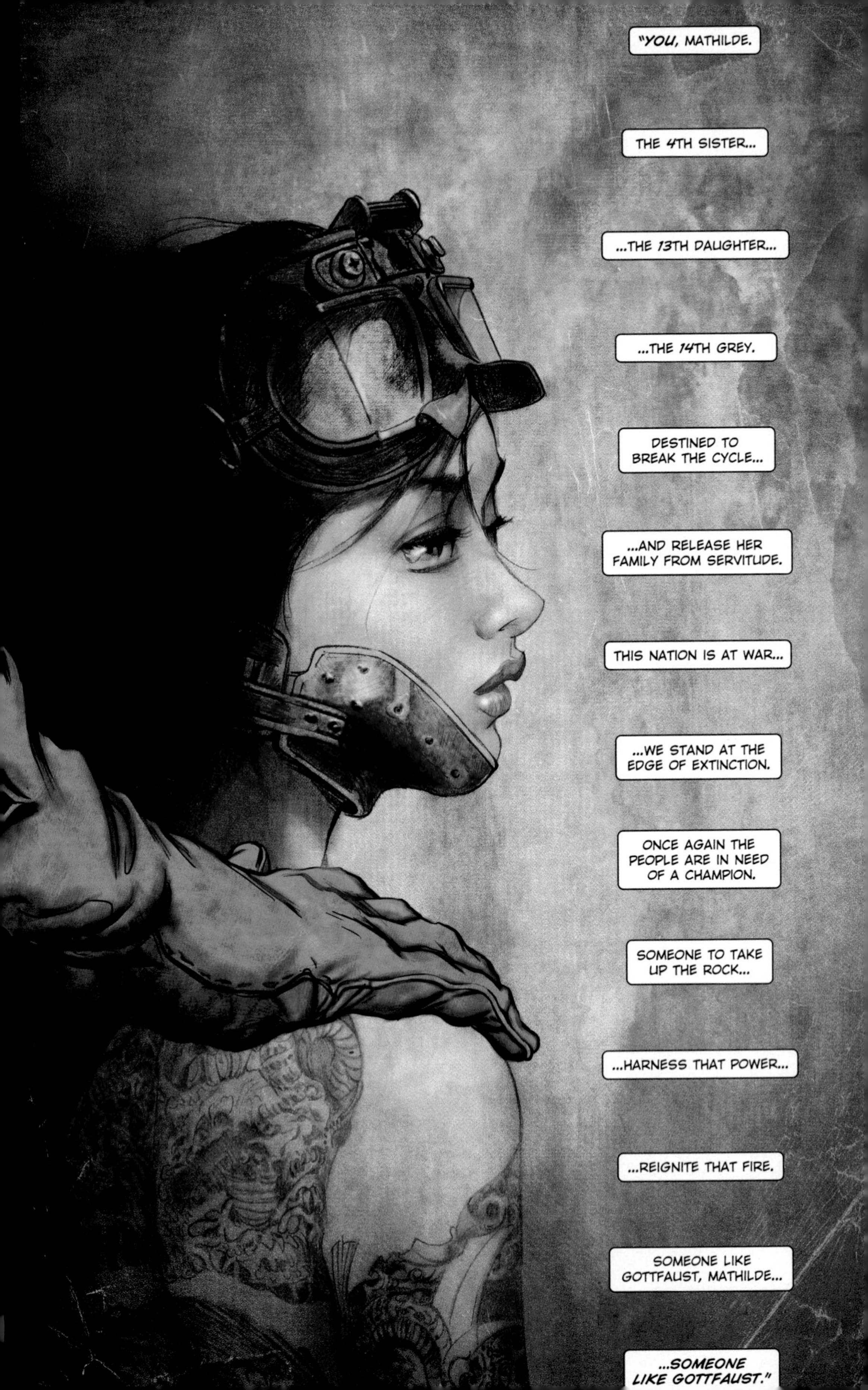
"YOU, MATHILDE.
THE 4TH SISTER...
...THE 13TH DAUGHTER...
...THE 14TH GREY.
DESTINED TO BREAK THE CYCLE...
...AND RELEASE HER FAMILY FROM SERVITUDE.
THIS NATION IS AT WAR...
...WE STAND AT THE EDGE OF EXTINCTION.
ONCE AGAIN THE PEOPLE ARE IN NEED OF A CHAMPION.
SOMEONE TO TAKE UP THE ROCK...
...HARNESS THAT POWER...
...REIGNITE THAT FIRE.
SOMEONE LIKE GOTTFAUST, MATHILDE...
...SOMEONE LIKE GOTTFAUST."

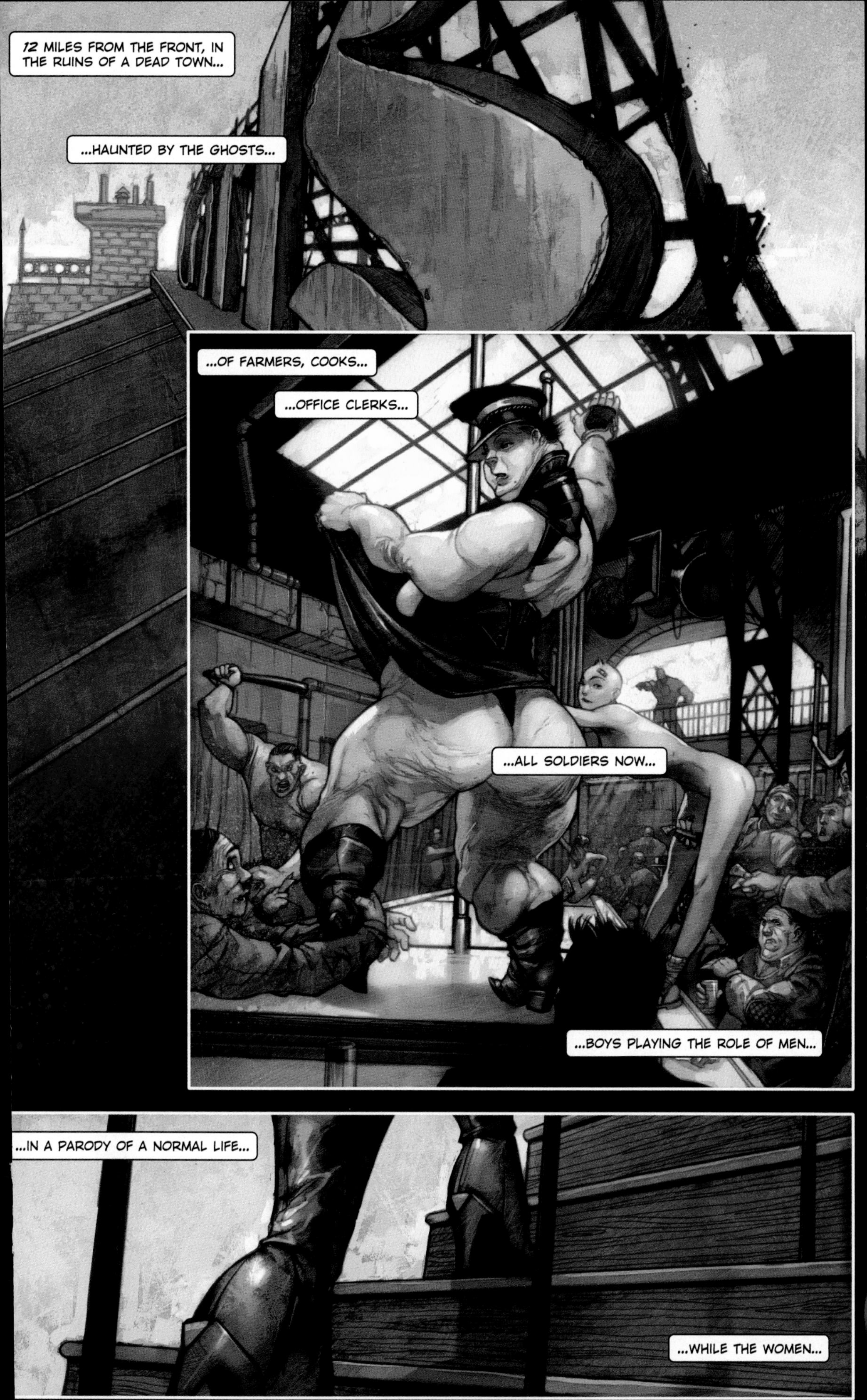
12 MILES FROM THE FRONT, IN THE RUINS OF A DEAD TOWN...
...HAUNTED BY THE GHOSTS...
...OF FARMERS, COOKS...
...OFFICE CLERKS...
...ALL SOLDIERS NOW...
...BOYS PLAYING THE ROLE OF MEN...
...IN A PARODY OF A NORMAL LIFE...
...WHILE THE WOMEN...

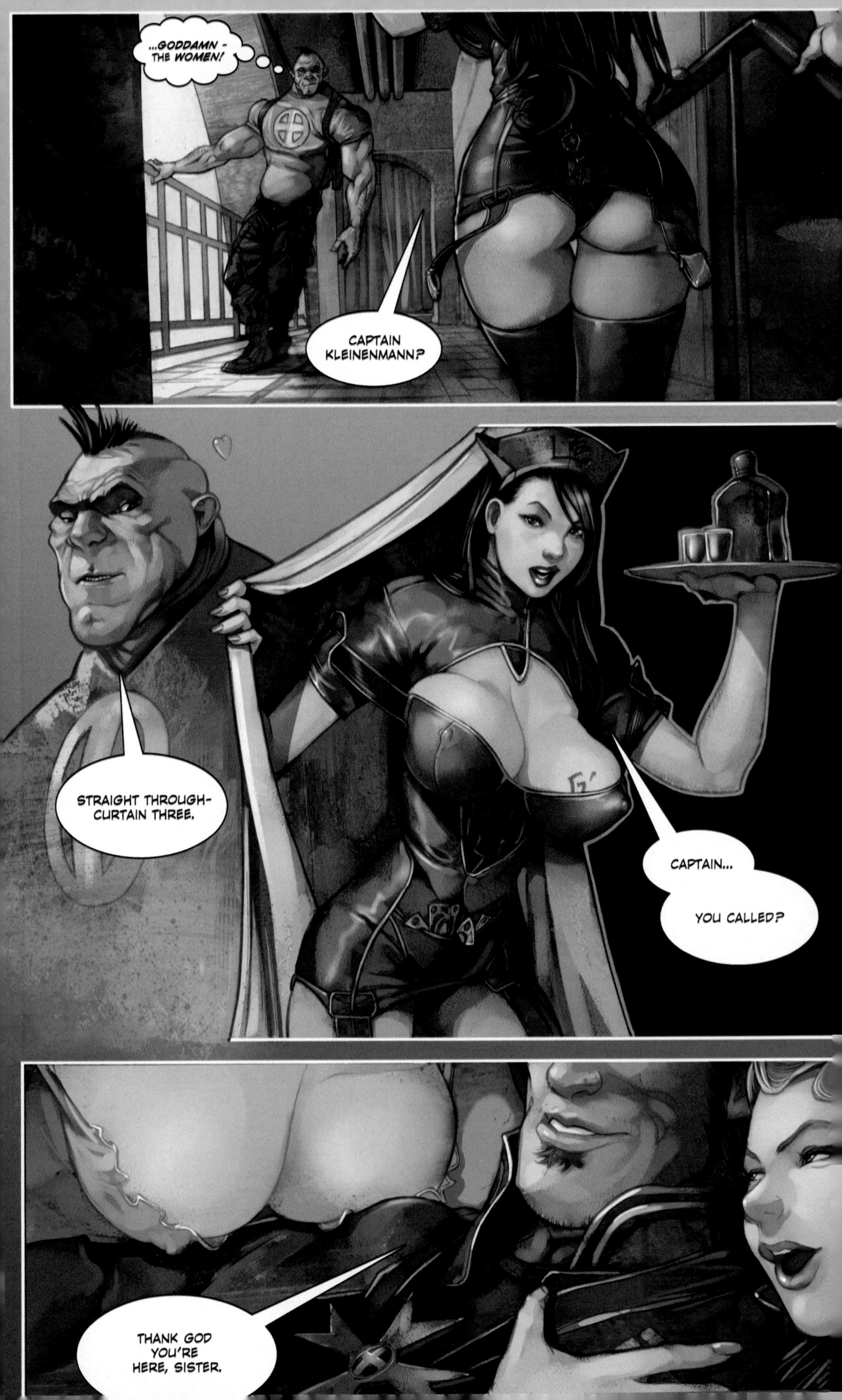
...GODDAMN - THE WOMEN!
CAPTAIN KLEINENMANN?
STRAIGHT THROUGH- CURTAIN THREE.
CAPTAIN...
YOU CALLED?
THANK GOD YOU'RE HERE, SISTER.

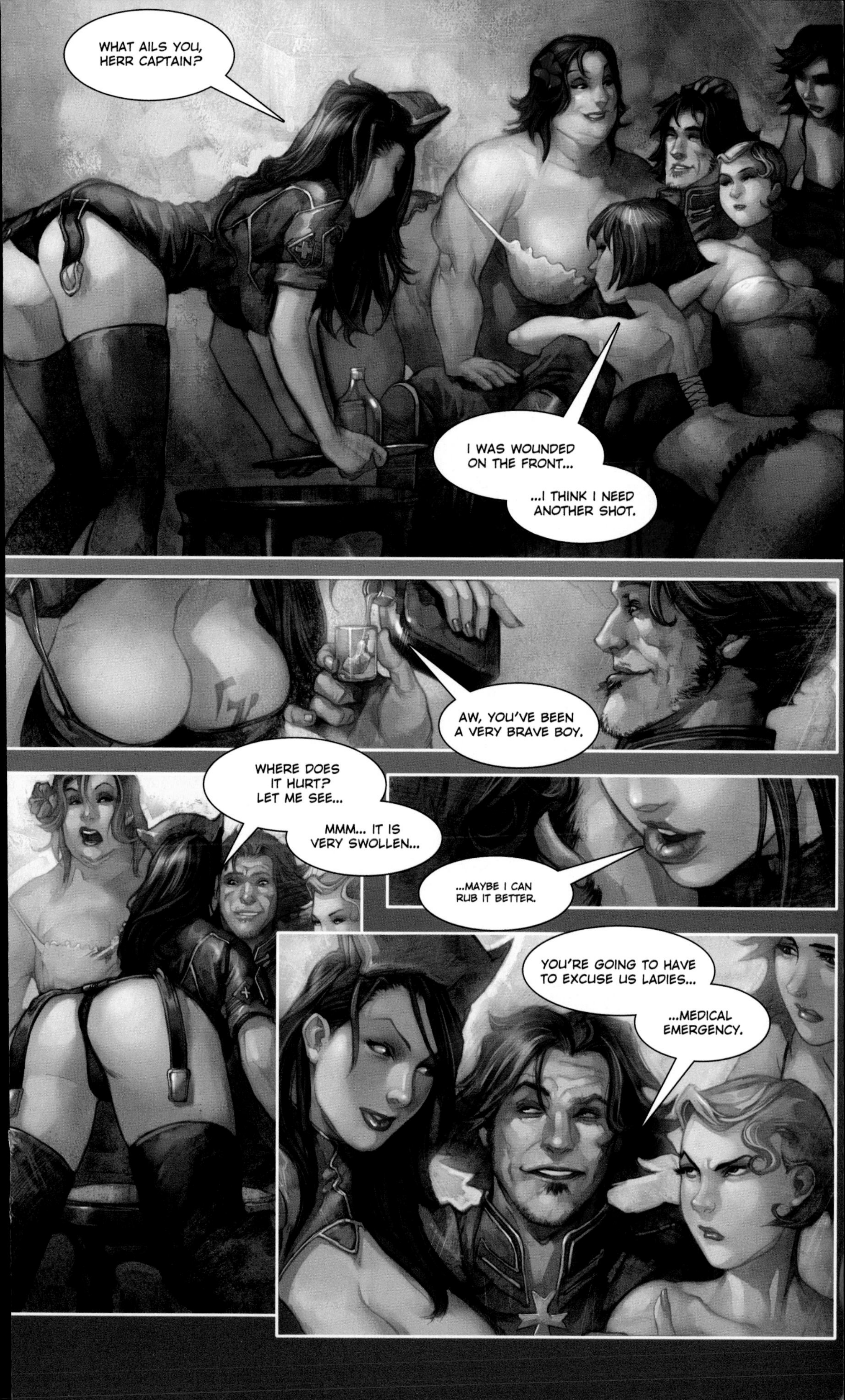
WHAT AILS YOU, HERR CAPTAIN?
I WAS WOUNDED ON THE FRONT...
...I THINK I NEED ANOTHER SHOT.
AW, YOU'VE BEEN A VERY BRAVE BOY.
WHERE DOES IT HURT? LET ME SEE...
MMM... IT IS VERY SWOLLEN...
...MAYBE I CAN RUB IT BETTER.
YOU'RE GOING TO HAVE TO EXCUSE US LADIES...
...MEDICAL EMERGENCY.

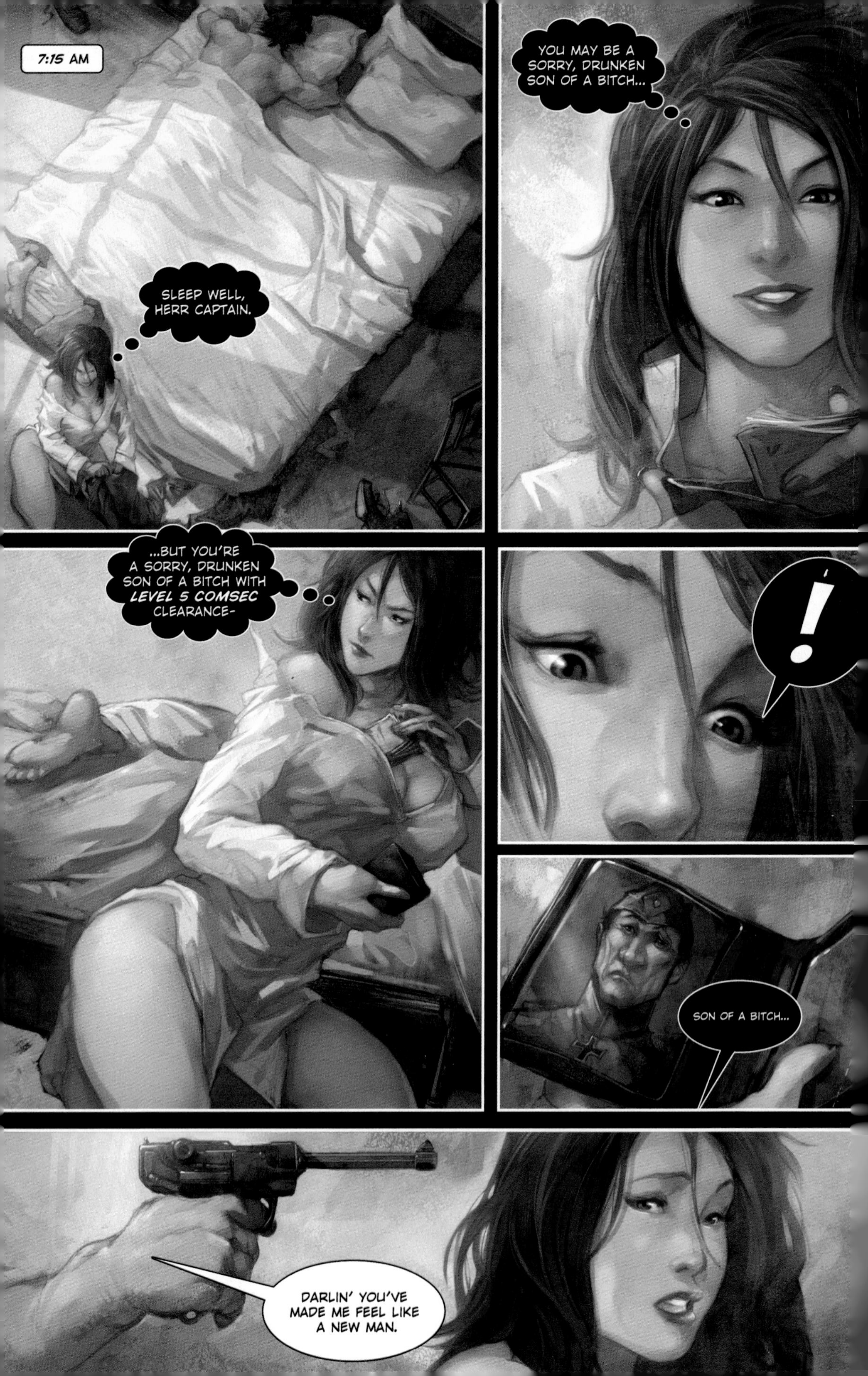
7:15 AM
SLEEP WELL, HERR CAPTAIN.
YOU MAY BE A SORRY, DRUNKEN SON OF A BITCH...
...BUT YOU'RE A SORRY, DRUNKEN SON OF A BITCH WITH LEVEL 5 COMSEC CLEARANCE-
!
SON OF A BITCH...
DARLIN' YOU'VE MADE ME FEEL LIKE A NEW MAN.

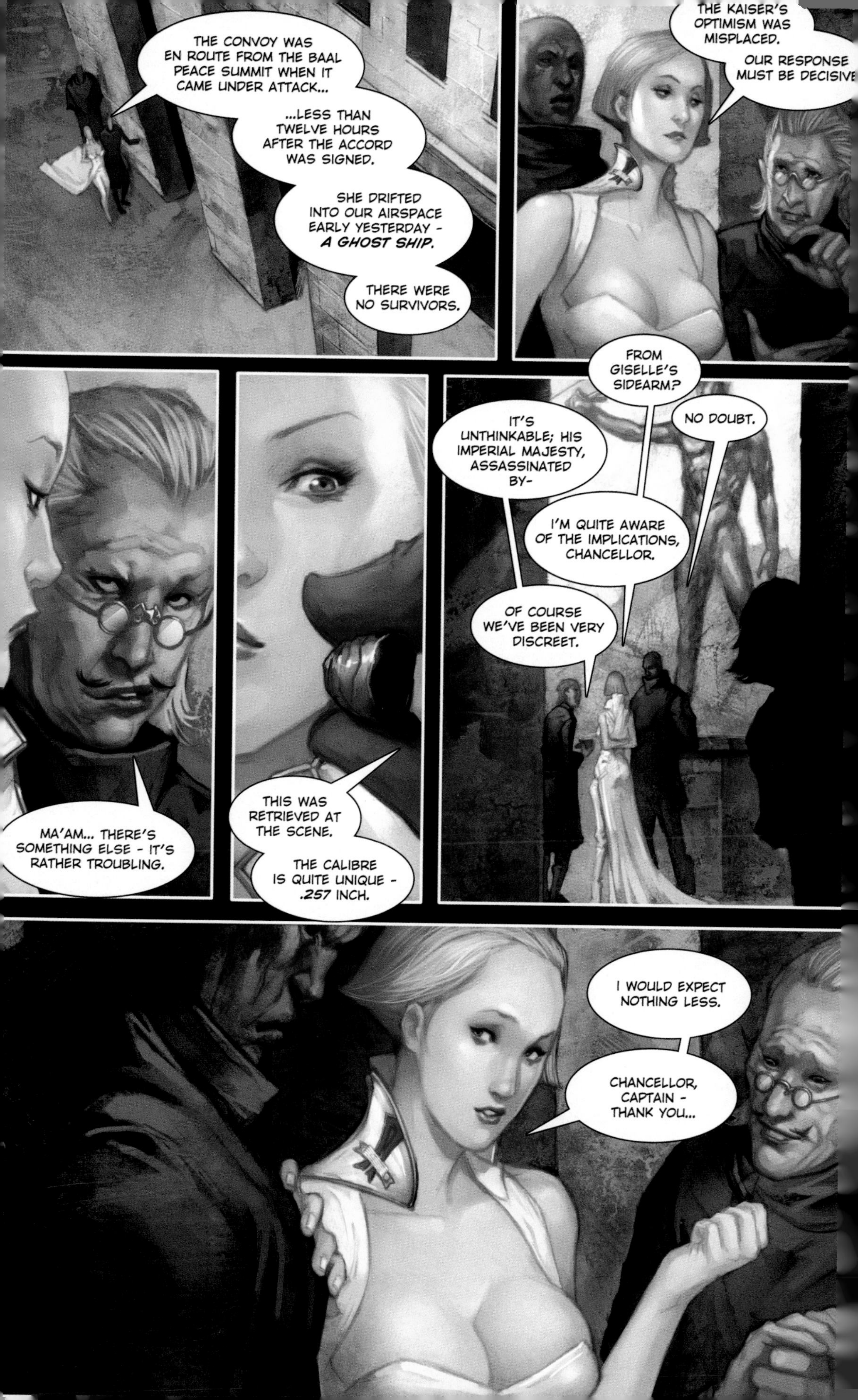
THE CONVOY WAS EN ROUTE FROM THE BAAL PEACE SUMMIT WHEN IT CAME UNDER ATTACK...
...LESS THAN TWELVE HOURS AFTER THE ACCORD WAS SIGNED.
SHE DRIFTED INTO OUR AIRSPACE EARLY YESTERDAY - *A GHOST SHIP.*
THERE WERE NO SURVIVORS.
THE KAISER'S OPTIMISM WAS MISPLACED.
OUR RESPONSE MUST BE DECISIVE
MA'AM... THERE'S SOMETHING ELSE - IT'S RATHER TROUBLING.
THIS WAS RETRIEVED AT THE SCENE.
THE CALIBRE IS QUITE UNIQUE - *.257* INCH.
FROM GISELLE'S SIDEARM?
NO DOUBT.
IT'S UNTHINKABLE; HIS IMPERIAL MAJESTY, ASSASSINATED BY-
I'M QUITE AWARE OF THE IMPLICATIONS, CHANCELLOR.
OF COURSE WE'VE BEEN VERY DISCREET.
I WOULD EXPECT NOTHING LESS.
CHANCELLOR, CAPTAIN - THANK YOU...

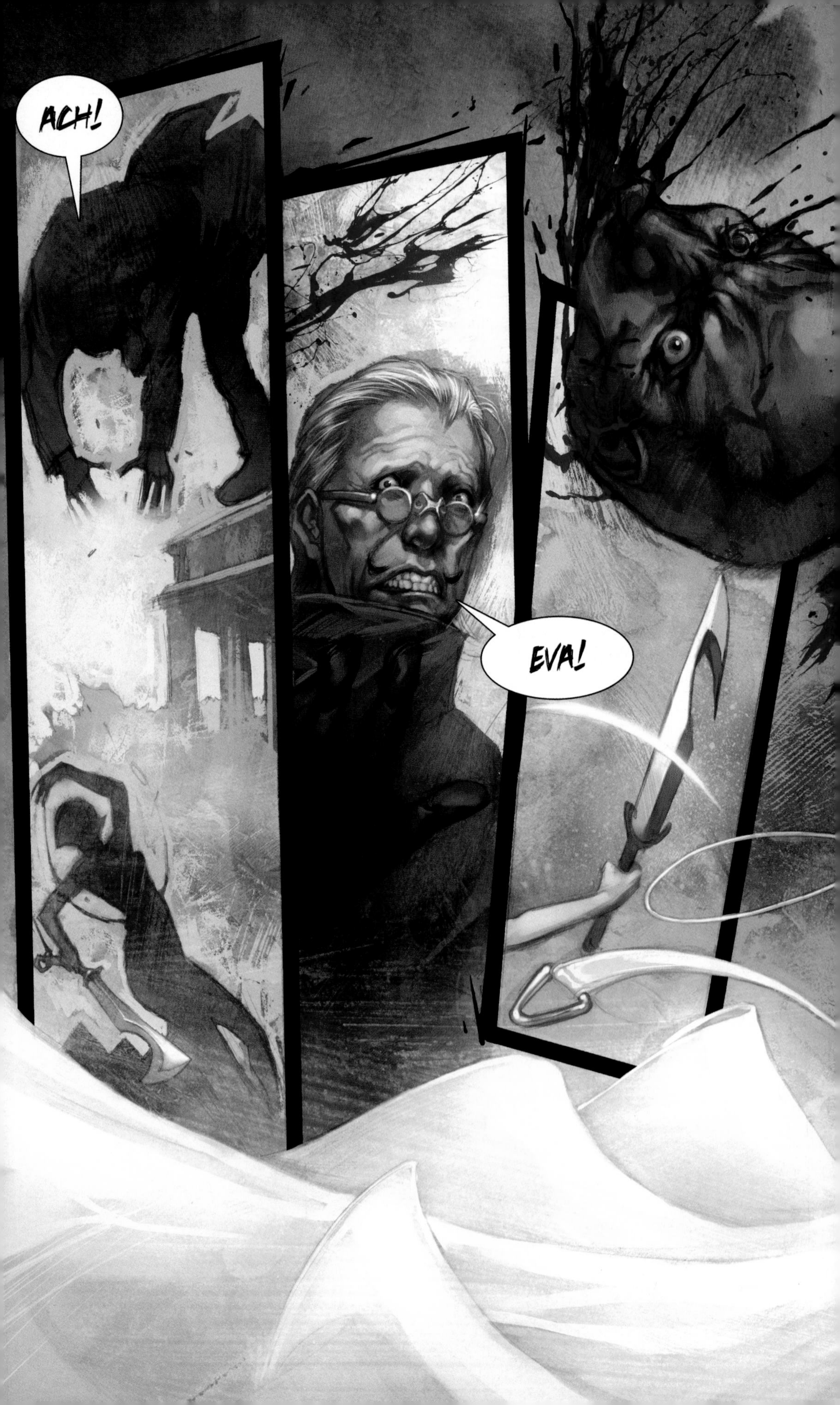
ACH!
EVA!

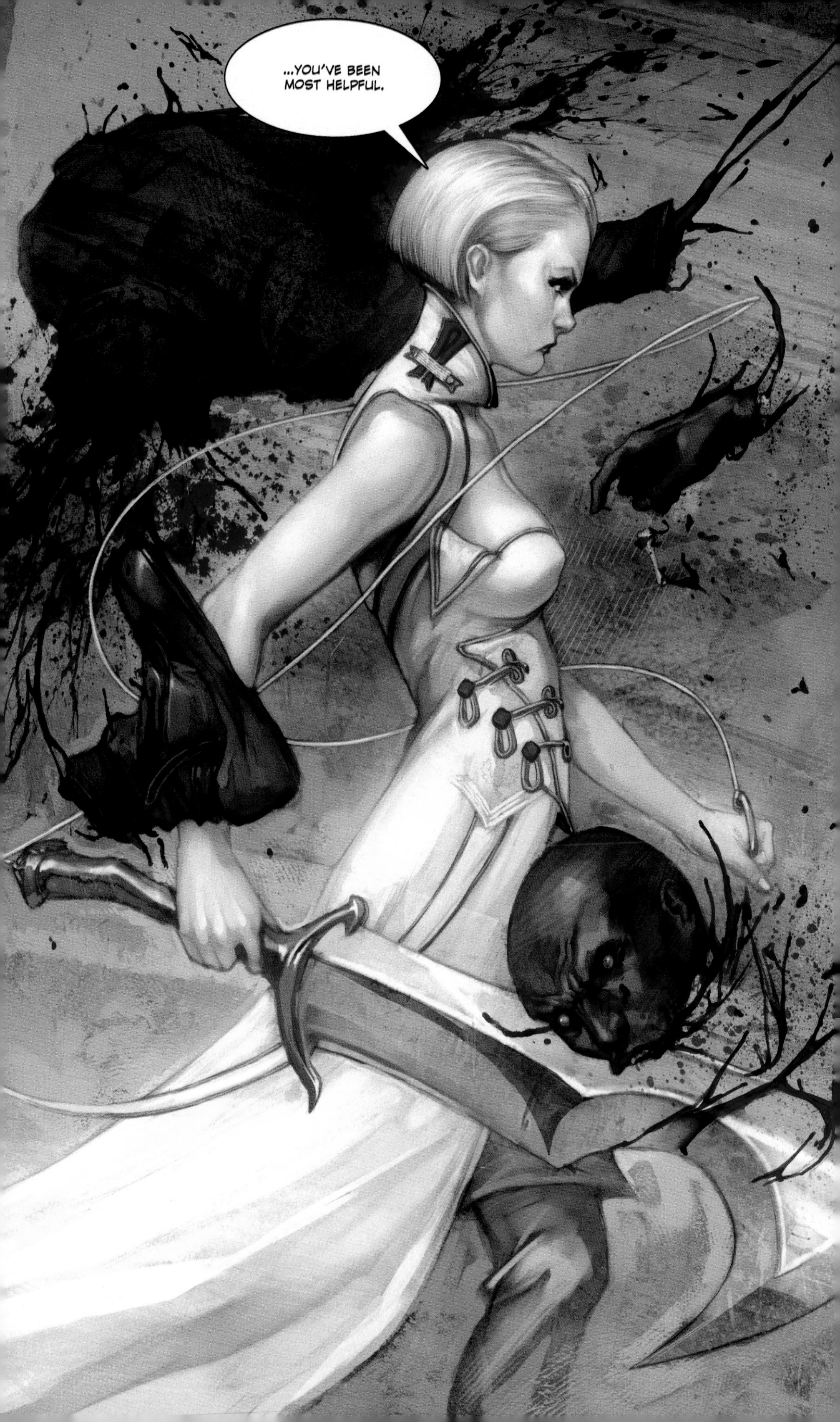
...YOU'VE BEEN MOST HELPFUL.

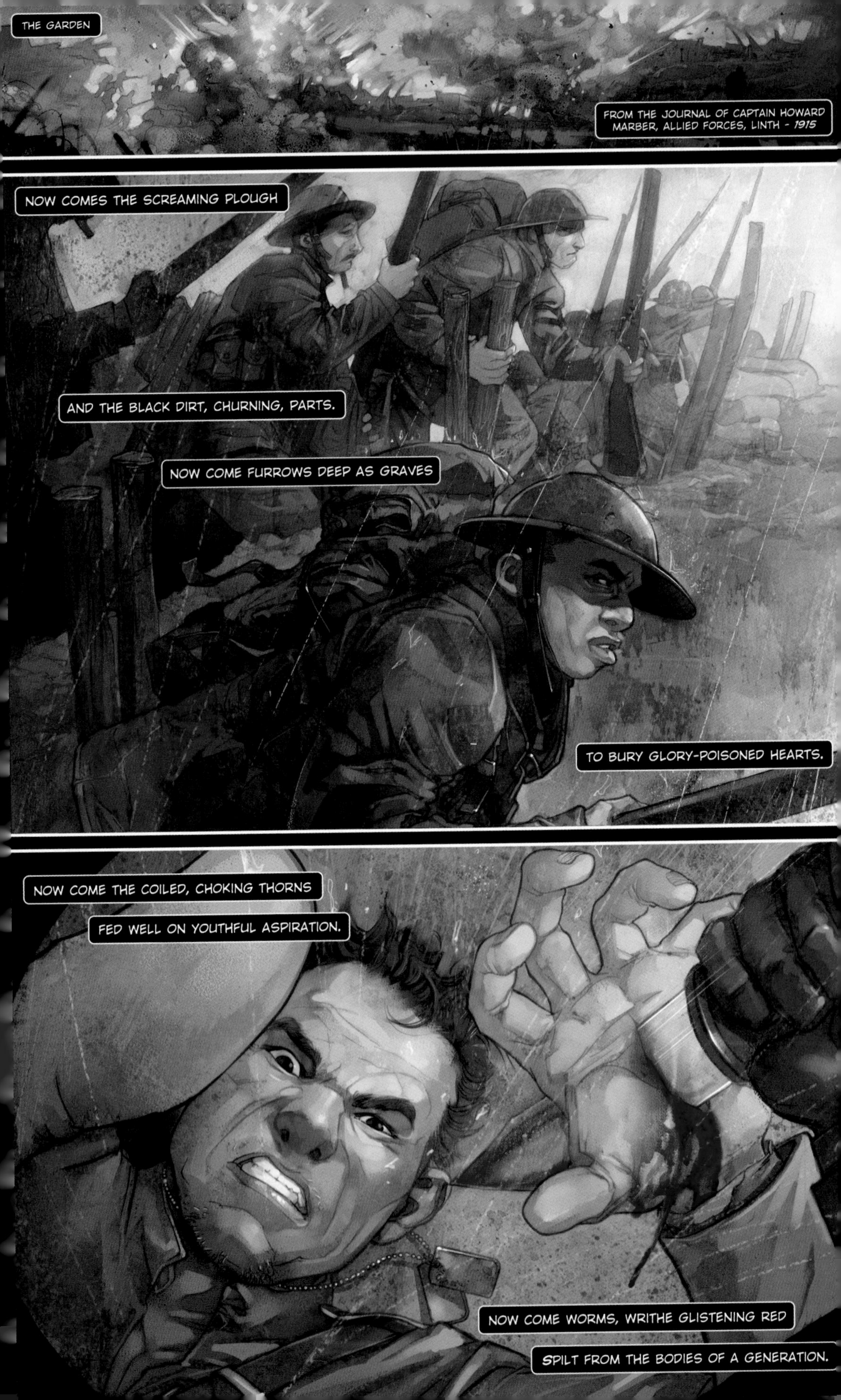
THE GARDEN
FROM THE JOURNAL OF CAPTAIN HOWARD MARBER, ALLIED FORCES, LINTH - 1915
NOW COMES THE SCREAMING PLOUGH
AND THE BLACK DIRT, CHURNING, PARTS.
NOW COME FURROWS DEEP AS GRAVES
TO BURY GLORY-POISONED HEARTS.
NOW COME THE COILED, CHOKING THORNS
FED WELL ON YOUTHFUL ASPIRATION.
NOW COME WORMS, WRITHE GLISTENING RED
SPILT FROM THE BODIES OF A GENERATION.

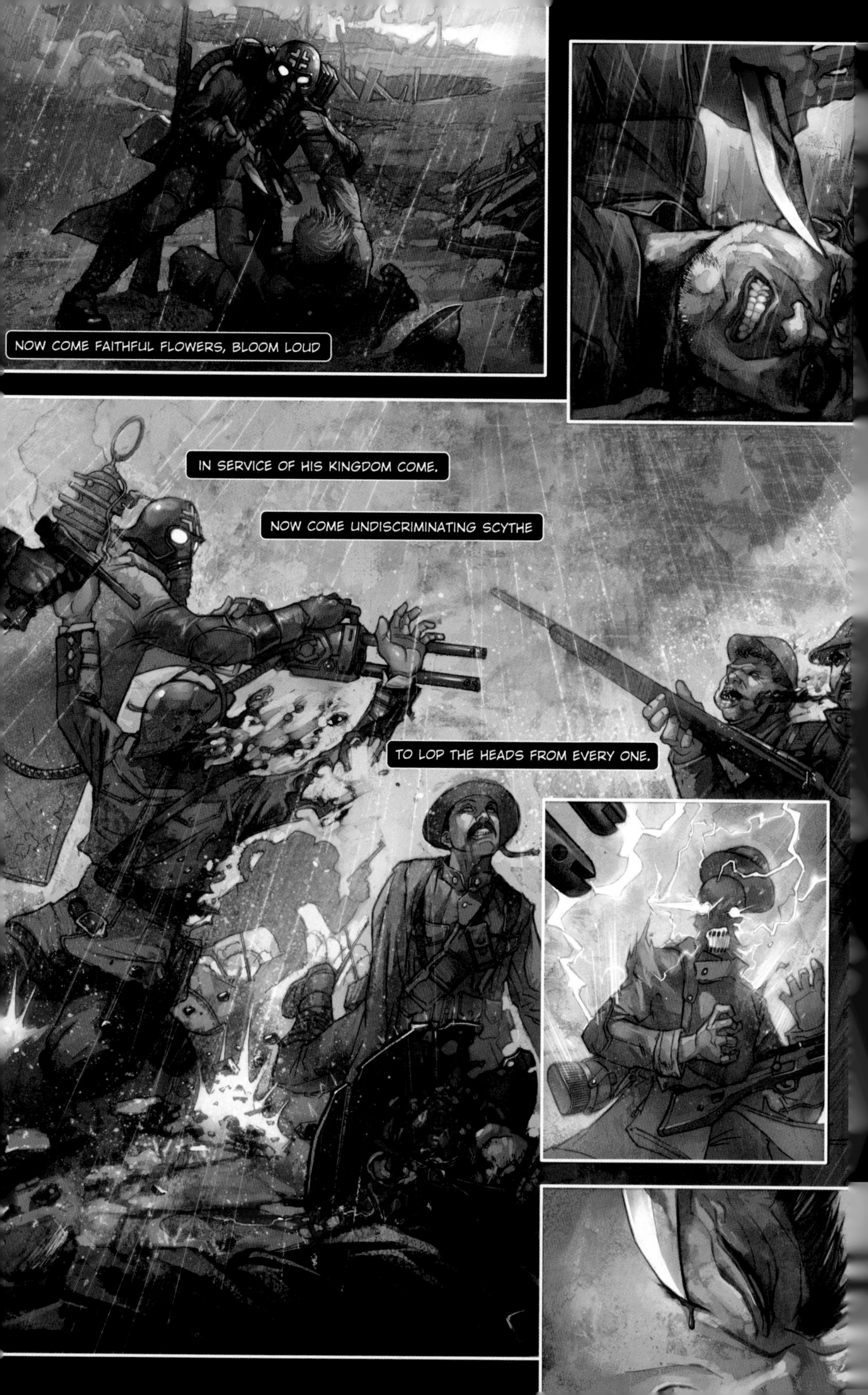
NOW COME FAITHFUL FLOWERS, BLOOM LOUD
IN SERVICE OF HIS KINGDOM COME.
NOW COME UNDISCRIMINATING SCYTHE
TO LOP THE HEADS FROM EVERY ONE.

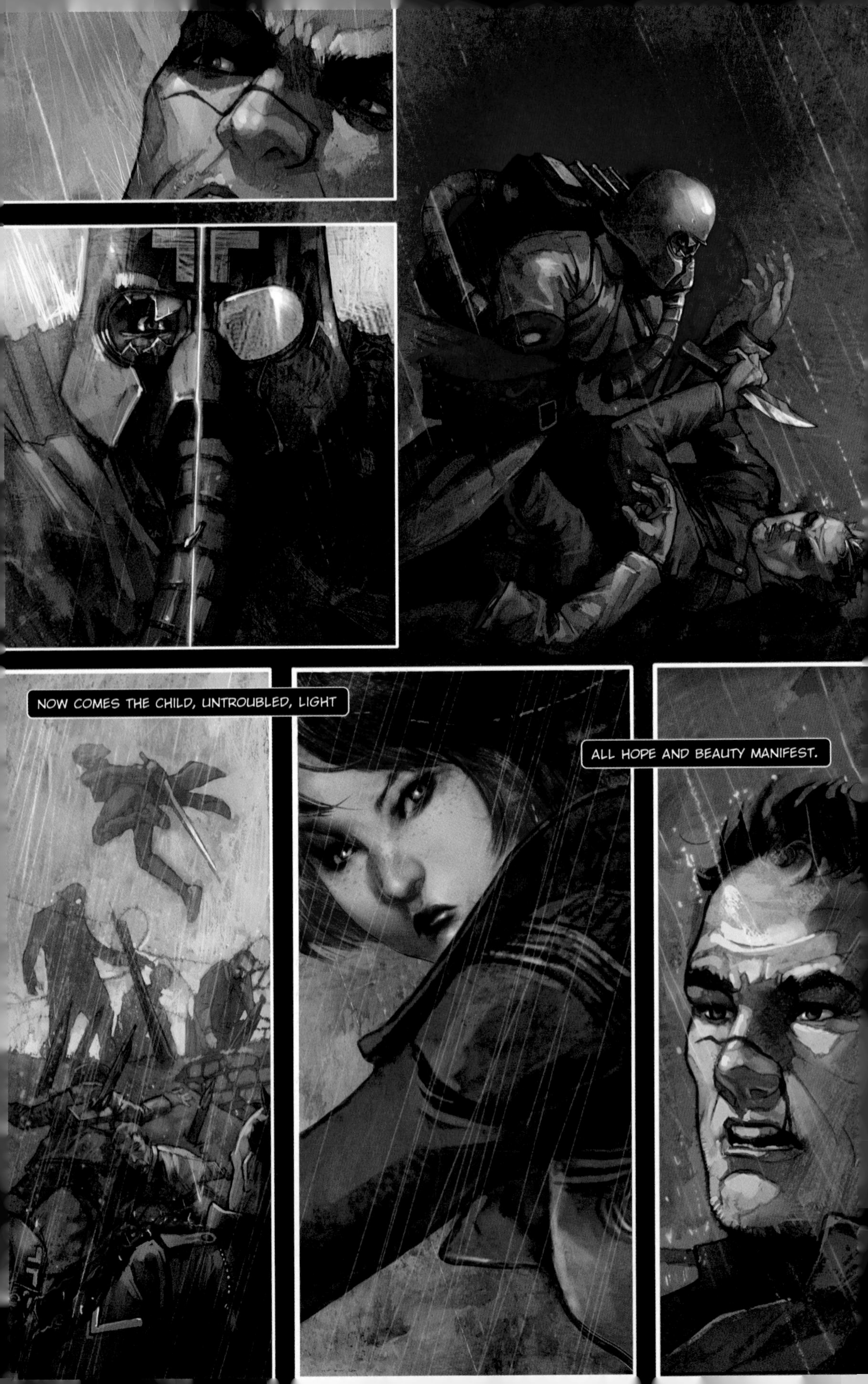
NOW COMES THE CHILD, UNTROUBLED, LIGHT
ALL HOPE AND BEAUTY MANIFEST.

HALT!

NOW COME RED BLOSSOM, SCATTER IN HER WAKE

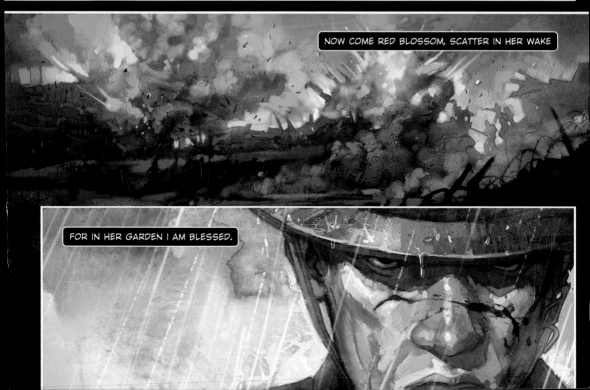

FOR IN HER GARDEN I AM BLESSED.

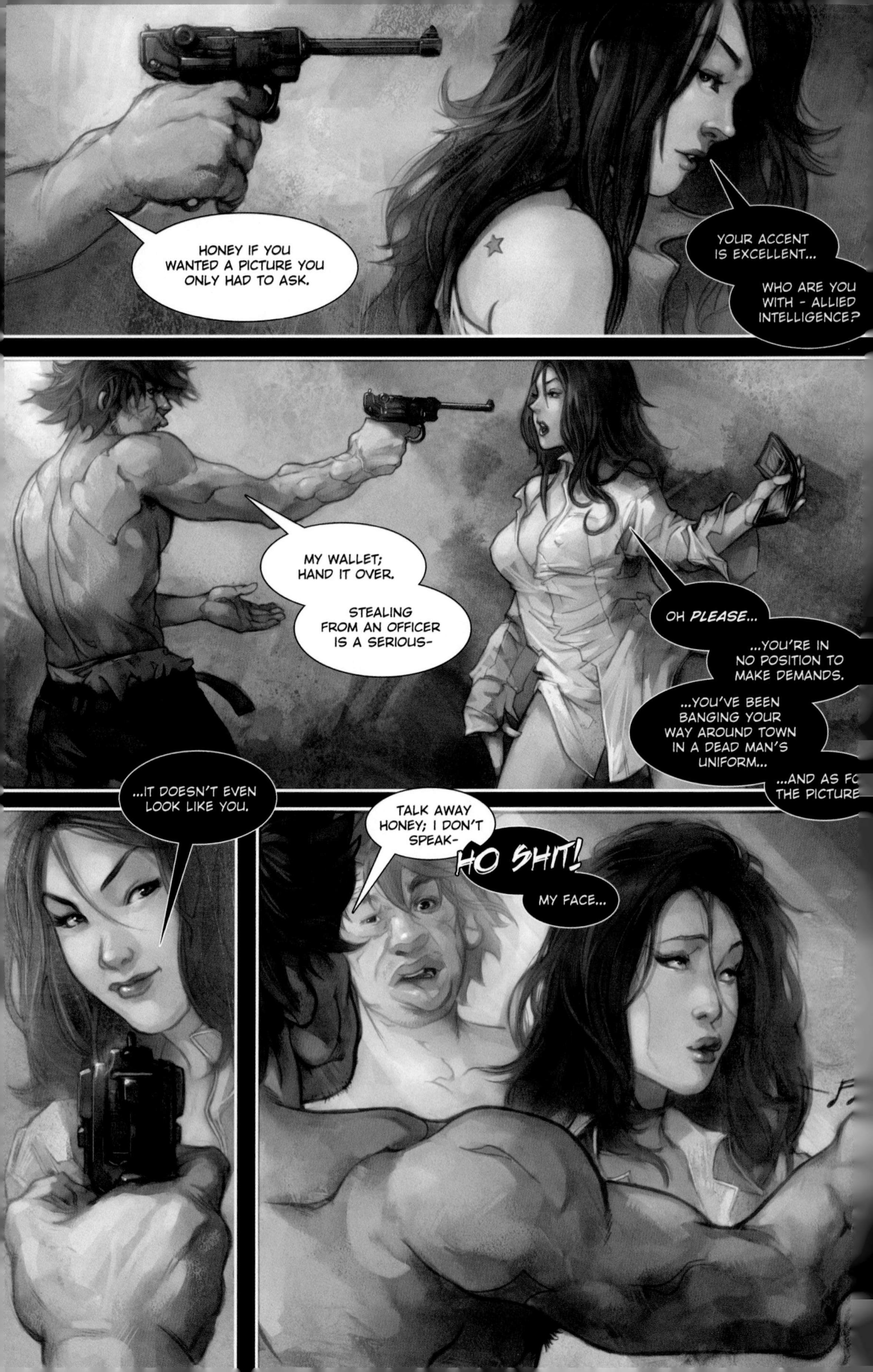
HONEY IF YOU WANTED A PICTURE YOU ONLY HAD TO ASK.
YOUR ACCENT IS EXCELLENT...
WHO ARE YOU WITH - ALLIED INTELLIGENCE?
MY WALLET; HAND IT OVER.
STEALING FROM AN OFFICER IS A SERIOUS-
OH PLEASE...
...YOU'RE IN NO POSITION TO MAKE DEMANDS.
...YOU'VE BEEN BANGING YOUR WAY AROUND TOWN IN A DEAD MAN'S UNIFORM...
...AND AS FO THE PICTURE
...IT DOESN'T EVEN LOOK LIKE YOU.
TALK AWAY HONEY; I DON'T SPEAK-
HO SHIT!
MY FACE...

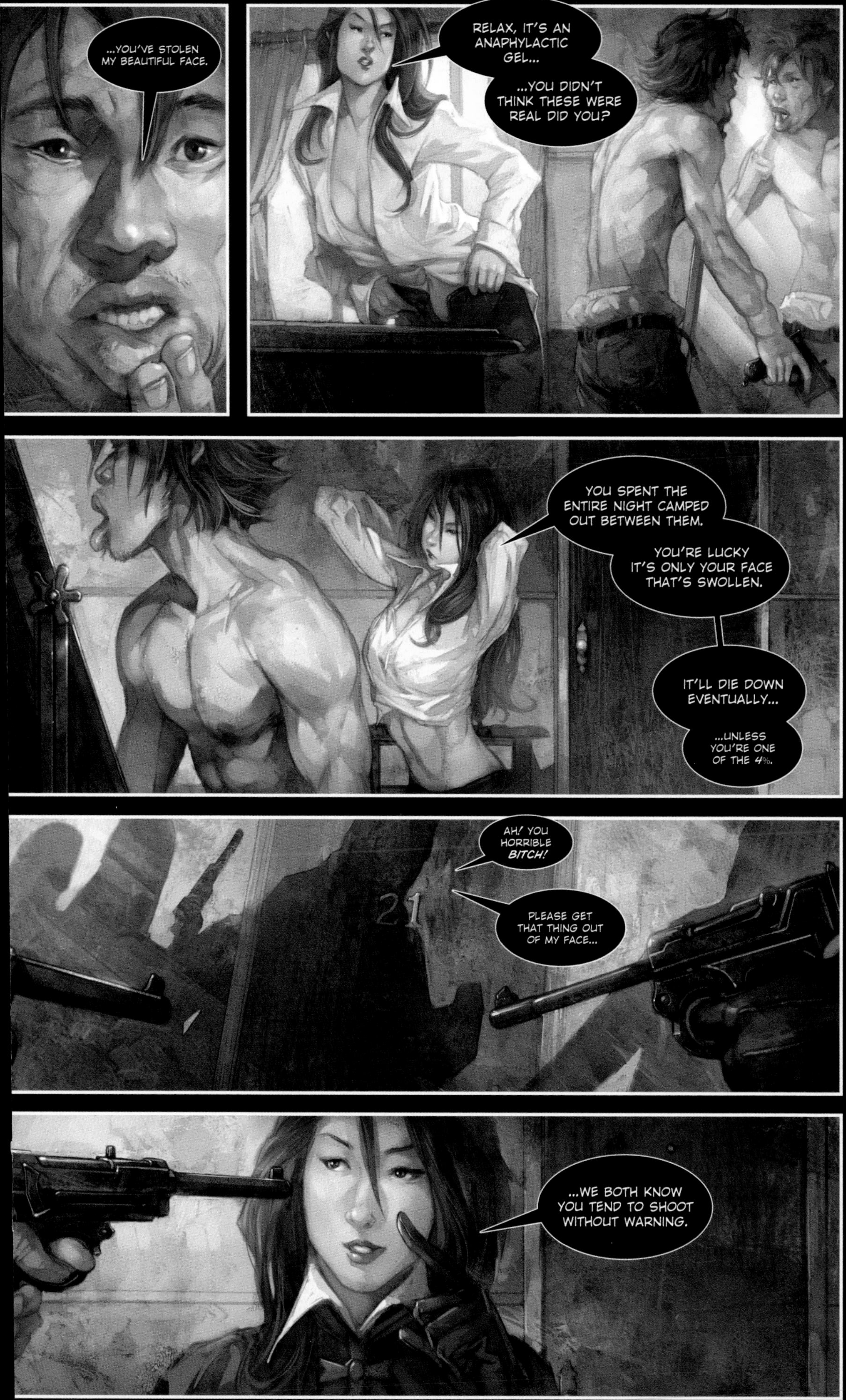
...YOU'VE STOLEN MY BEAUTIFUL FACE.
RELAX, IT'S AN ANAPHYLACTIC GEL...
...YOU DIDN'T THINK THESE WERE REAL DID YOU?
YOU SPENT THE ENTIRE NIGHT CAMPED OUT BETWEEN THEM.
YOU'RE LUCKY IT'S ONLY YOUR FACE THAT'S SWOLLEN.
IT'LL DIE DOWN EVENTUALLY...
...UNLESS YOU'RE ONE OF THE 4%.
AH! YOU HORRIBLE *BITCH!*
21
PLEASE GET THAT THING OUT OF MY FACE...
...WE BOTH KNOW YOU TEND TO SHOOT WITHOUT WARNING.

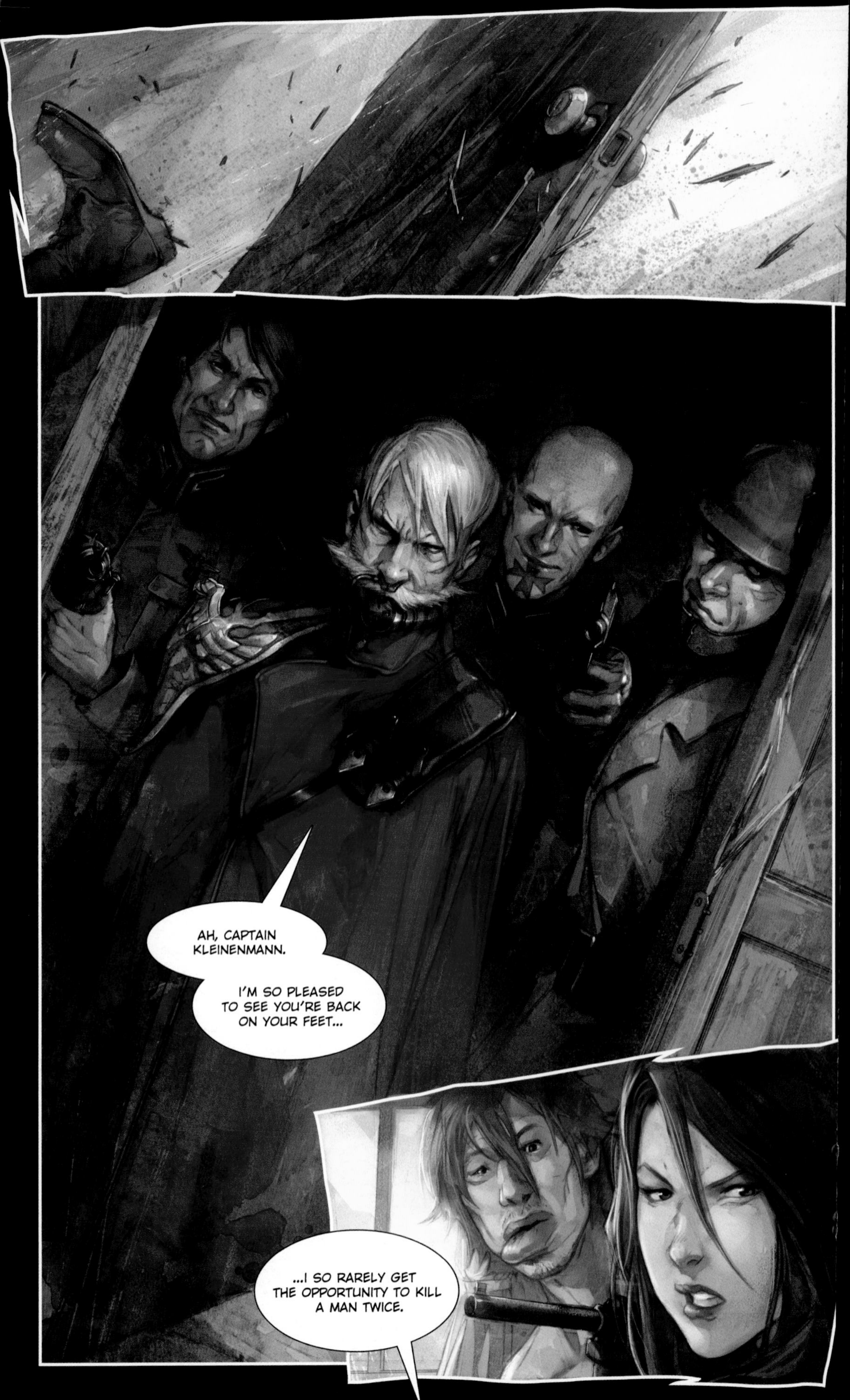
AH, CAPTAIN KLEINENMANN.
I'M SO PLEASED TO SEE YOU'RE BACK ON YOUR FEET...
...I SO RARELY GET THE OPPORTUNITY TO KILL A MAN TWICE.

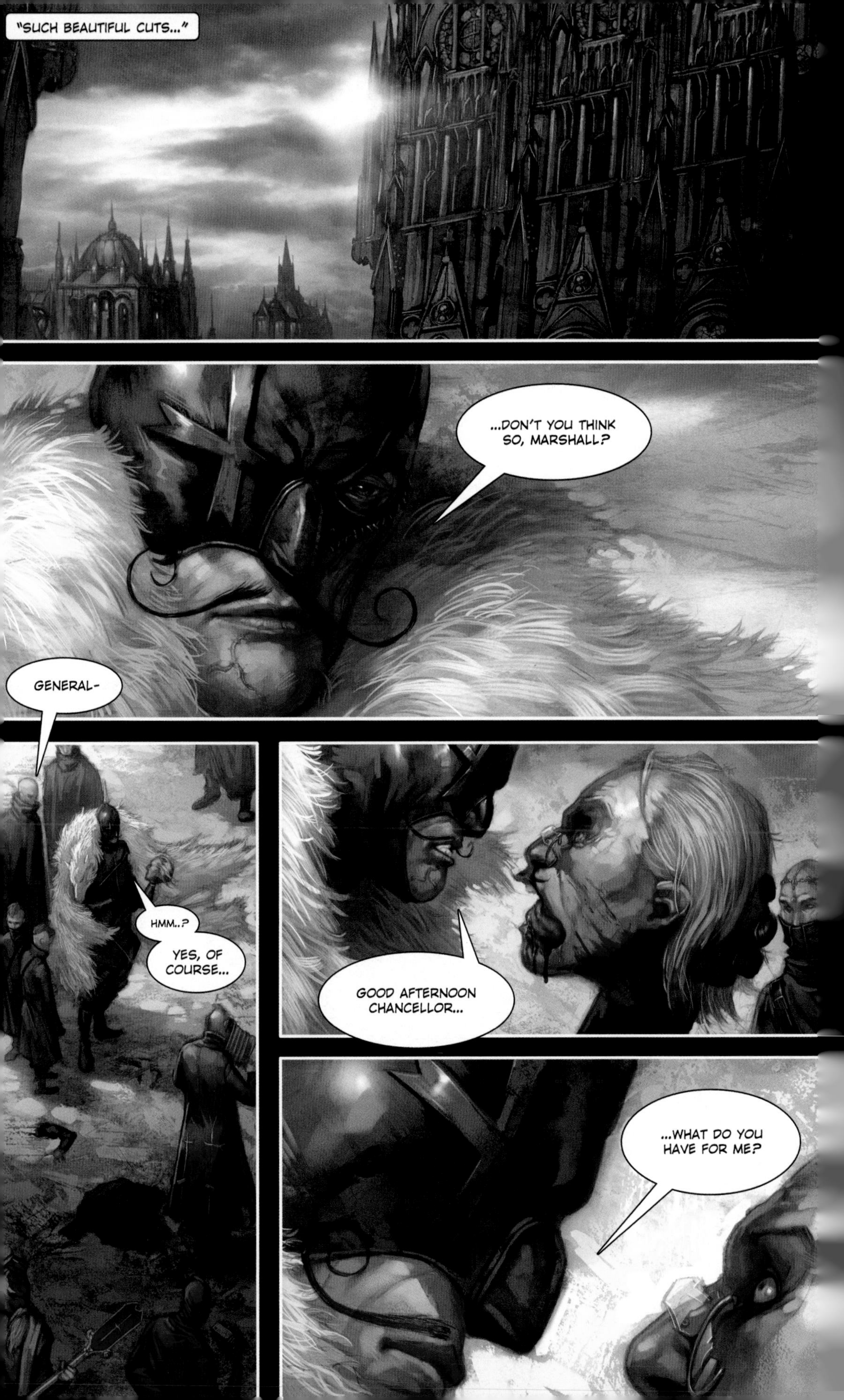
"SUCH BEAUTIFUL CUTS..."
...DON'T YOU THINK SO, MARSHALL?
GENERAL-
HMM..?
YES, OF COURSE...
GOOD AFTERNOON CHANCELLOR...
...WHAT DO YOU HAVE FOR ME?

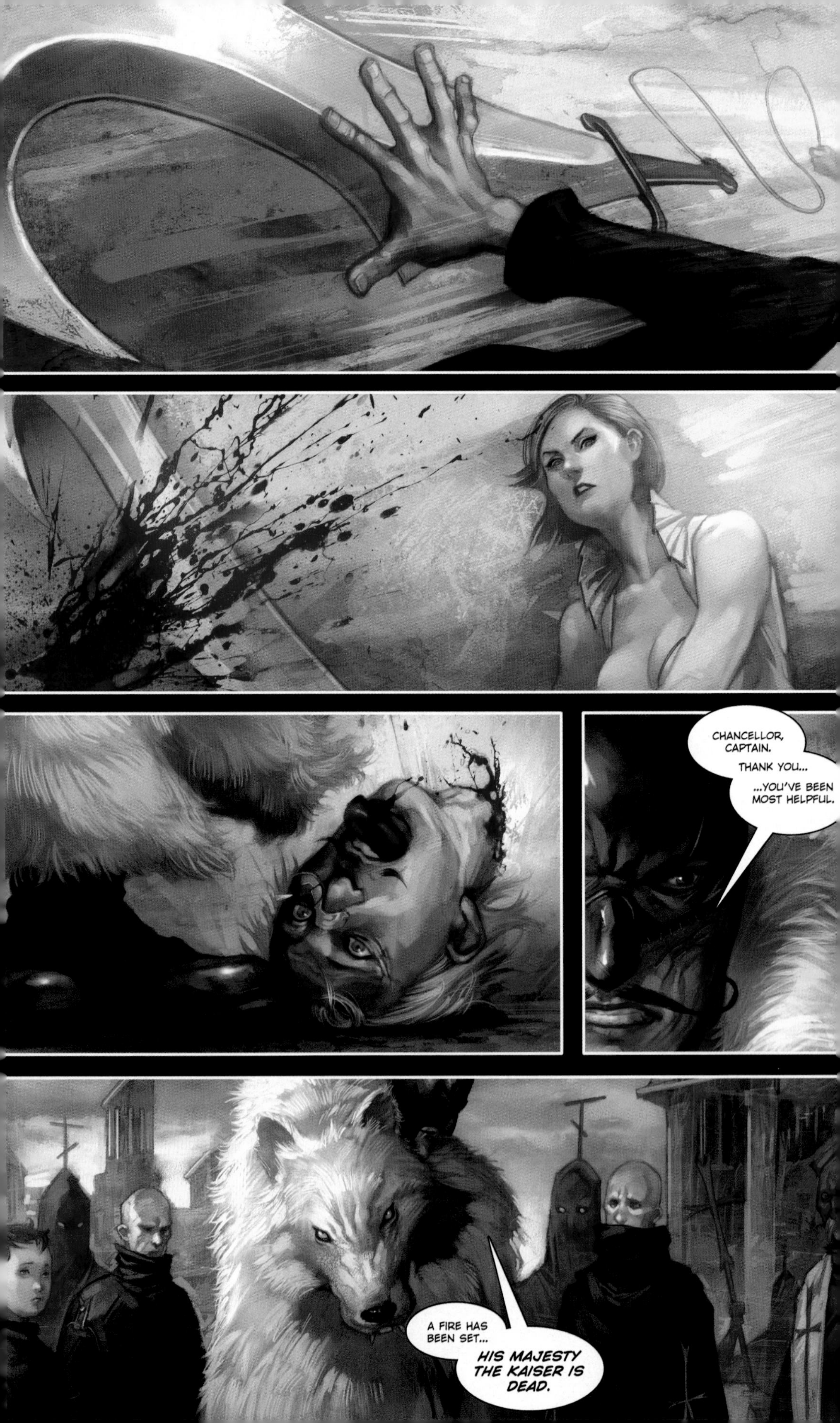
CHANCELLOR, CAPTAIN.
THANK YOU...
...YOU'VE BEEN MOST HELPFUL.
A FIRE HAS BEEN SET...
HIS MAJESTY THE KAISER IS DEAD.

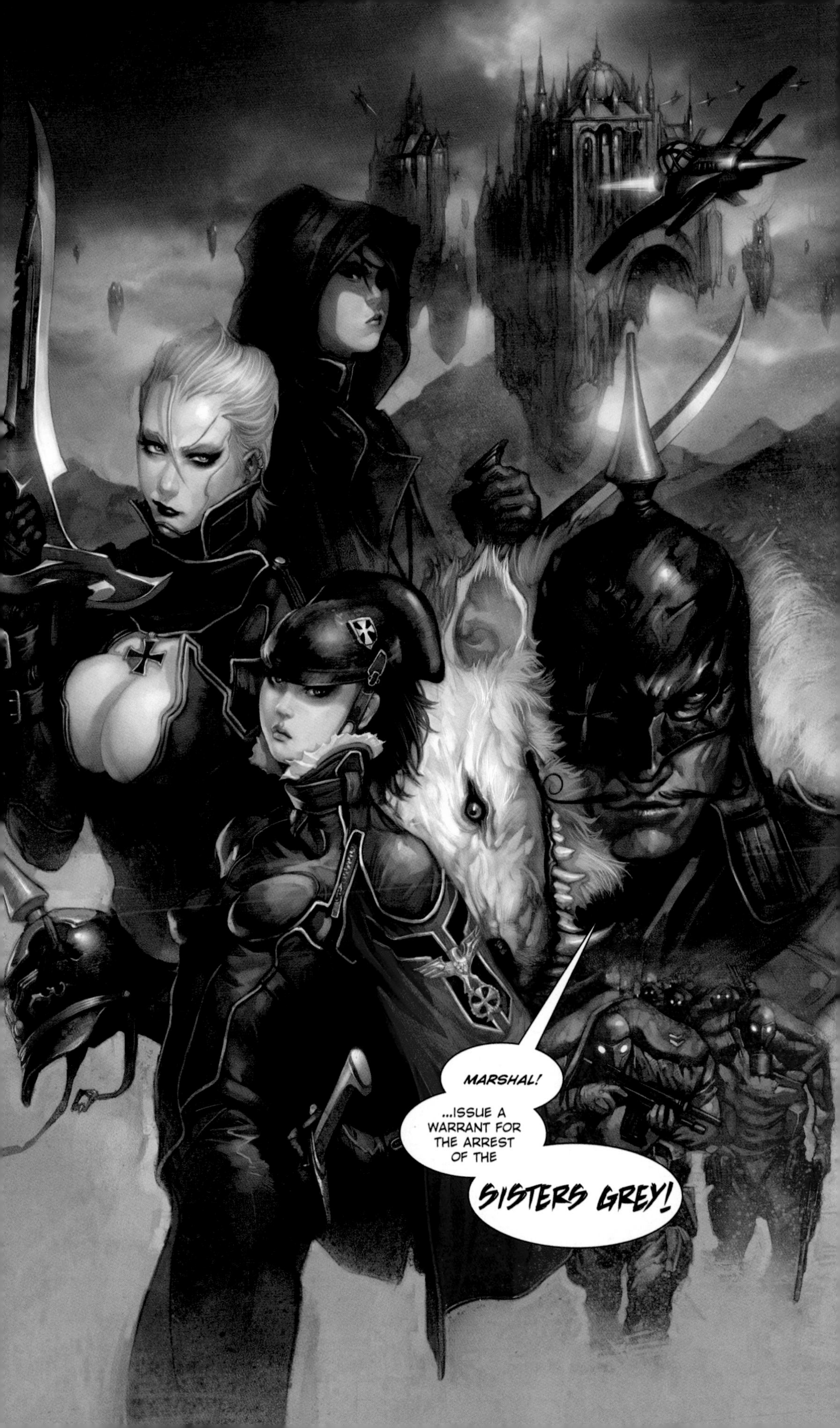
MARSHAL!
...ISSUE A WARRANT FOR THE ARREST OF THE
SISTERS GREY!

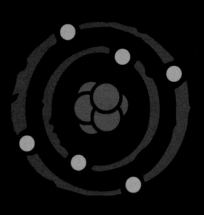

II

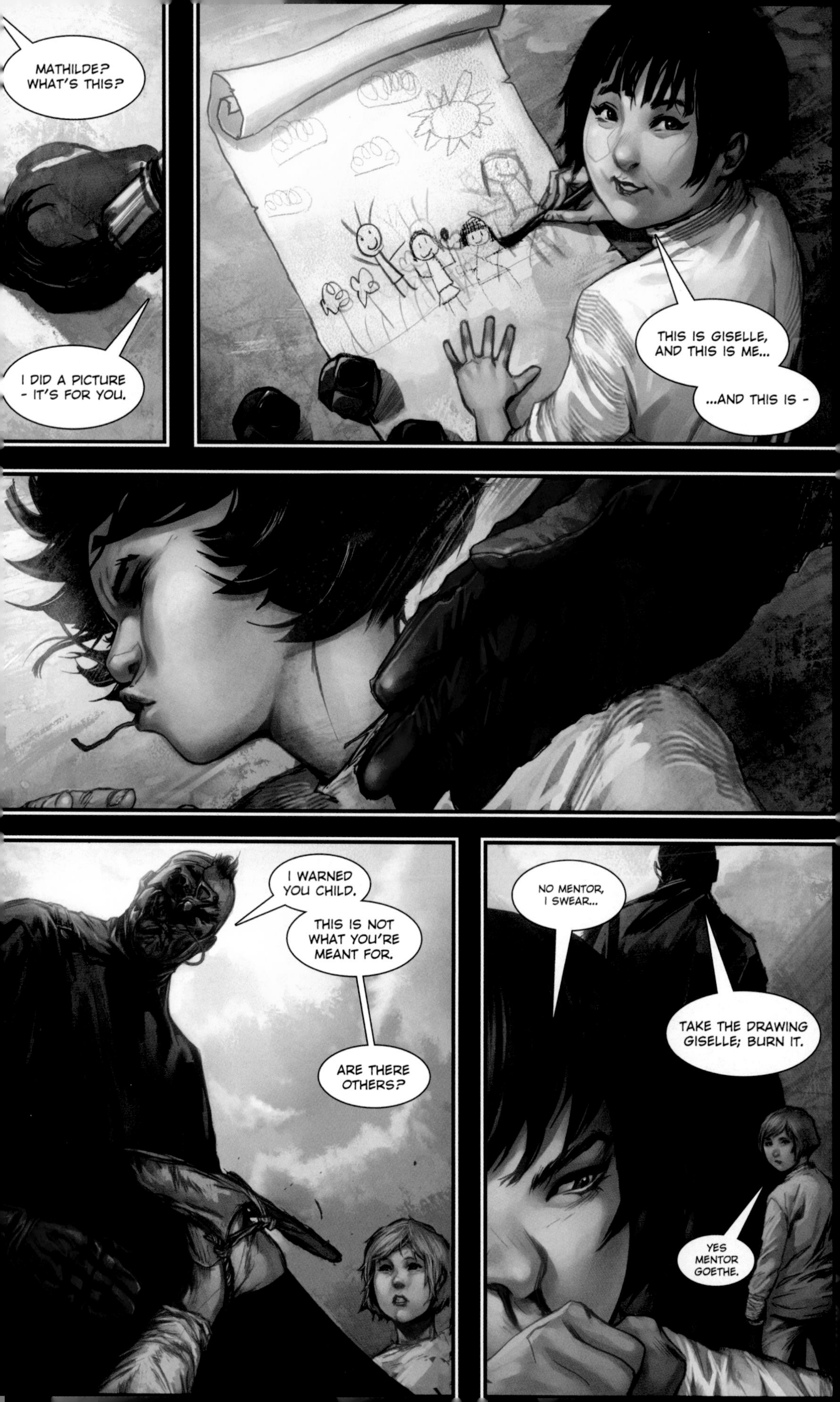
MATHILDE? WHAT'S THIS?
I DID A PICTURE - IT'S FOR YOU.
THIS IS GISELLE, AND THIS IS ME...
...AND THIS IS -
I WARNED YOU CHILD.
THIS IS NOT WHAT YOU'RE MEANT FOR.
ARE THERE OTHERS?
NO MENTOR, I SWEAR...
TAKE THE DRAWING GISELLE; BURN IT.
YES MENTOR GOETHE.

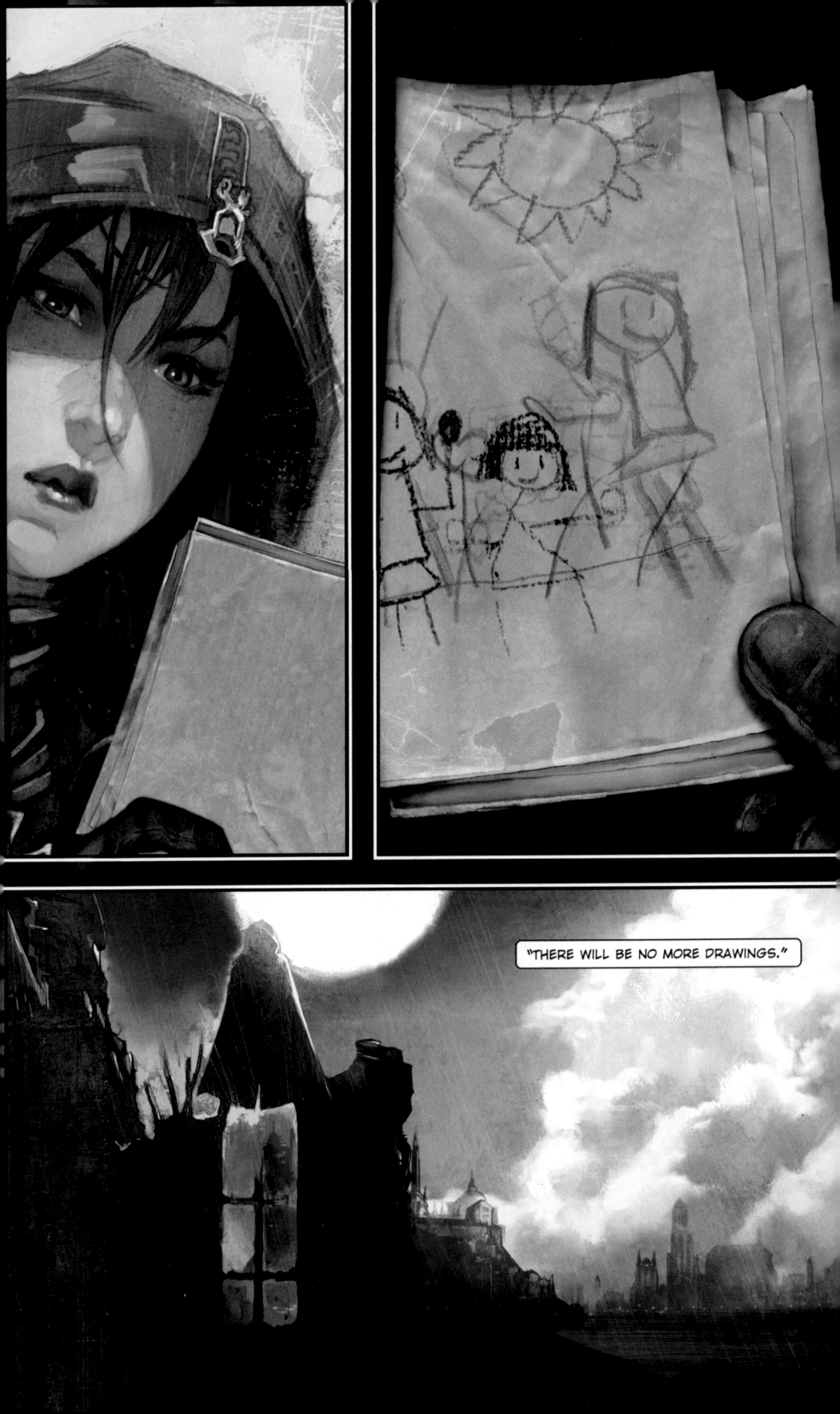
"THERE WILL BE NO MORE DRAWINGS."

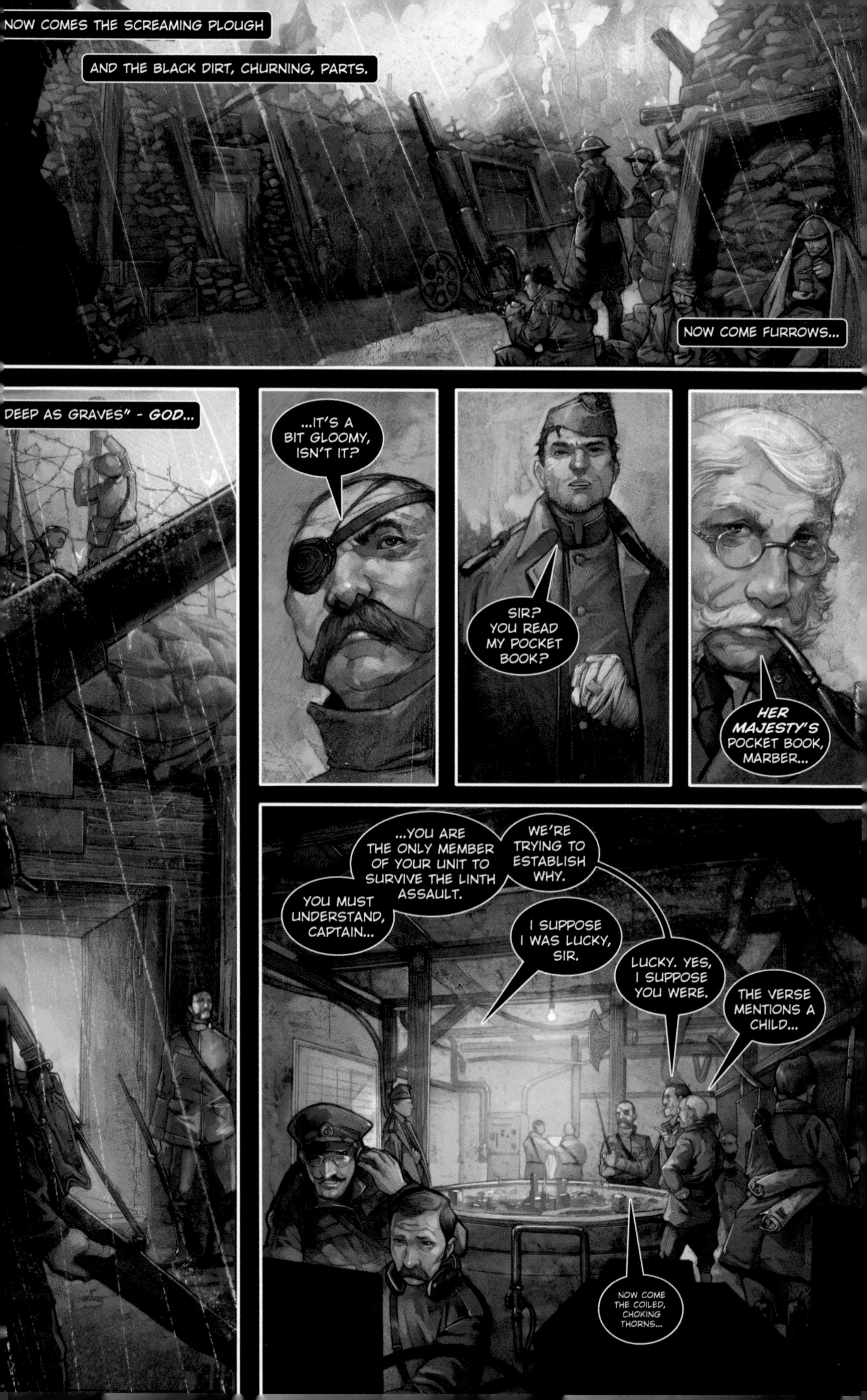

NOW COMES THE SCREAMING PLOUGH
AND THE BLACK DIRT, CHURNING, PARTS.
NOW COME FURROWS...
DEEP AS GRAVES" - GOD...
...IT'S A BIT GLOOMY, ISN'T IT?
SIR? YOU READ MY POCKET BOOK?
HER MAJESTY'S POCKET BOOK, MARBER...
YOU MUST UNDERSTAND, CAPTAIN...
...YOU ARE THE ONLY MEMBER OF YOUR UNIT TO SURVIVE THE LINTH ASSAULT.
WE'RE TRYING TO ESTABLISH WHY.
I SUPPOSE I WAS LUCKY, SIR.
LUCKY. YES, I SUPPOSE YOU WERE.
THE VERSE MENTIONS A CHILD...
NOW COME THE COILED, CHOKING THORNS...

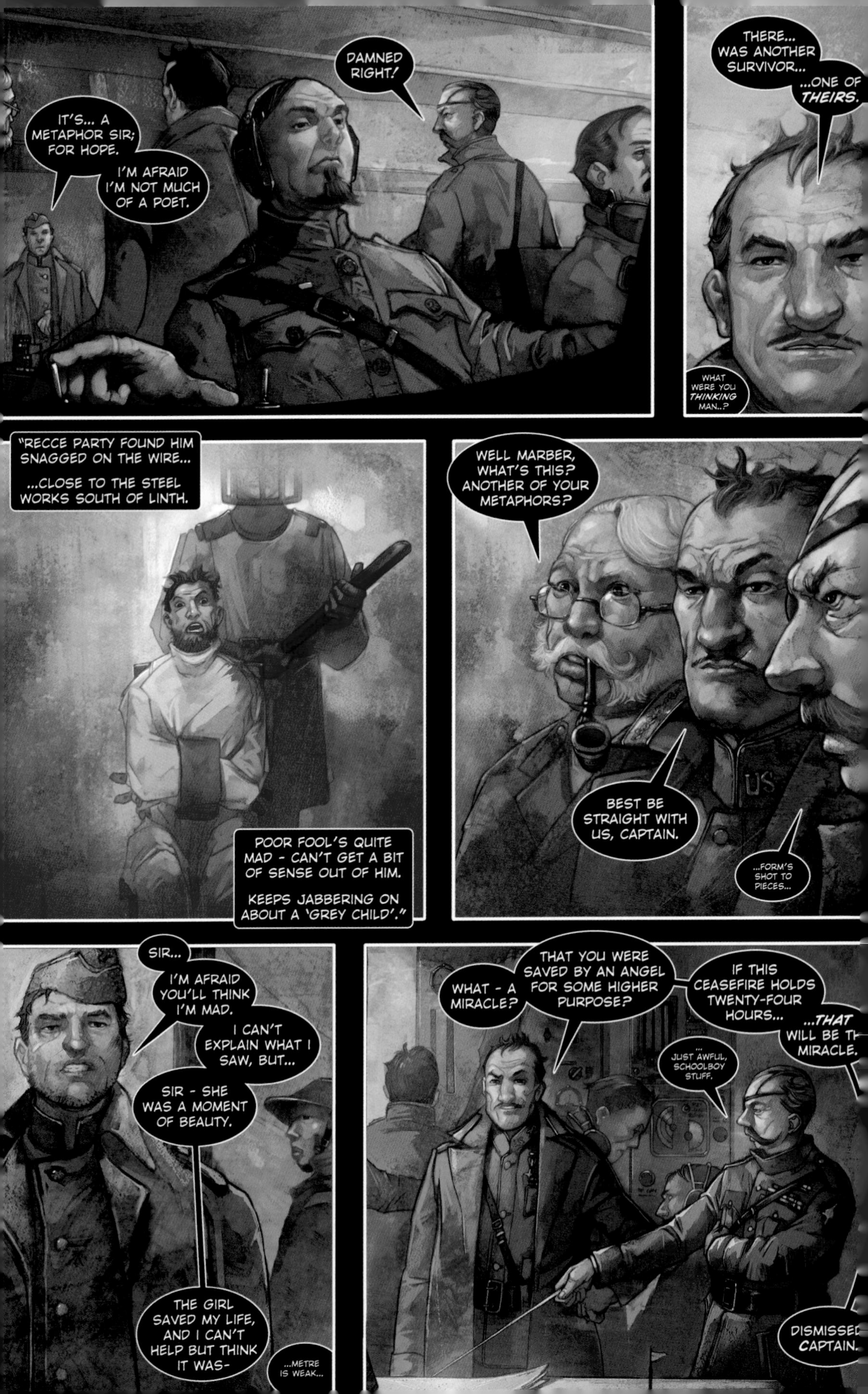

IT'S... A METAPHOR SIR; FOR HOPE.
I'M AFRAID I'M NOT MUCH OF A POET.
DAMNED RIGHT!
THERE... WAS ANOTHER SURVIVOR...
...ONE OF *THEIRS*.
WHAT WERE YOU *THINKING* MAN..?
"RECCE PARTY FOUND HIM SNAGGED ON THE WIRE...
...CLOSE TO THE STEEL WORKS SOUTH OF LINTH.
POOR FOOL'S QUITE MAD - CAN'T GET A BIT OF SENSE OUT OF HIM.
KEEPS JABBERING ON ABOUT A 'GREY CHILD'."
WELL MARBER, WHAT'S THIS? ANOTHER OF YOUR METAPHORS?
BEST BE STRAIGHT WITH US, CAPTAIN.
...FORM'S SHOT TO PIECES...
SIR...
I'M AFRAID YOU'LL THINK I'M MAD.
I CAN'T EXPLAIN WHAT I SAW, BUT...
SIR - SHE WAS A MOMENT OF BEAUTY.
THE GIRL SAVED MY LIFE, AND I CAN'T HELP BUT THINK IT WAS-
...METRE IS WEAK...
WHAT - A MIRACLE?
THAT YOU WERE SAVED BY AN ANGEL FOR SOME HIGHER PURPOSE?
...JUST AWFUL, SCHOOLBOY STUFF.
IF THIS CEASEFIRE HOLDS TWENTY-FOUR HOURS...
...*THAT* WILL BE T
MIRACLE.
DISMISSE
CAPTAIN.

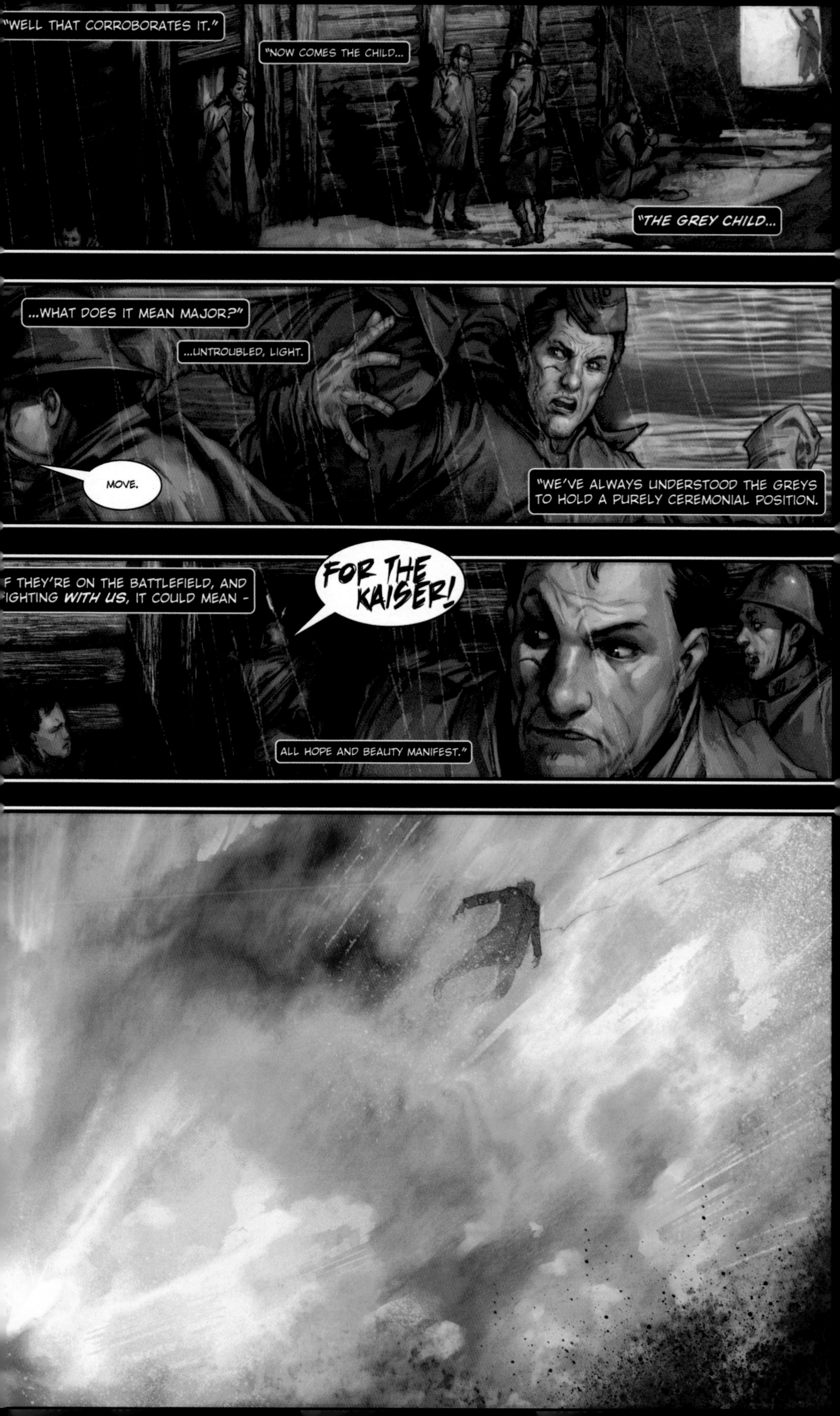
"WELL THAT CORROBORATES IT."
"NOW COMES THE CHILD...
"THE GREY CHILD...
...WHAT DOES IT MEAN MAJOR?"
...UNTROUBLED, LIGHT.
MOVE.
"WE'VE ALWAYS UNDERSTOOD THE GREYS TO HOLD A PURELY CEREMONIAL POSITION.
F THEY'RE ON THE BATTLEFIELD, AND IGHTING WITH US, IT COULD MEAN -
FOR THE KAISER!
ALL HOPE AND BEAUTY MANIFEST."

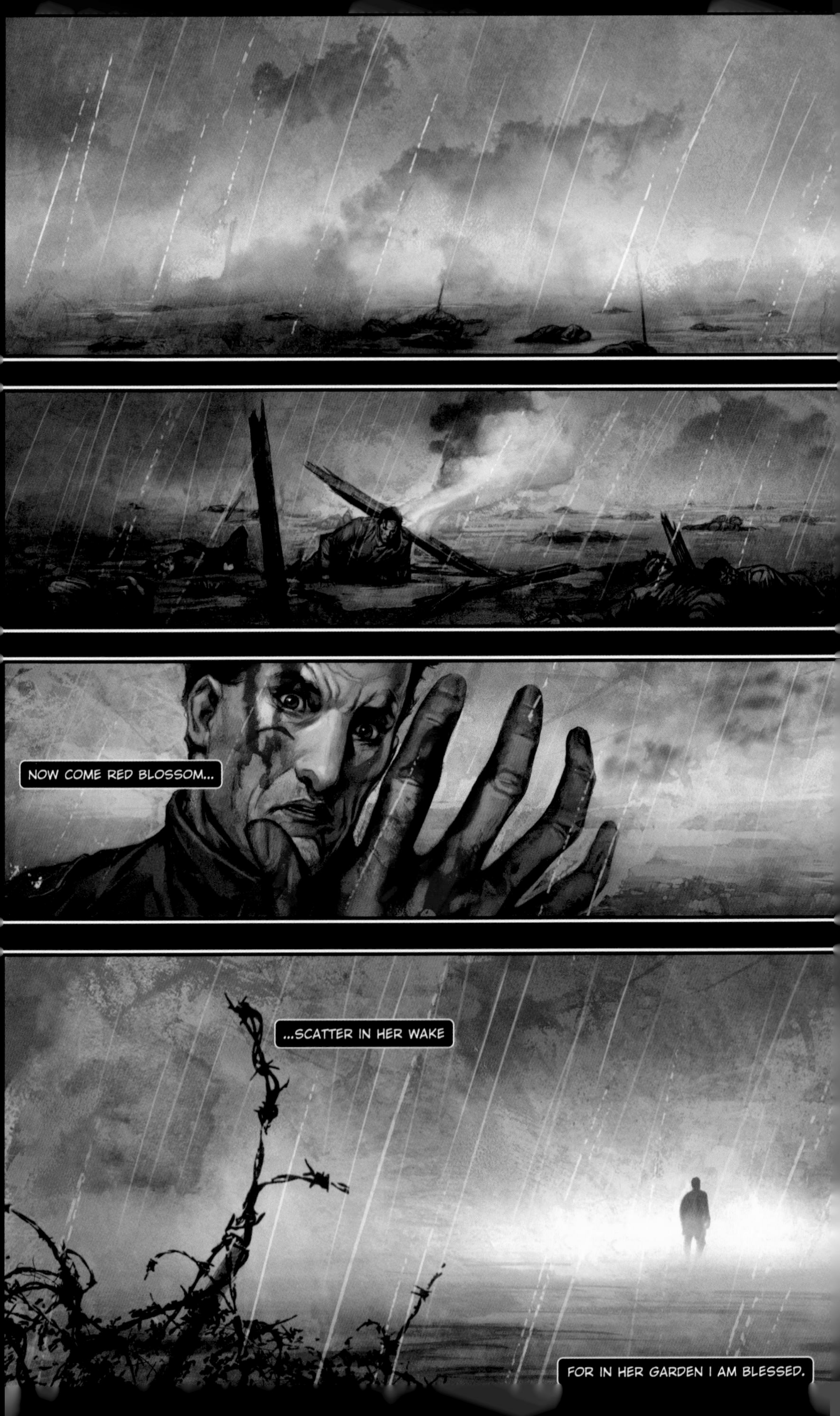
NOW COME RED BLOSSOM...
...SCATTER IN HER WAKE
FOR IN HER GARDEN I AM BLESSED.

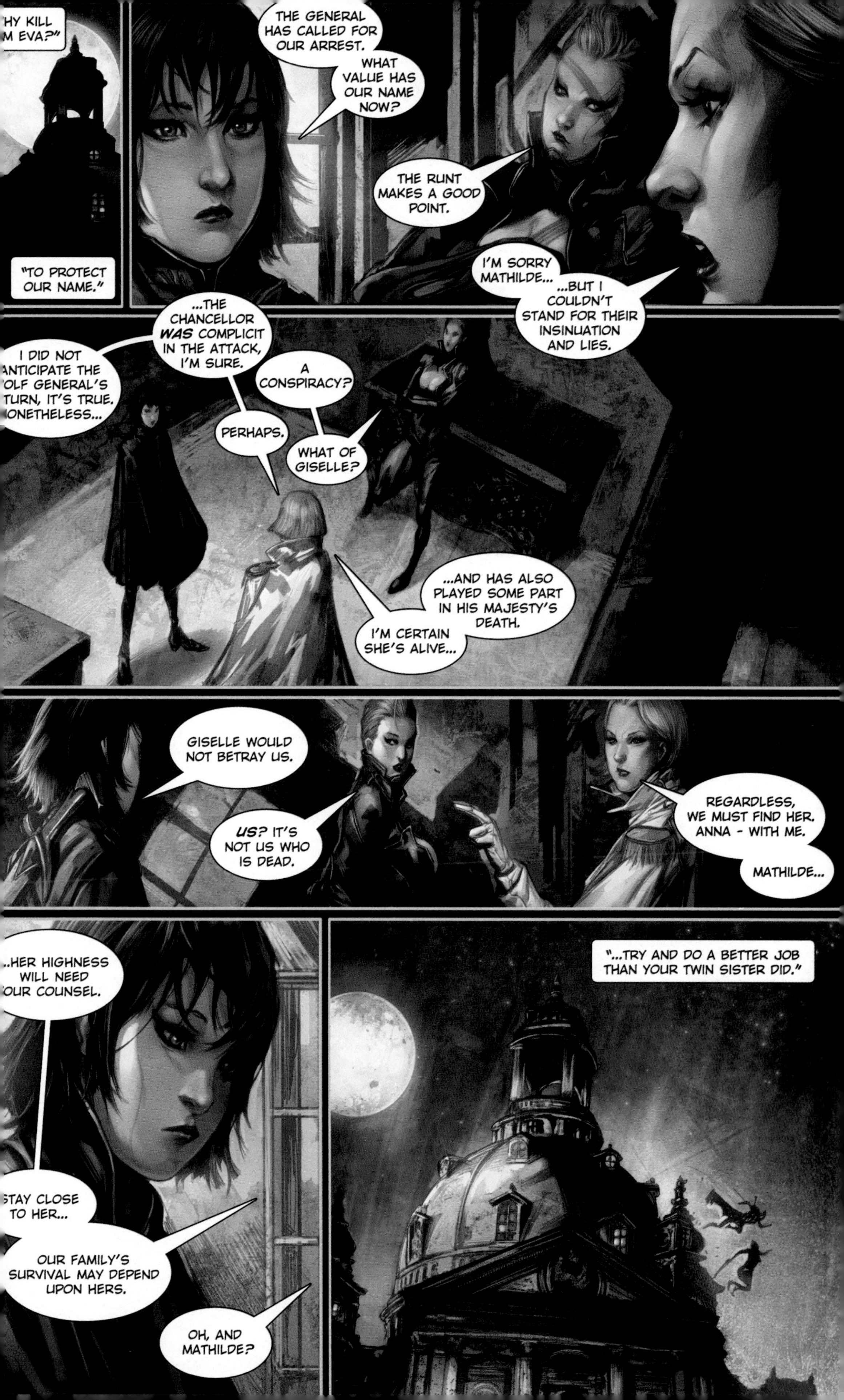
"HY KILL
M EVA?"
"TO PROTECT OUR NAME."
THE GENERAL HAS CALLED FOR OUR ARREST.
WHAT VALUE HAS OUR NAME NOW?
THE RUNT MAKES A GOOD POINT.
I'M SORRY MATHILDE...
...BUT I COULDN'T STAND FOR THEIR INSINUATION AND LIES.
I DID NOT ANTICIPATE THE OLF GENERAL'S TURN, IT'S TRUE. ONETHELESS...
...THE CHANCELLOR WAS COMPLICIT IN THE ATTACK, I'M SURE.
A CONSPIRACY?
PERHAPS.
WHAT OF GISELLE?
I'M CERTAIN SHE'S ALIVE...
...AND HAS ALSO PLAYED SOME PART IN HIS MAJESTY'S DEATH.
GISELLE WOULD NOT BETRAY US.
US? IT'S NOT US WHO IS DEAD.
REGARDLESS, WE MUST FIND HER. ANNA - WITH ME.
MATHILDE...
..HER HIGHNESS WILL NEED OUR COUNSEL.
STAY CLOSE TO HER...
OUR FAMILY'S SURVIVAL MAY DEPEND UPON HERS.
OH, AND MATHILDE?
"...TRY AND DO A BETTER JOB THAN YOUR TWIN SISTER DID."

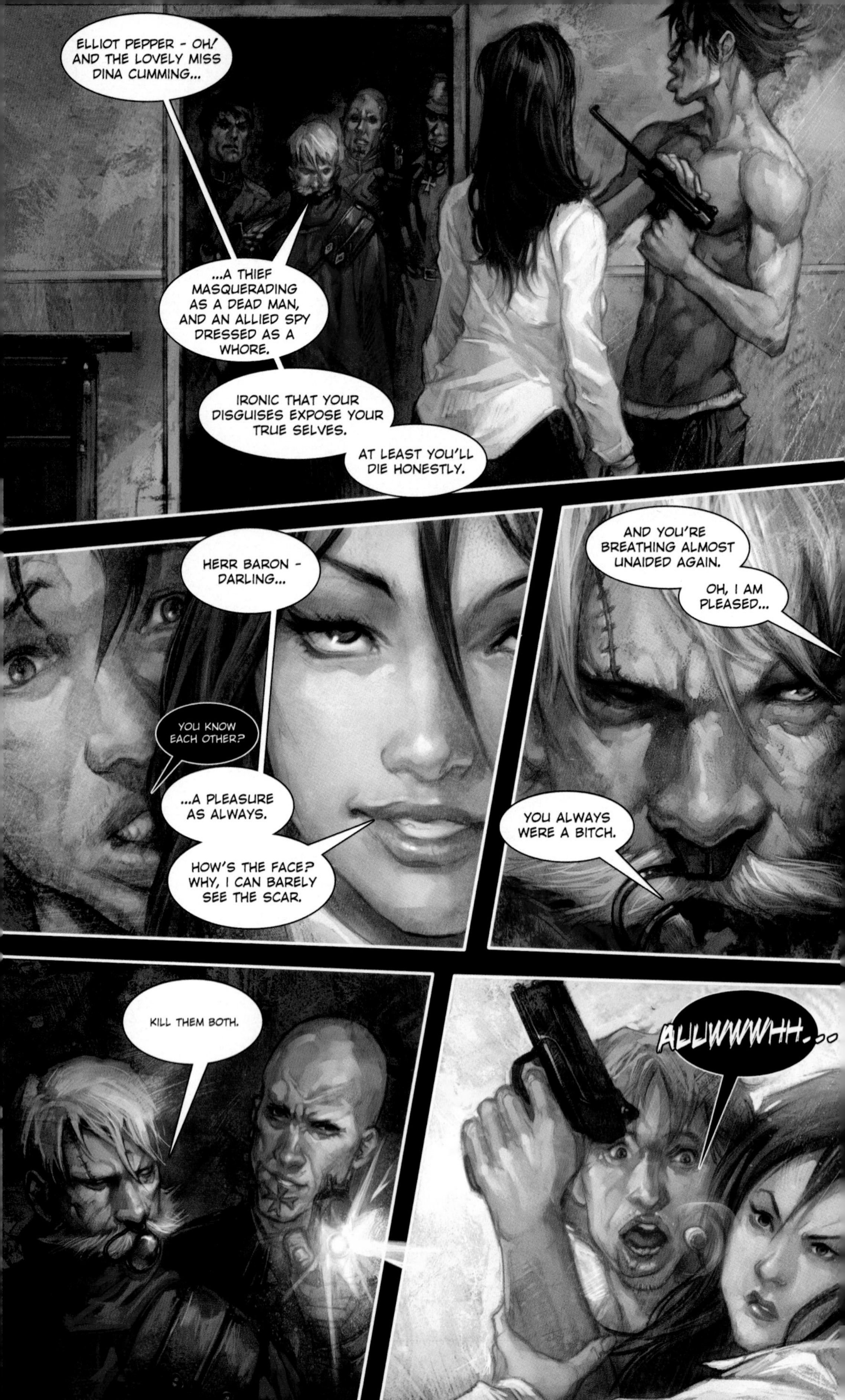
ELLIOT PEPPER - OH! AND THE LOVELY MISS DINA CUMMING...
...A THIEF MASQUERADING AS A DEAD MAN, AND AN ALLIED SPY DRESSED AS A WHORE.
IRONIC THAT YOUR DISGUISES EXPOSE YOUR TRUE SELVES.
AT LEAST YOU'LL DIE HONESTLY.
HERR BARON - DARLING...
YOU KNOW EACH OTHER?
...A PLEASURE AS ALWAYS.
HOW'S THE FACE? WHY, I CAN BARELY SEE THE SCAR.
AND YOU'RE BREATHING ALMOST UNAIDED AGAIN.
OH, I AM PLEASED...
YOU ALWAYS WERE A BITCH.
KILL THEM BOTH.
AUUWWWHH...

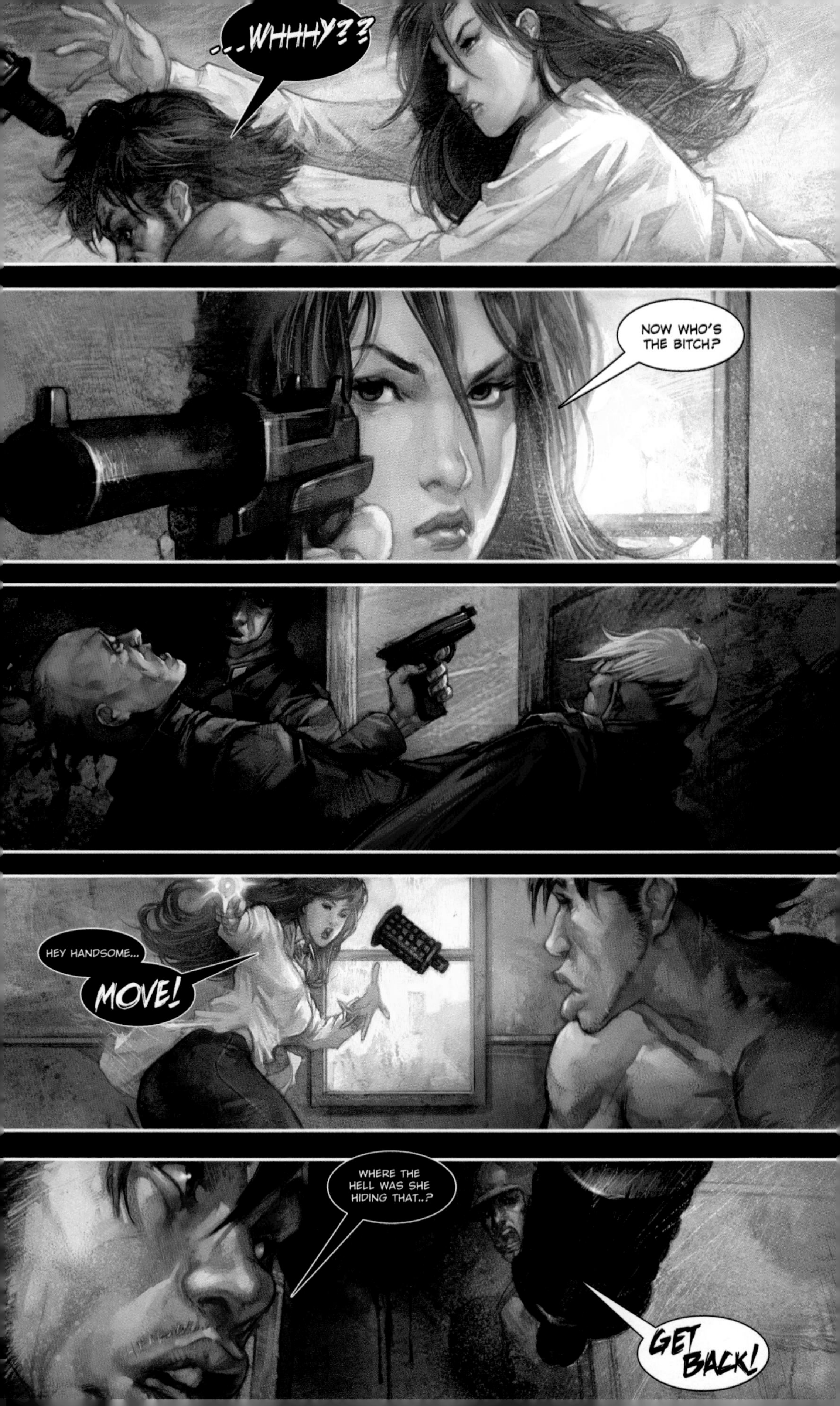
...WHHHY??
NOW WHO'S THE BITCH?
HEY HANDSOME...
MOVE!
WHERE THE HELL WAS SHE HIDING THAT..?
GET BACK!

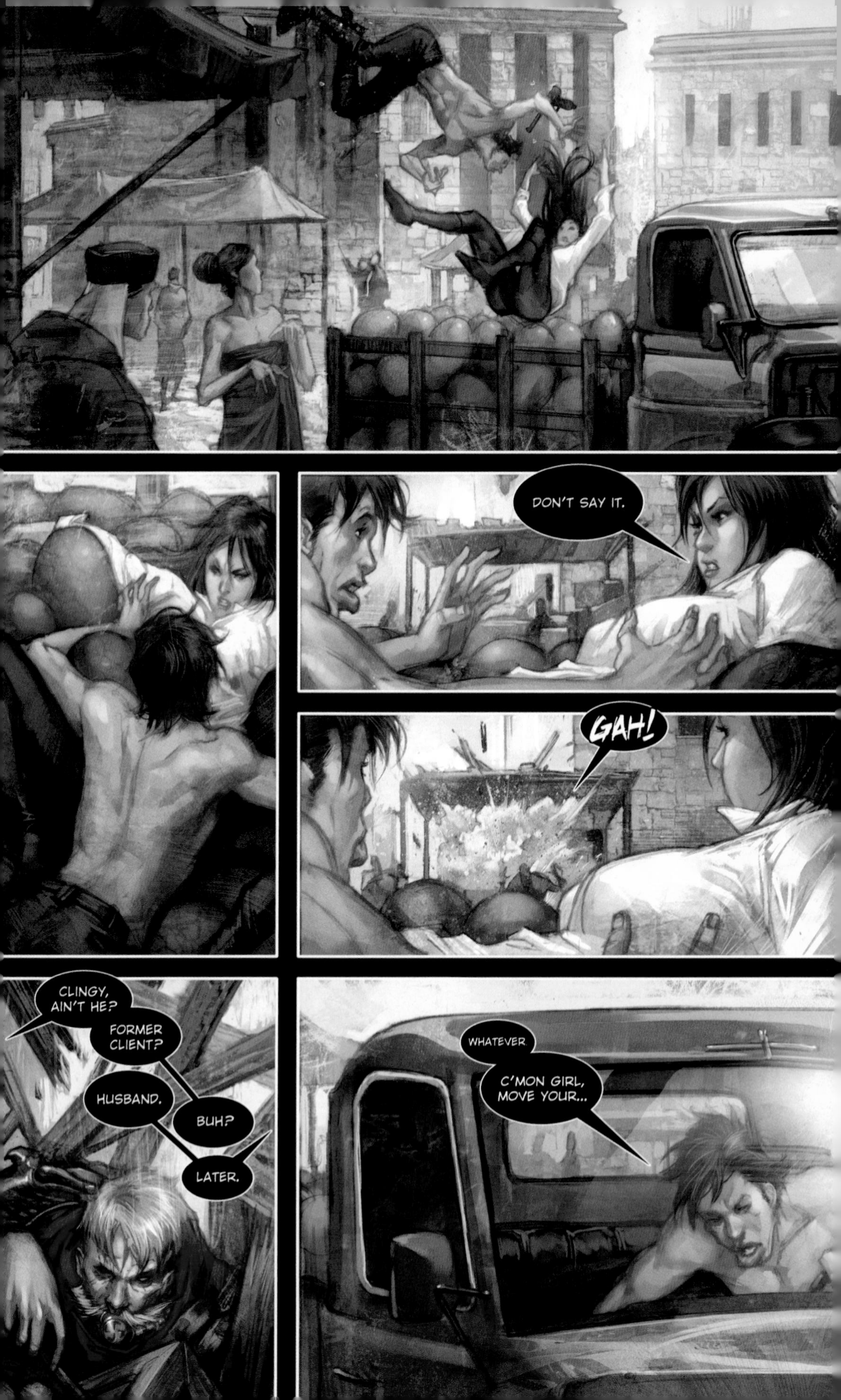
DON'T SAY IT.
GAH!
CLINGY, AIN'T HE?
FORMER CLIENT?
HUSBAND.
BUH?
LATER.
WHATEVER.
C'MON GIRL, MOVE YOUR...

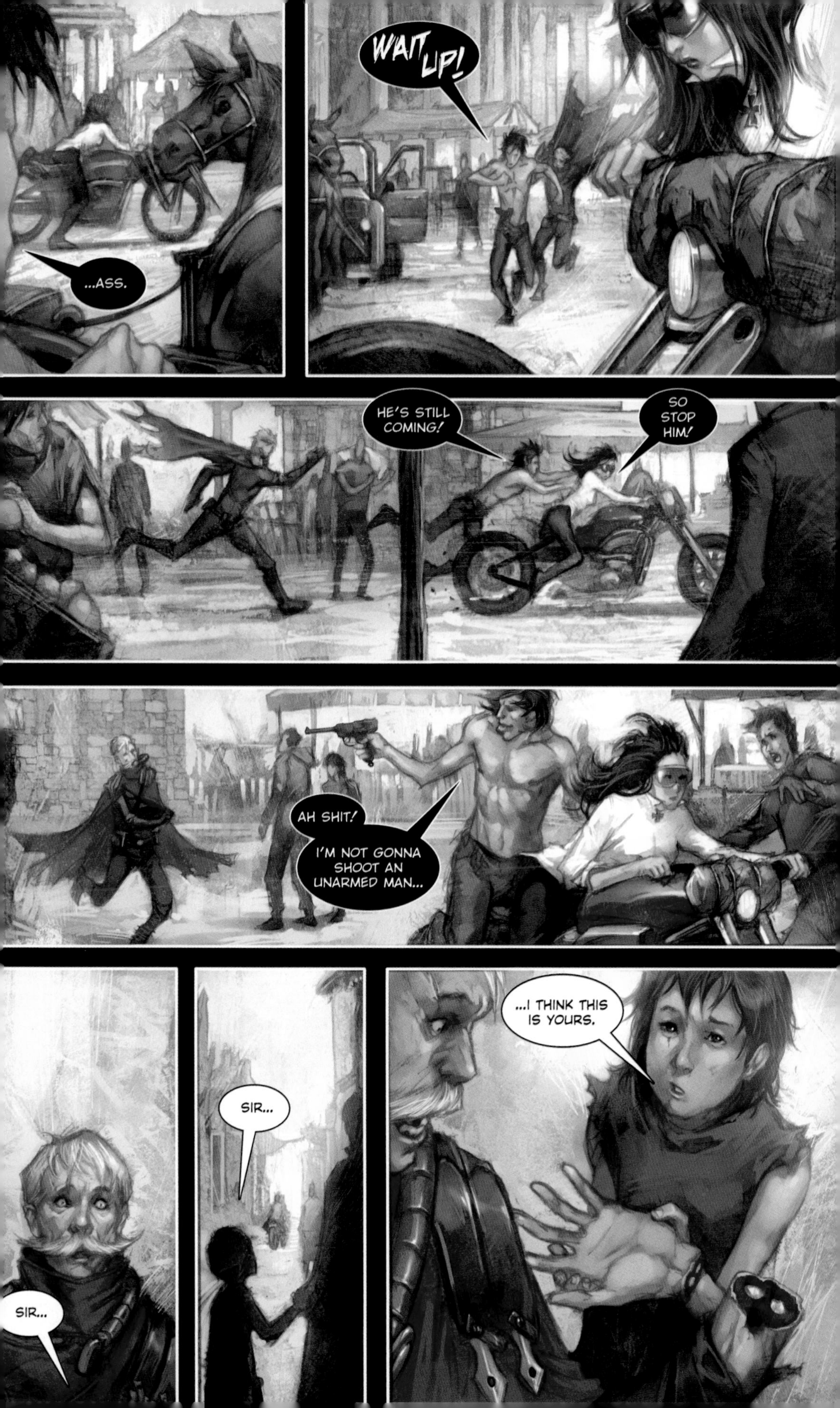
...ASS.
WAIT UP!
HE'S STILL COMING!
SO STOP HIM!
AH SHIT!
I'M NOT GONNA SHOOT AN UNARMED MAN...
SIR...
SIR...
...I THINK THIS IS YOURS.

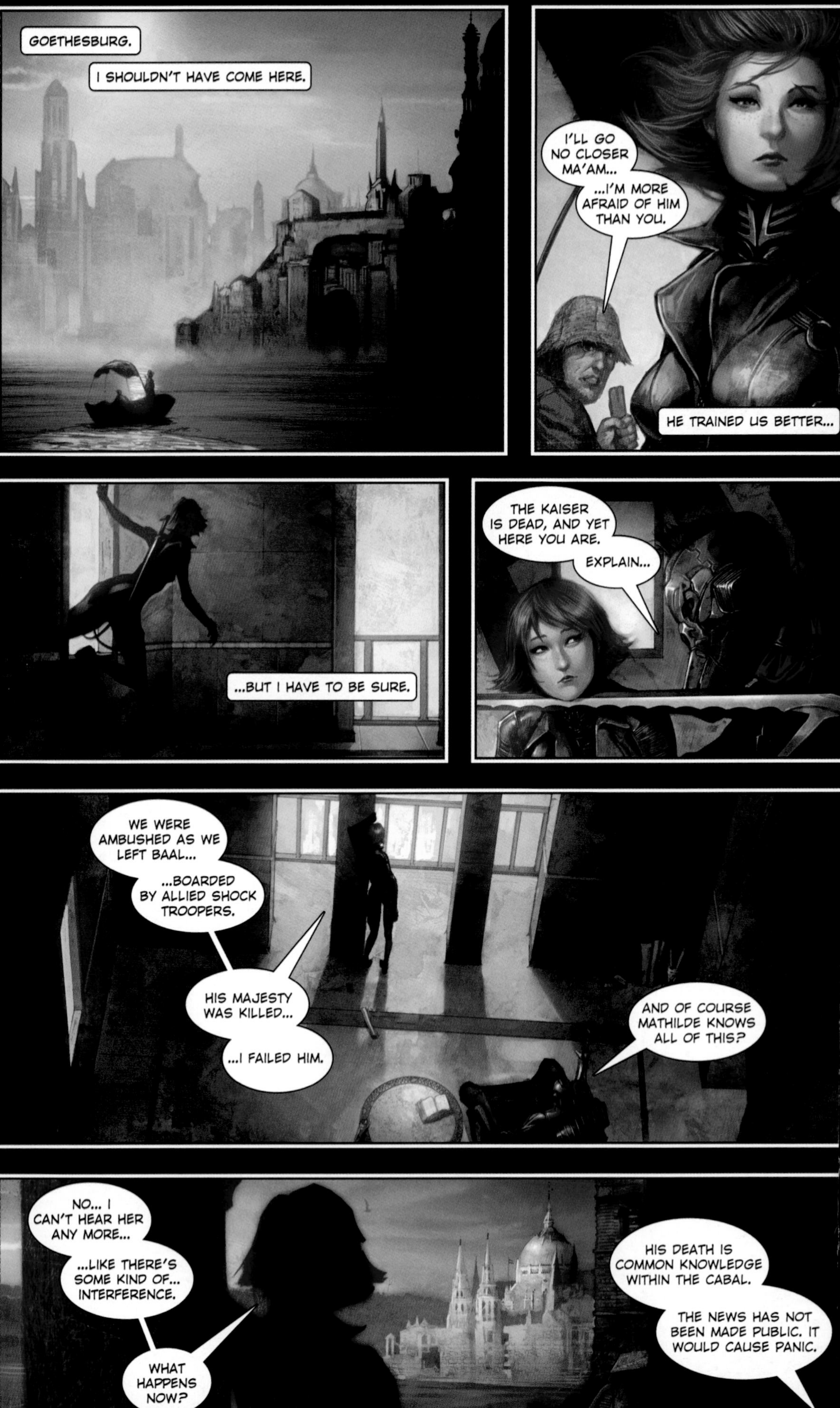
GOETHESBURG.
I SHOULDN'T HAVE COME HERE.
I'LL GO NO CLOSER MA'AM...
...I'M MORE AFRAID OF HIM THAN YOU.
HE TRAINED US BETTER...
...BUT I HAVE TO BE SURE.
THE KAISER IS DEAD, AND YET HERE YOU ARE.
EXPLAIN...
WE WERE AMBUSHED AS WE LEFT BAAL...
...BOARDED BY ALLIED SHOCK TROOPERS.
HIS MAJESTY WAS KILLED...
...I FAILED HIM.
AND OF COURSE MATHILDE KNOWS ALL OF THIS?
NO... I CAN'T HEAR HER ANY MORE...
...LIKE THERE'S SOME KIND OF... INTERFERENCE.
WHAT HAPPENS NOW?
HIS DEATH IS COMMON KNOWLEDGE WITHIN THE CABAL.
THE NEWS HAS NOT BEEN MADE PUBLIC. IT WOULD CAUSE PANIC.

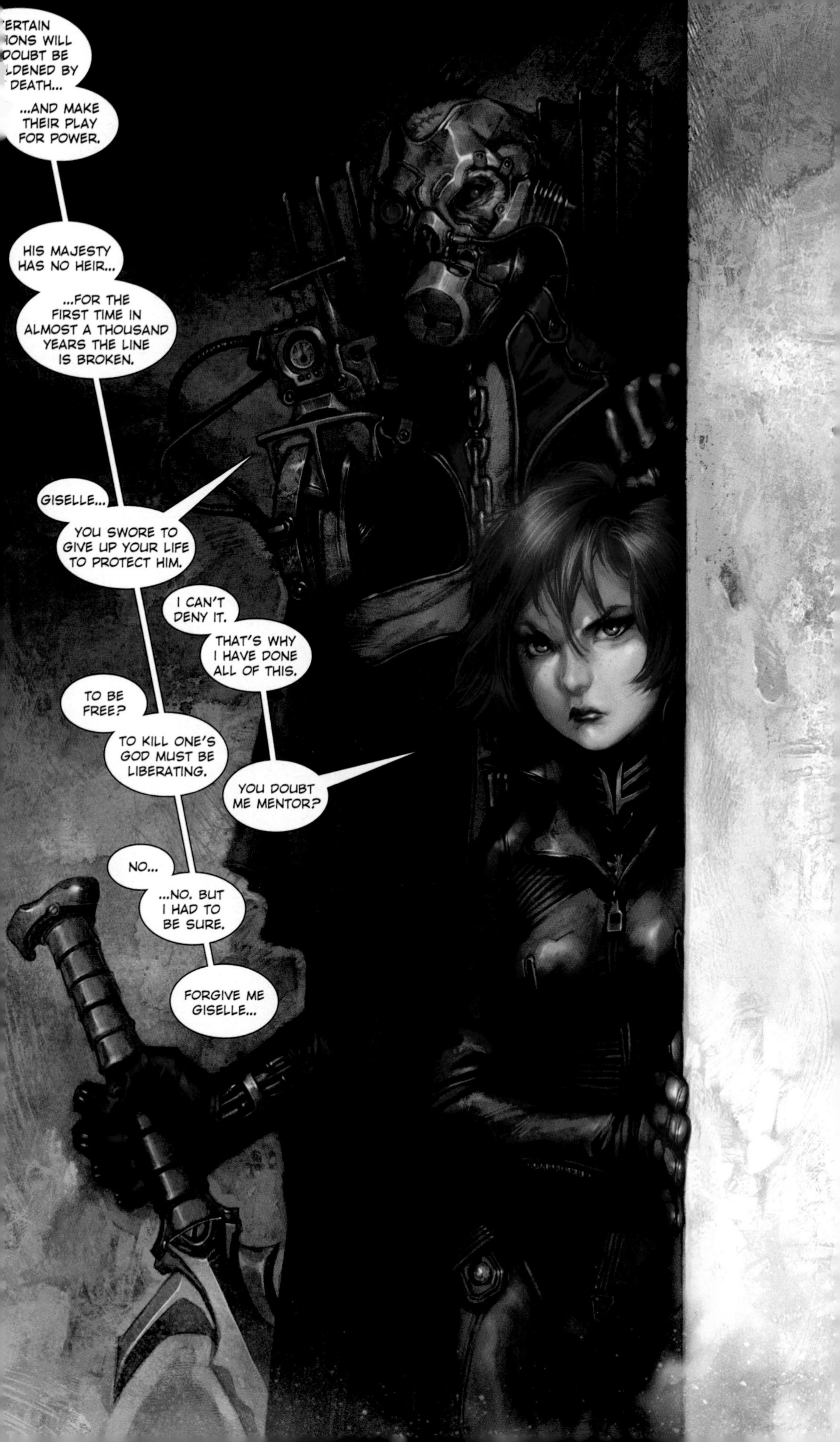

ERTAIN IONS WILL DOUBT BE LDENED BY DEATH...
...AND MAKE THEIR PLAY FOR POWER.
HIS MAJESTY HAS NO HEIR...
...FOR THE FIRST TIME IN ALMOST A THOUSAND YEARS THE LINE IS BROKEN.
GISELLE...
YOU SWORE TO GIVE UP YOUR LIFE TO PROTECT HIM.
I CAN'T DENY IT.
THAT'S WHY I HAVE DONE ALL OF THIS.
TO BE FREE?
TO KILL ONE'S GOD MUST BE LIBERATING.
YOU DOUBT ME MENTOR?
NO...
...NO. BUT I HAD TO BE SURE.
FORGIVE ME GISELLE...

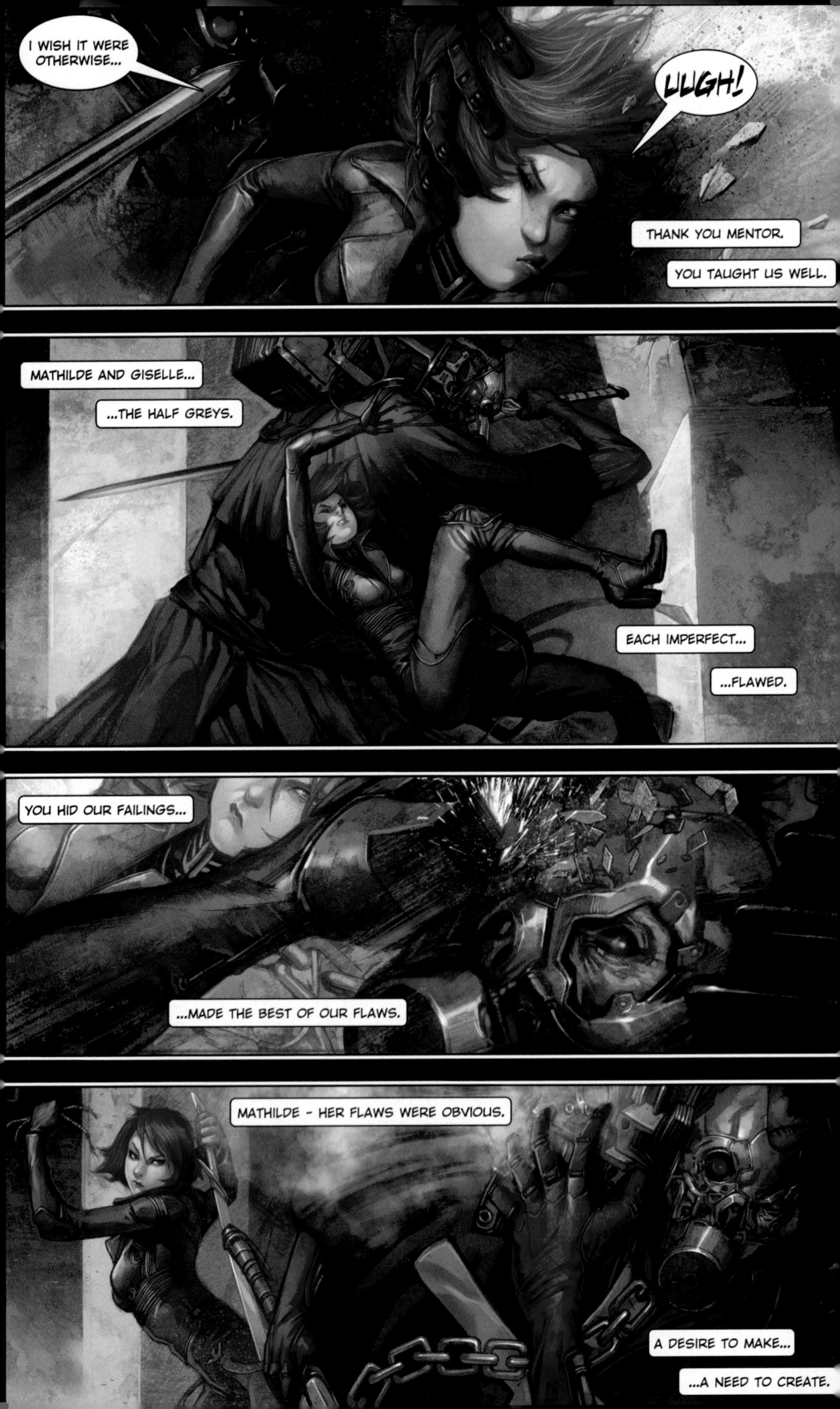
I WISH IT WERE OTHERWISE...
UUGH!
THANK YOU MENTOR.
YOU TAUGHT US WELL.
MATHILDE AND GISELLE...
...THE HALF GREYS.
EACH IMPERFECT...
...FLAWED.
YOU HID OUR FAILINGS...
...MADE THE BEST OF OUR FLAWS.
MATHILDE - HER FLAWS WERE OBVIOUS.
A DESIRE TO MAKE...
...A NEED TO CREATE.

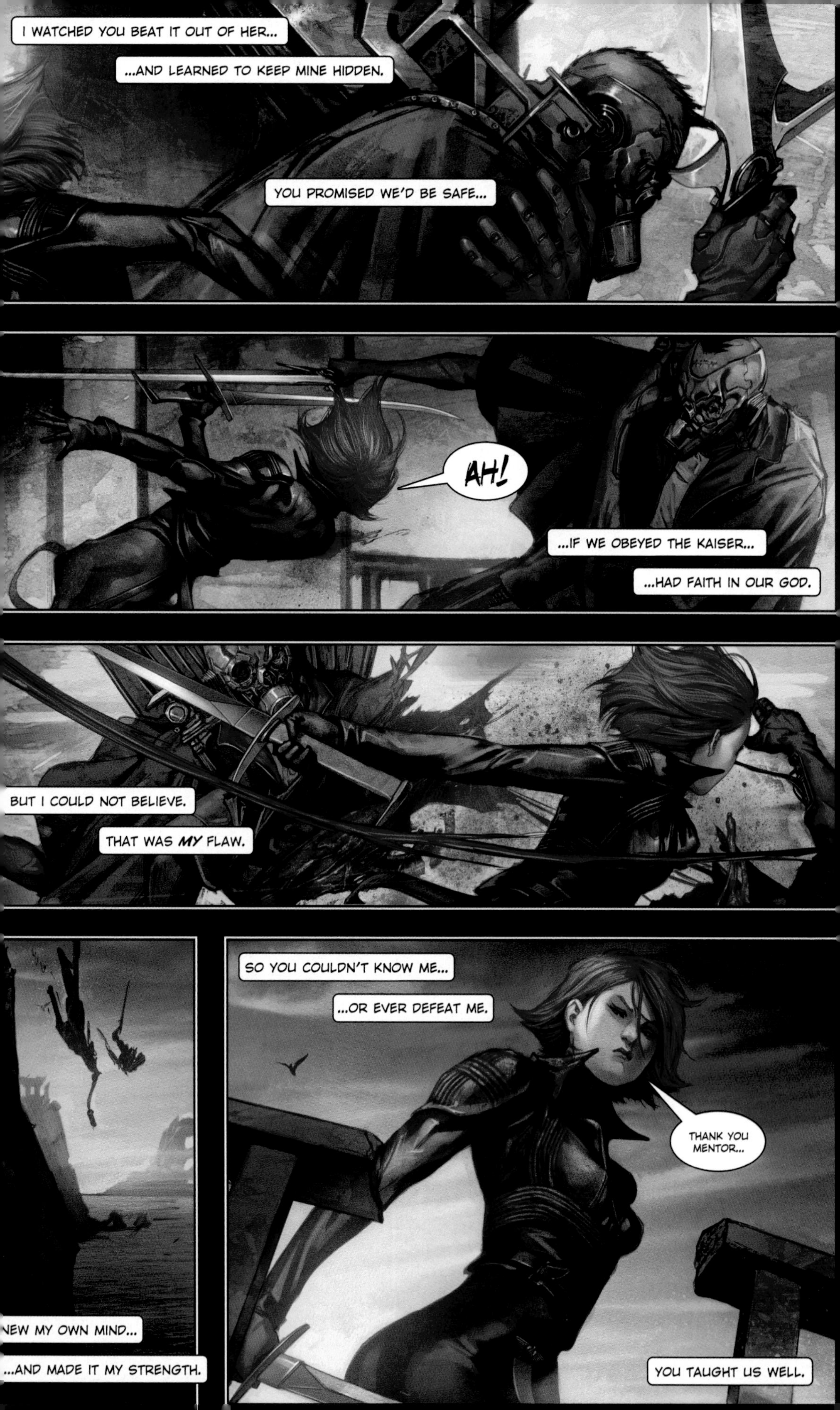
I WATCHED YOU BEAT IT OUT OF HER...
...AND LEARNED TO KEEP MINE HIDDEN.
YOU PROMISED WE'D BE SAFE...
AH!
...IF WE OBEYED THE KAISER...
...HAD FAITH IN OUR GOD.
BUT I COULD NOT BELIEVE.
THAT WAS *MY* FLAW.
NEW MY OWN MIND...
...AND MADE IT MY STRENGTH.
SO YOU COULDN'T KNOW ME...
...OR EVER DEFEAT ME.
THANK YOU MENTOR...
YOU TAUGHT US WELL.

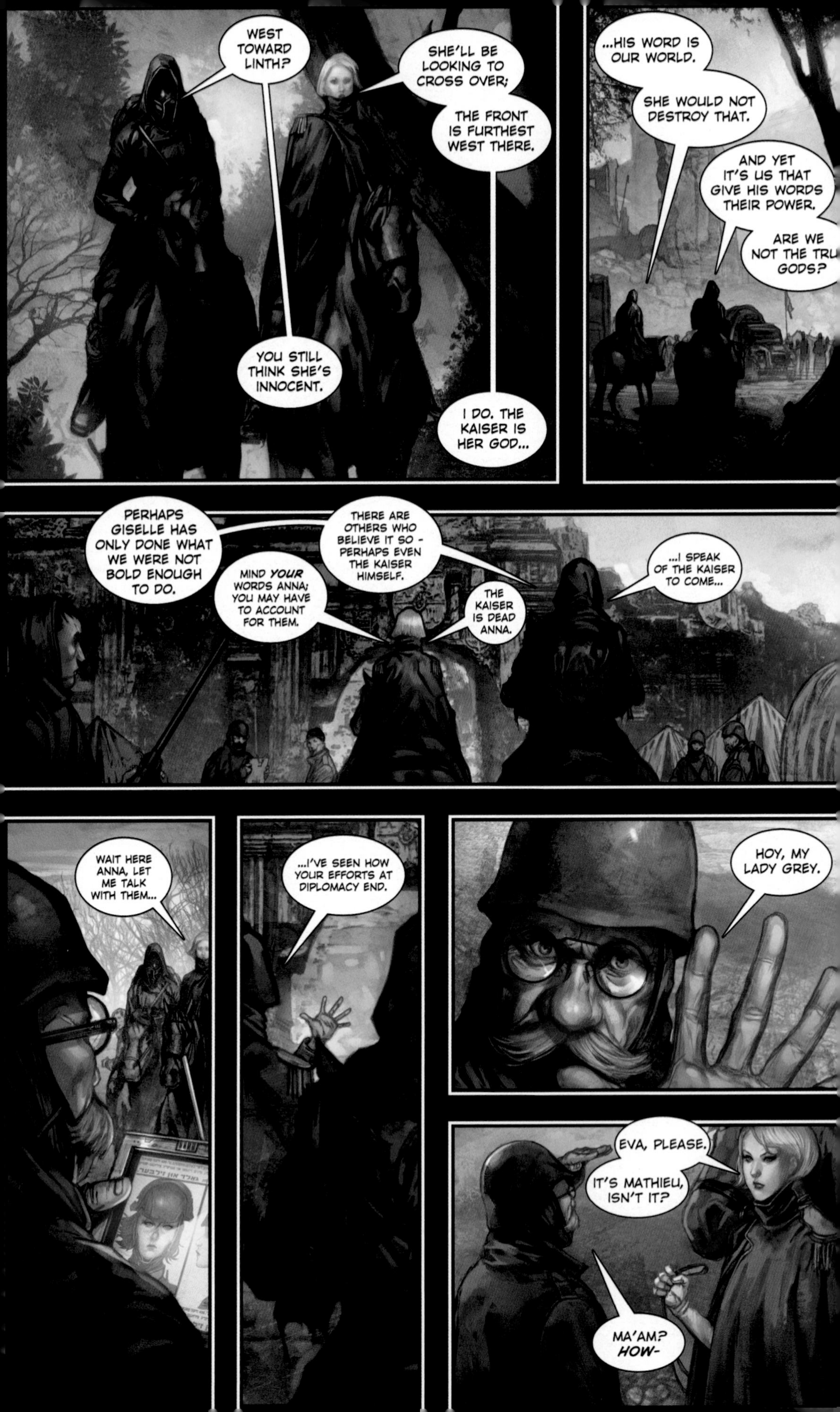

WEST TOWARD LINTH?
SHE'LL BE LOOKING TO CROSS OVER;
THE FRONT IS FURTHEST WEST THERE.
YOU STILL THINK SHE'S INNOCENT.
I DO. THE KAISER IS HER GOD...
...HIS WORD IS OUR WORLD.
SHE WOULD NOT DESTROY THAT.
AND YET IT'S US THAT GIVE HIS WORDS THEIR POWER.
ARE WE NOT THE TRU GODS?
PERHAPS GISELLE HAS ONLY DONE WHAT WE WERE NOT BOLD ENOUGH TO DO.
MIND *YOUR* WORDS ANNA; YOU MAY HAVE TO ACCOUNT FOR THEM.
THERE ARE OTHERS WHO BELIEVE IT SO - PERHAPS EVEN THE KAISER HIMSELF.
THE KAISER IS DEAD ANNA.
...I SPEAK OF THE KAISER TO COME...
WAIT HERE ANNA, LET ME TALK WITH THEM...
...I'VE SEEN HOW YOUR EFFORTS AT DIPLOMACY END.
HOY, MY LADY GREY.
EVA, PLEASE.
IT'S MATHIEU, ISN'T IT?
MA'AM? *HOW-*

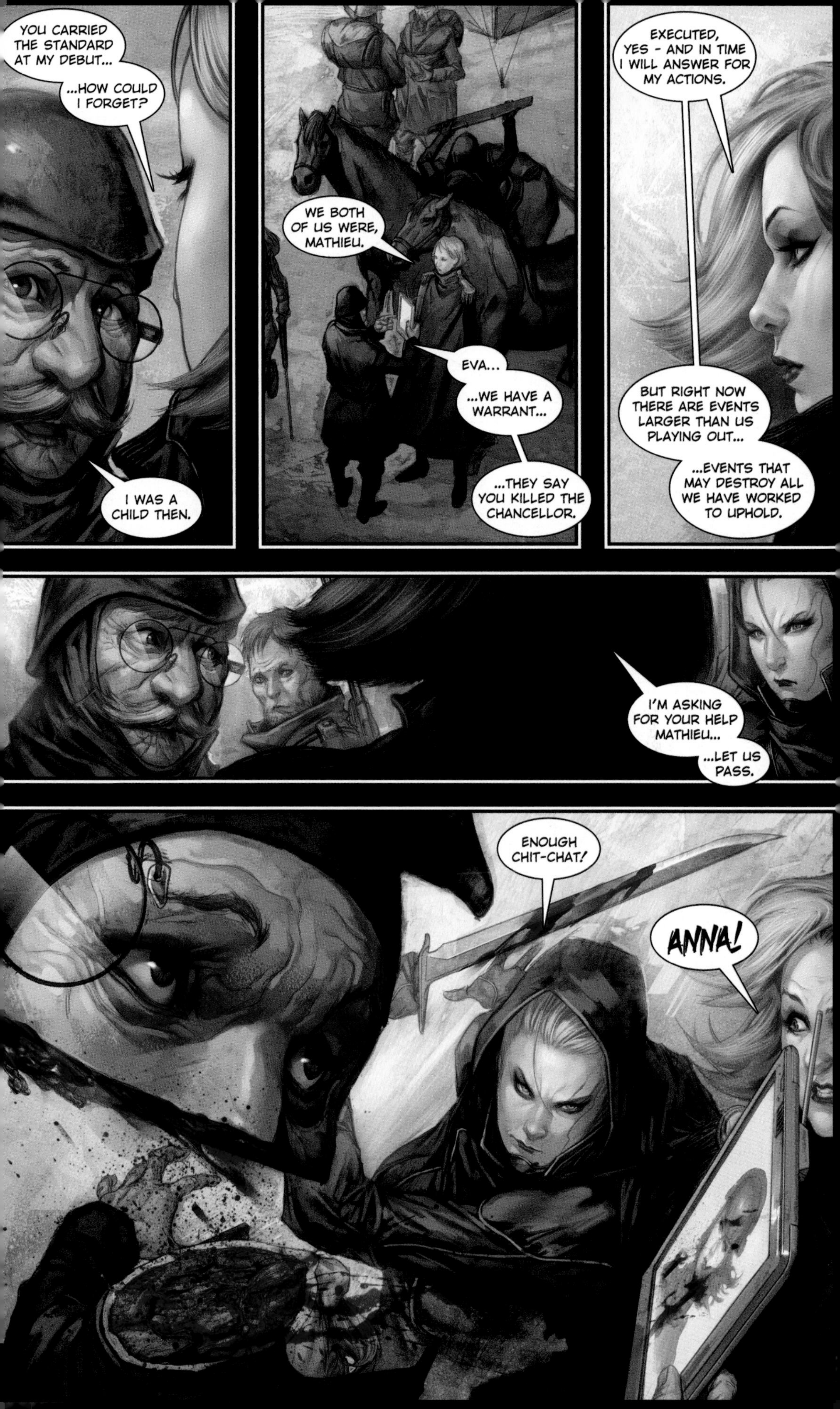
YOU CARRIED THE STANDARD AT MY DEBUT...
...HOW COULD I FORGET?
I WAS A CHILD THEN.
WE BOTH OF US WERE, MATHIEU.
EVA...
...WE HAVE A WARRANT...
...THEY SAY YOU KILLED THE CHANCELLOR.
EXECUTED, YES - AND IN TIME I WILL ANSWER FOR MY ACTIONS.
BUT RIGHT NOW THERE ARE EVENTS LARGER THAN US PLAYING OUT...
...EVENTS THAT MAY DESTROY ALL WE HAVE WORKED TO UPHOLD.
I'M ASKING FOR YOUR HELP MATHIEU...
...LET US PASS.
ENOUGH CHIT-CHAT!
ANNA!

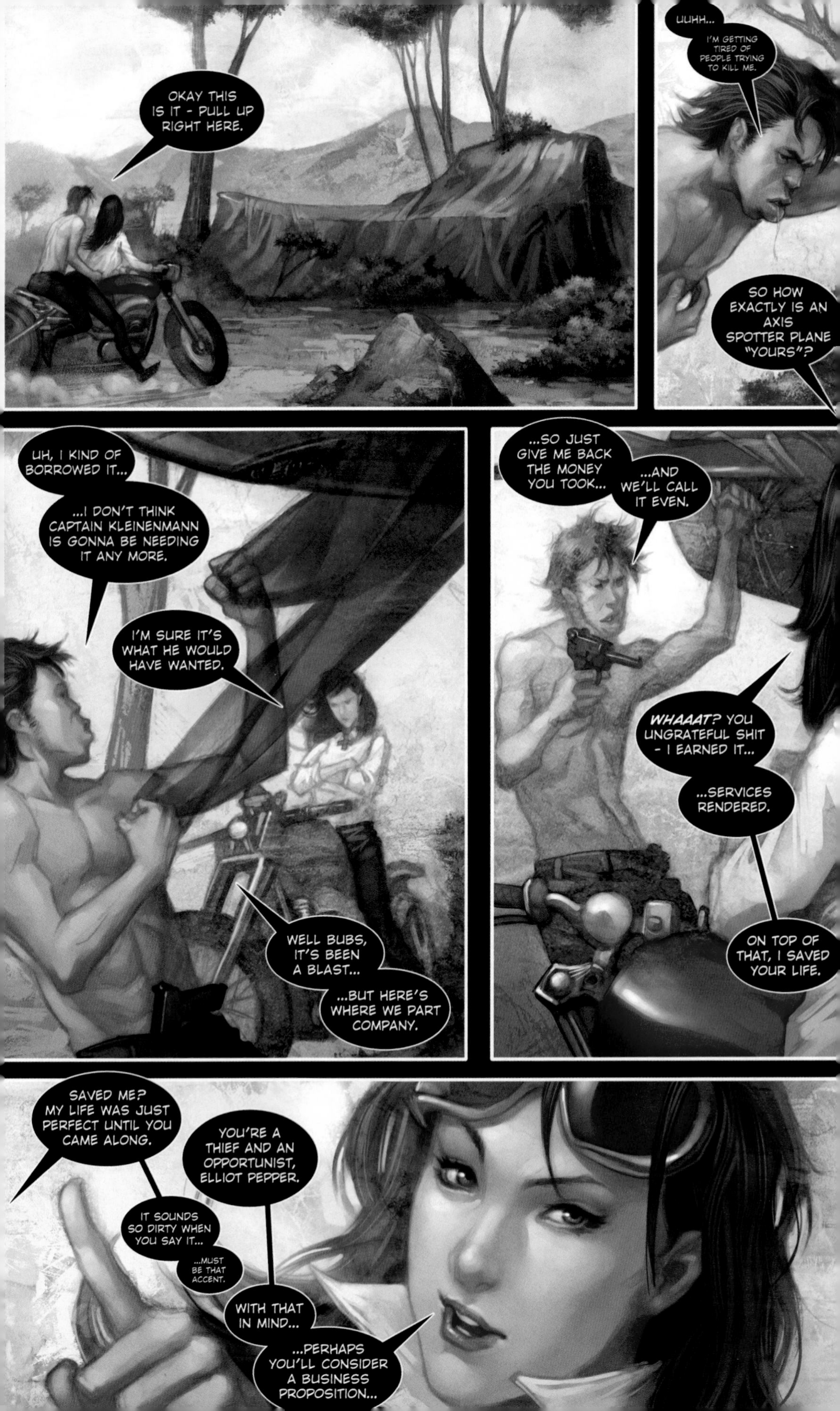

OKAY THIS IS IT - PULL UP RIGHT HERE.
UUHH...
I'M GETTING TIRED OF PEOPLE TRYING TO KILL ME.
SO HOW EXACTLY IS AN AXIS SPOTTER PLANE "YOURS"?
UH, I KIND OF BORROWED IT...
...I DON'T THINK CAPTAIN KLEINENMANN IS GONNA BE NEEDING IT ANY MORE.
I'M SURE IT'S WHAT HE WOULD HAVE WANTED.
WELL BUBS, IT'S BEEN A BLAST...
...BUT HERE'S WHERE WE PART COMPANY.
...SO JUST GIVE ME BACK THE MONEY YOU TOOK...
...AND WE'LL CALL IT EVEN.
WHAAAT? YOU UNGRATEFUL SHIT - I EARNED IT...
...SERVICES RENDERED.
ON TOP OF THAT, I SAVED YOUR LIFE.
SAVED ME? MY LIFE WAS JUST PERFECT UNTIL YOU CAME ALONG.
YOU'RE A THIEF AND AN OPPORTUNIST, ELLIOT PEPPER.
IT SOUNDS SO DIRTY WHEN YOU SAY IT...
...MUST BE THAT ACCENT.
WITH THAT IN MIND...
...PERHAPS YOU'LL CONSIDER A BUSINESS PROPOSITION...

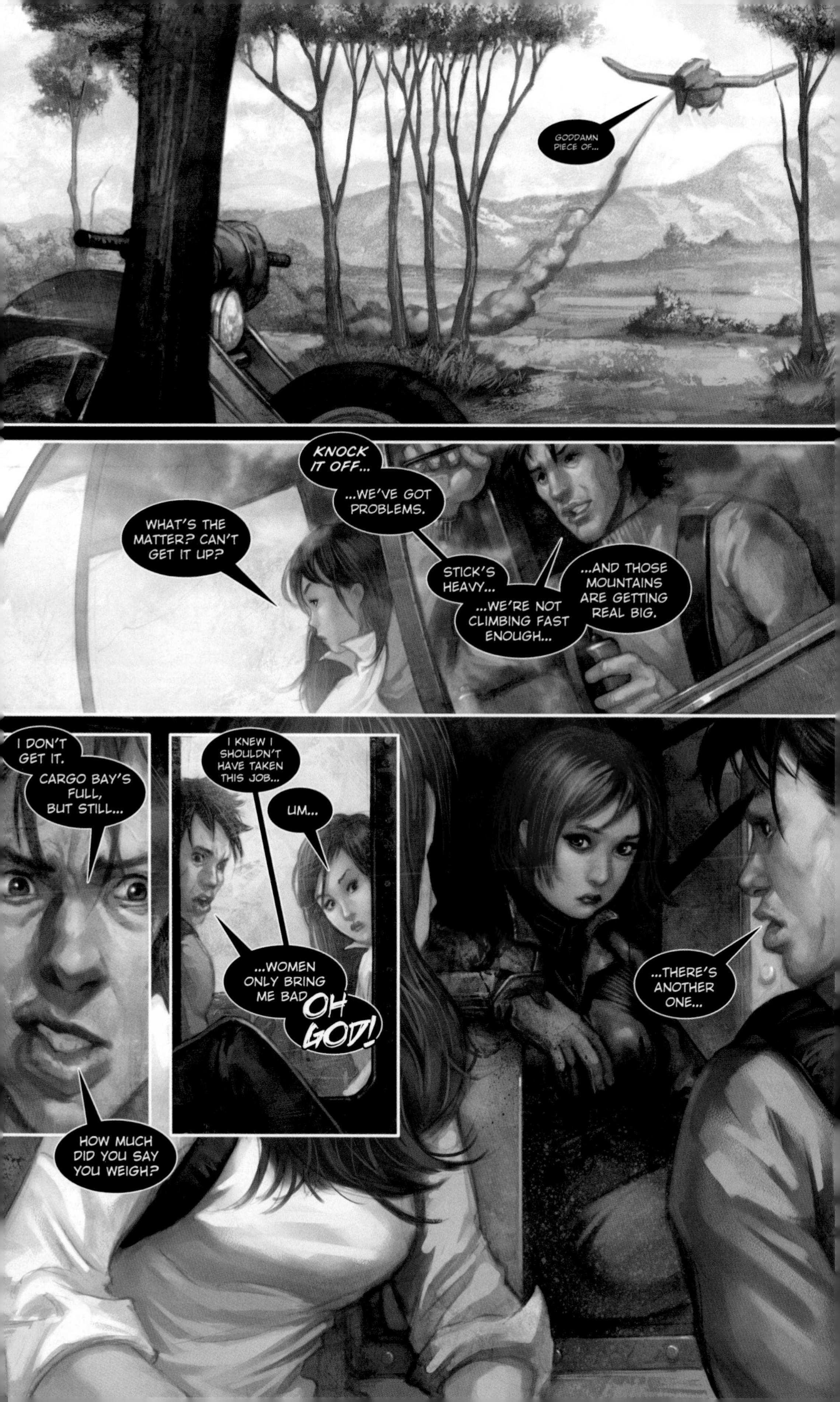
GODDAMN PIECE OF...
KNOCK IT OFF...
...WE'VE GOT PROBLEMS.
WHAT'S THE MATTER? CAN'T GET IT UP?
STICK'S HEAVY...
...WE'RE NOT CLIMBING FAST ENOUGH...
...AND THOSE MOUNTAINS ARE GETTING REAL BIG.
I DON'T GET IT.
CARGO BAY'S FULL, BUT STILL...
HOW MUCH DID YOU SAY YOU WEIGH?
I KNEW I SHOULDN'T HAVE TAKEN THIS JOB...
UM...
...WOMEN ONLY BRING ME BAD
OH GOD!
...THERE'S ANOTHER ONE...

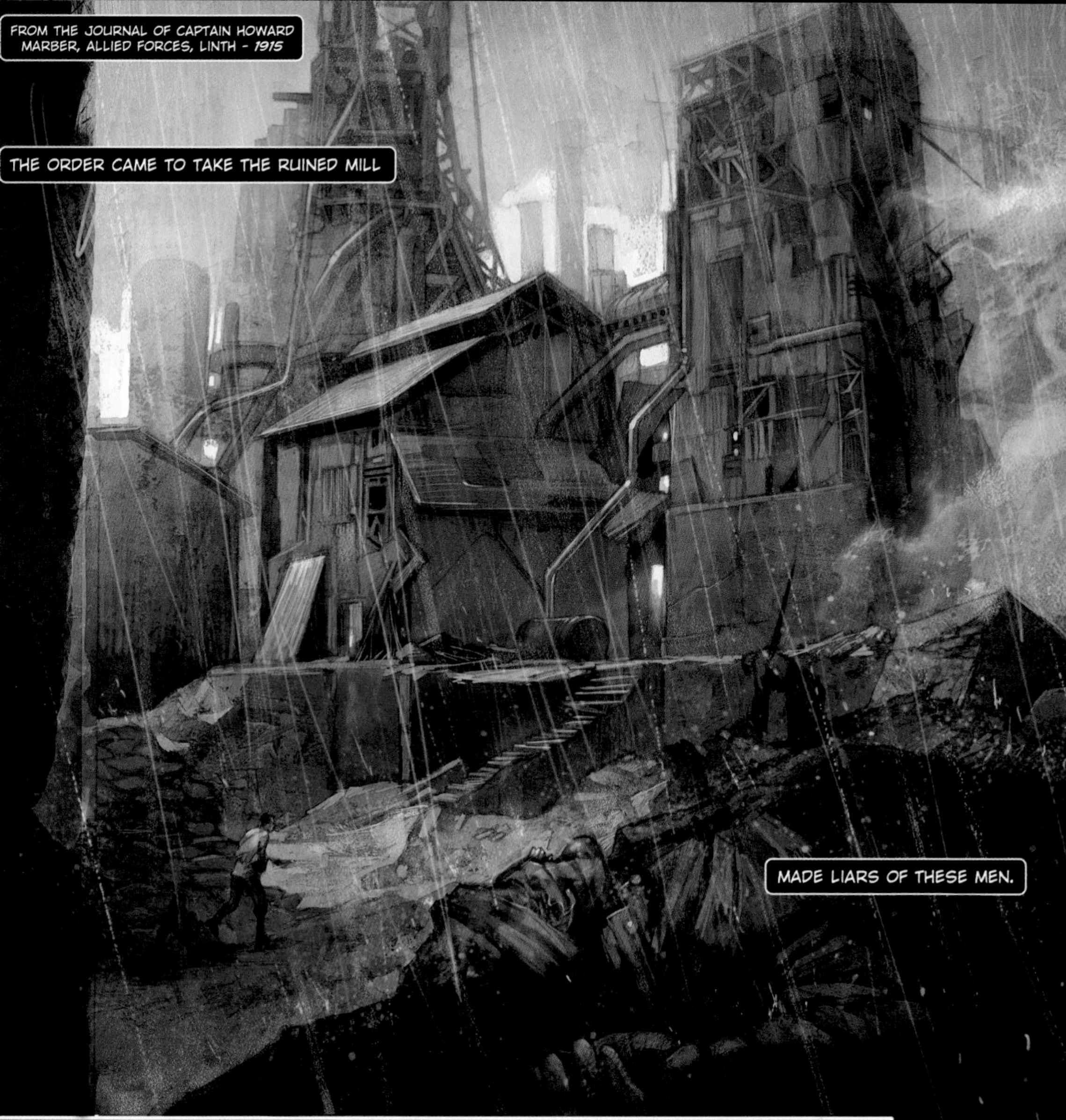
FROM THE JOURNAL OF CAPTAIN HOWARD MARBER, ALLIED FORCES, LINTH - *1915*
THE ORDER CAME TO TAKE THE RUINED MILL
MADE LIARS OF THESE MEN.

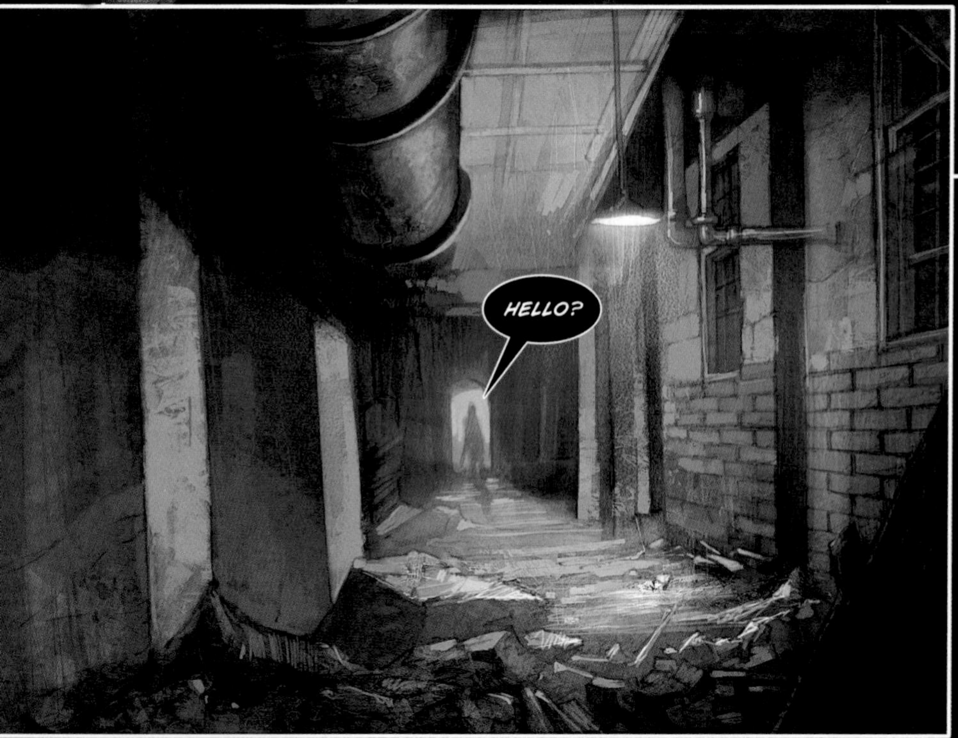
HELLO?

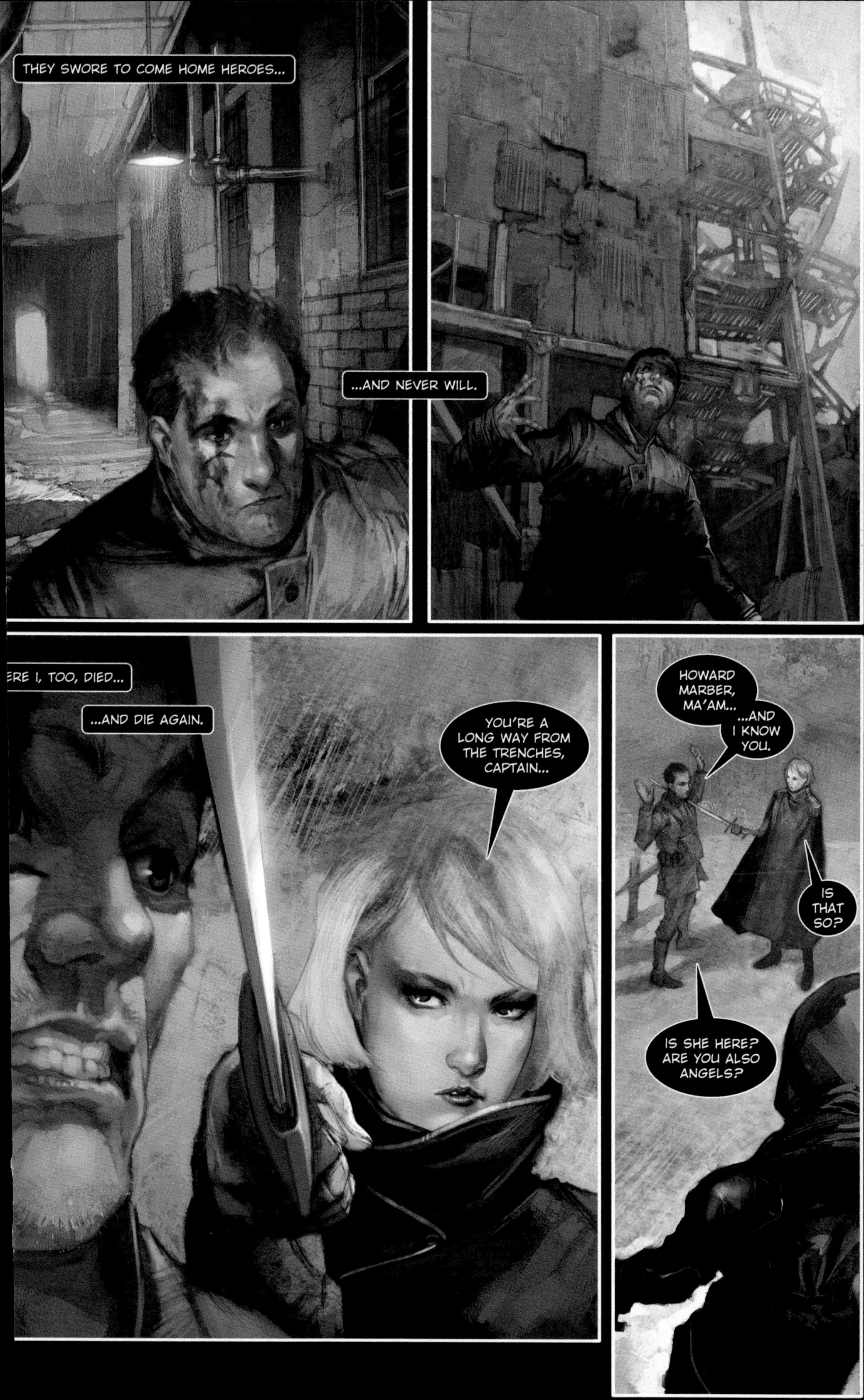
THEY SWORE TO COME HOME HEROES...
...AND NEVER WILL.
ERE I, TOO, DIED...
...AND DIE AGAIN.
YOU'RE A LONG WAY FROM THE TRENCHES, CAPTAIN...
HOWARD MARBER, MA'AM...
...AND I KNOW YOU.
IS THAT SO?
IS SHE HERE? ARE YOU ALSO ANGELS?

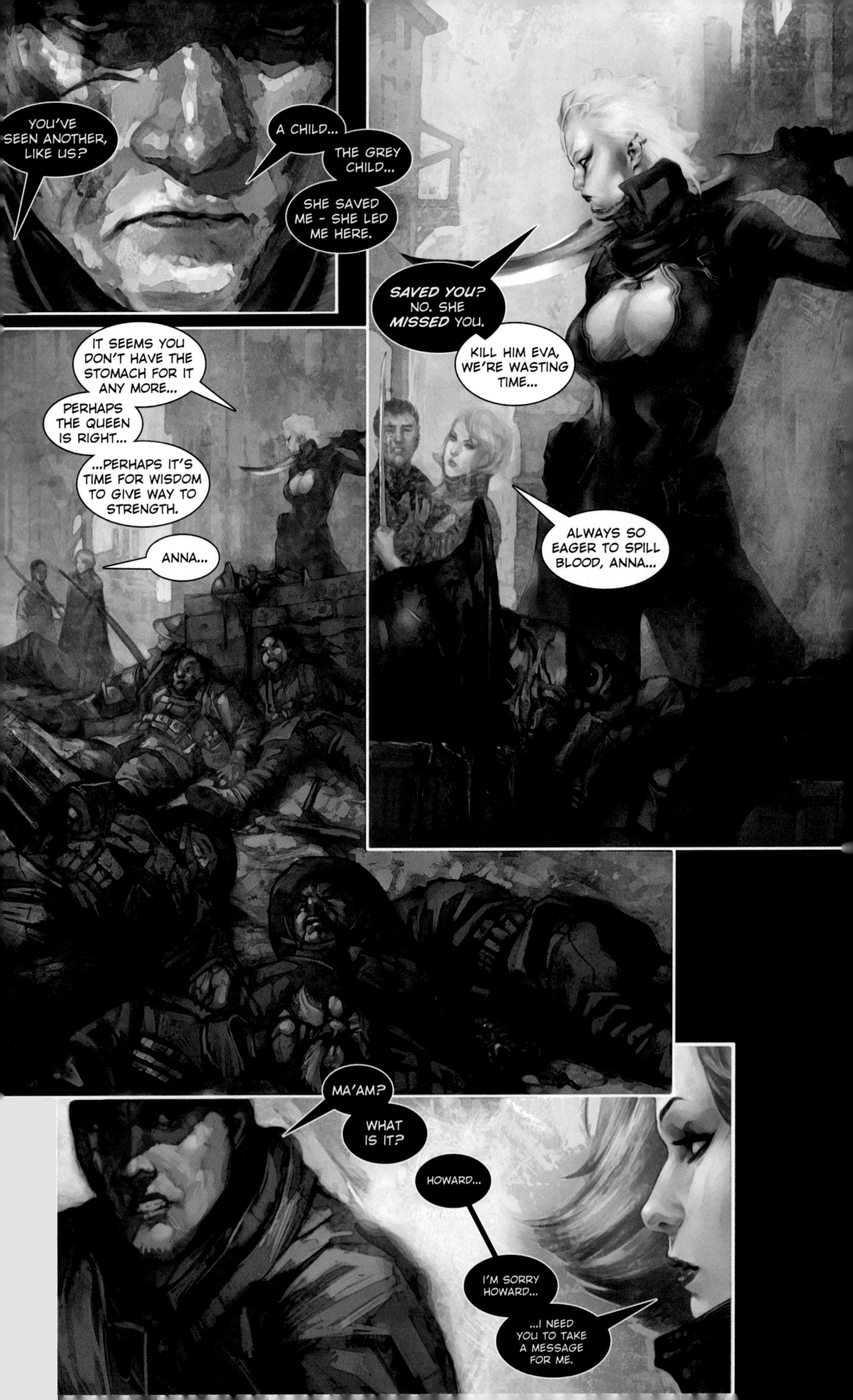
YOU'VE SEEN ANOTHER, LIKE US?
A CHILD...
THE GREY CHILD...
SHE SAVED ME - SHE LED ME HERE.
SAVED YOU? NO. SHE *MISSED* YOU.
KILL HIM EVA, WE'RE WASTING TIME...
ALWAYS SO EAGER TO SPILL BLOOD, ANNA...
IT SEEMS YOU DON'T HAVE THE STOMACH FOR IT ANY MORE...
PERHAPS THE QUEEN IS RIGHT...
...PERHAPS IT'S TIME FOR WISDOM TO GIVE WAY TO STRENGTH.
ANNA...
MA'AM?
WHAT IS IT?
HOWARD...
I'M SORRY HOWARD...
...I NEED YOU TO TAKE A MESSAGE FOR ME.

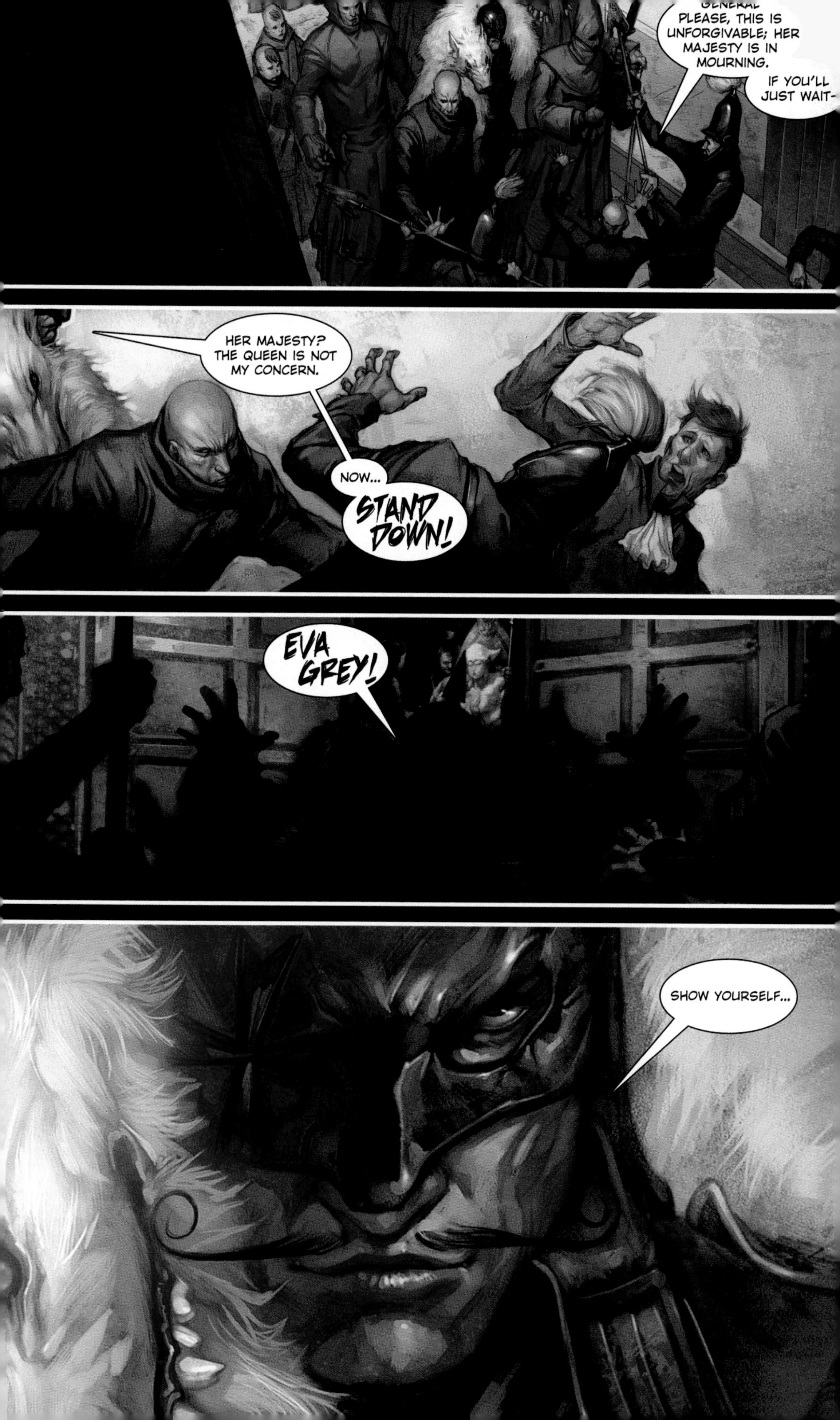
PLEASE, THIS IS UNFORGIVABLE; HER MAJESTY IS IN MOURNING.
IF YOU'LL JUST WAIT-
HER MAJESTY? THE QUEEN IS NOT MY CONCERN.
NOW...
STAND DOWN!
EVA GREY!
SHOW YOURSELF...

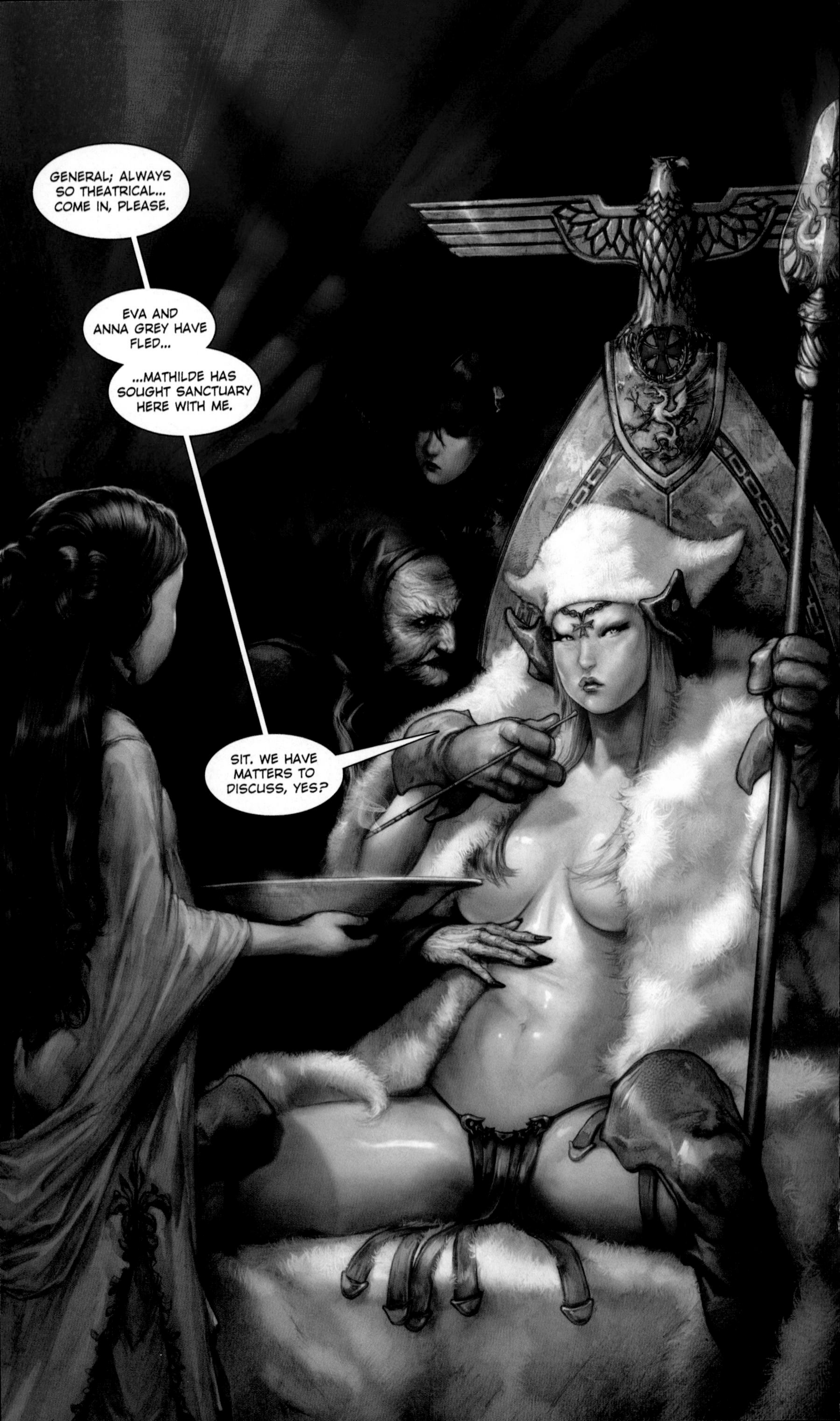
GENERAL; ALWAYS SO THEATRICAL... COME IN, PLEASE.
EVA AND ANNA GREY HAVE FLED...
...MATHILDE HAS SOUGHT SANCTUARY HERE WITH ME.
SIT. WE HAVE MATTERS TO DISCUSS, YES?

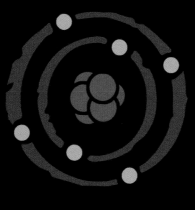

III

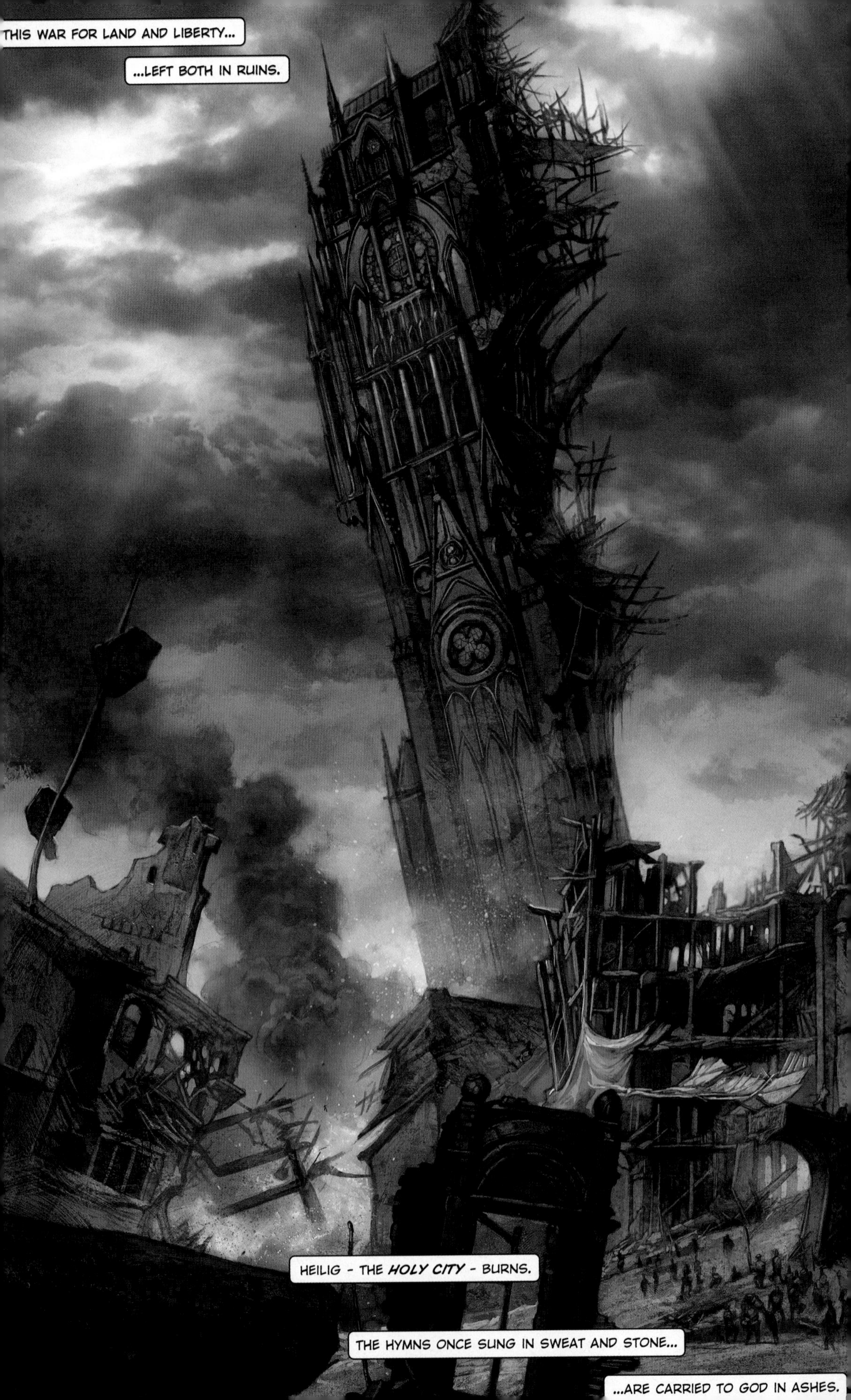
THIS WAR FOR LAND AND LIBERTY...
...LEFT BOTH IN RUINS.
HEILIG - THE *HOLY CITY* - BURNS.
THE HYMNS ONCE SUNG IN SWEAT AND STONE...
...ARE CARRIED TO GOD IN ASHES.

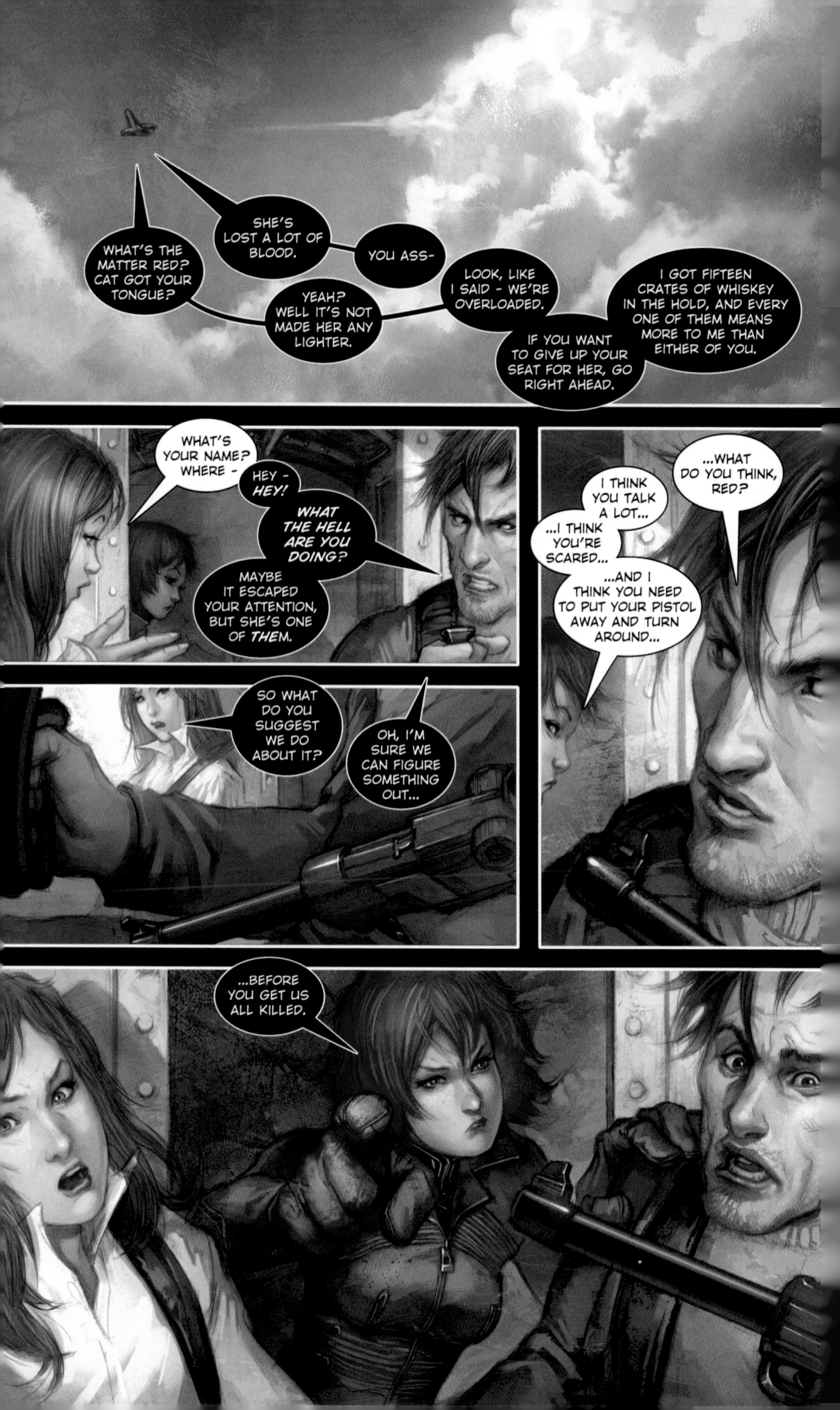

WHAT'S THE MATTER RED? CAT GOT YOUR TONGUE?
SHE'S LOST A LOT OF BLOOD.
YOU ASS-
YEAH? WELL IT'S NOT MADE HER ANY LIGHTER.
LOOK, LIKE I SAID - WE'RE OVERLOADED.
IF YOU WANT TO GIVE UP YOUR SEAT FOR HER, GO RIGHT AHEAD.
I GOT FIFTEEN CRATES OF WHISKEY IN THE HOLD, AND EVERY ONE OF THEM MEANS MORE TO ME THAN EITHER OF YOU.
WHAT'S YOUR NAME? WHERE -
HEY - *HEY!*
WHAT THE HELL ARE YOU DOING?
MAYBE IT ESCAPED YOUR ATTENTION, BUT SHE'S ONE OF *THEM*.
SO WHAT DO YOU SUGGEST WE DO ABOUT IT?
OH, I'M SURE WE CAN FIGURE SOMETHING OUT...
...WHAT DO YOU THINK, RED?
I THINK YOU TALK A LOT...
...I THINK YOU'RE SCARED...
...AND I THINK YOU NEED TO PUT YOUR PISTOL AWAY AND TURN AROUND...
...BEFORE YOU GET US ALL KILLED.

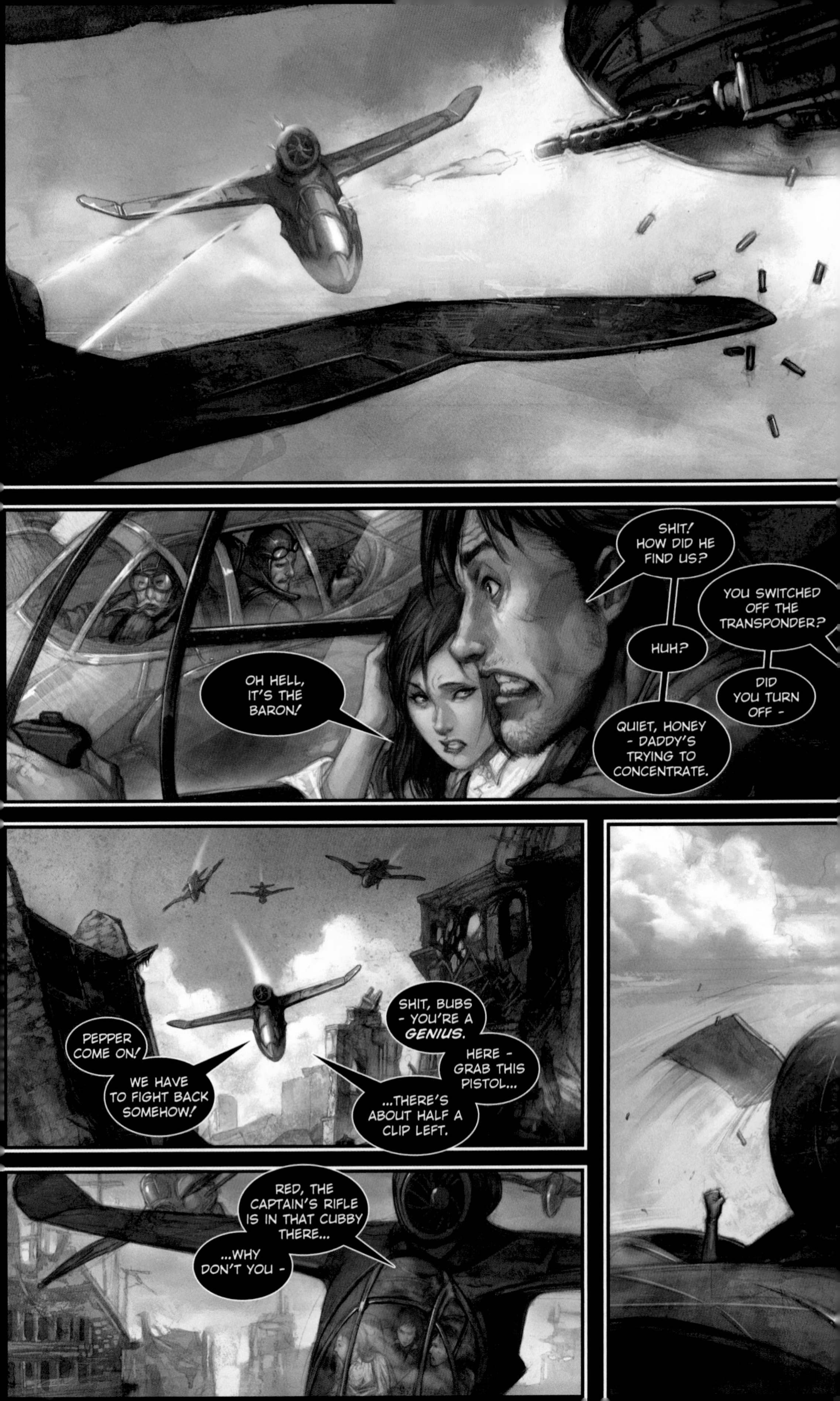
SHIT! HOW DID HE FIND US?
YOU SWITCHED OFF THE TRANSPONDER?
HUH?
DID YOU TURN OFF -
OH HELL, IT'S THE BARON!
QUIET, HONEY - DADDY'S TRYING TO CONCENTRATE.
PEPPER COME ON!
WE HAVE TO FIGHT BACK SOMEHOW!
SHIT, BUBS - YOU'RE A GENIUS.
HERE - GRAB THIS PISTOL...
...THERE'S ABOUT HALF A CLIP LEFT.
RED, THE CAPTAIN'S RIFLE IS IN THAT CUBBY THERE...
...WHY DON'T YOU -

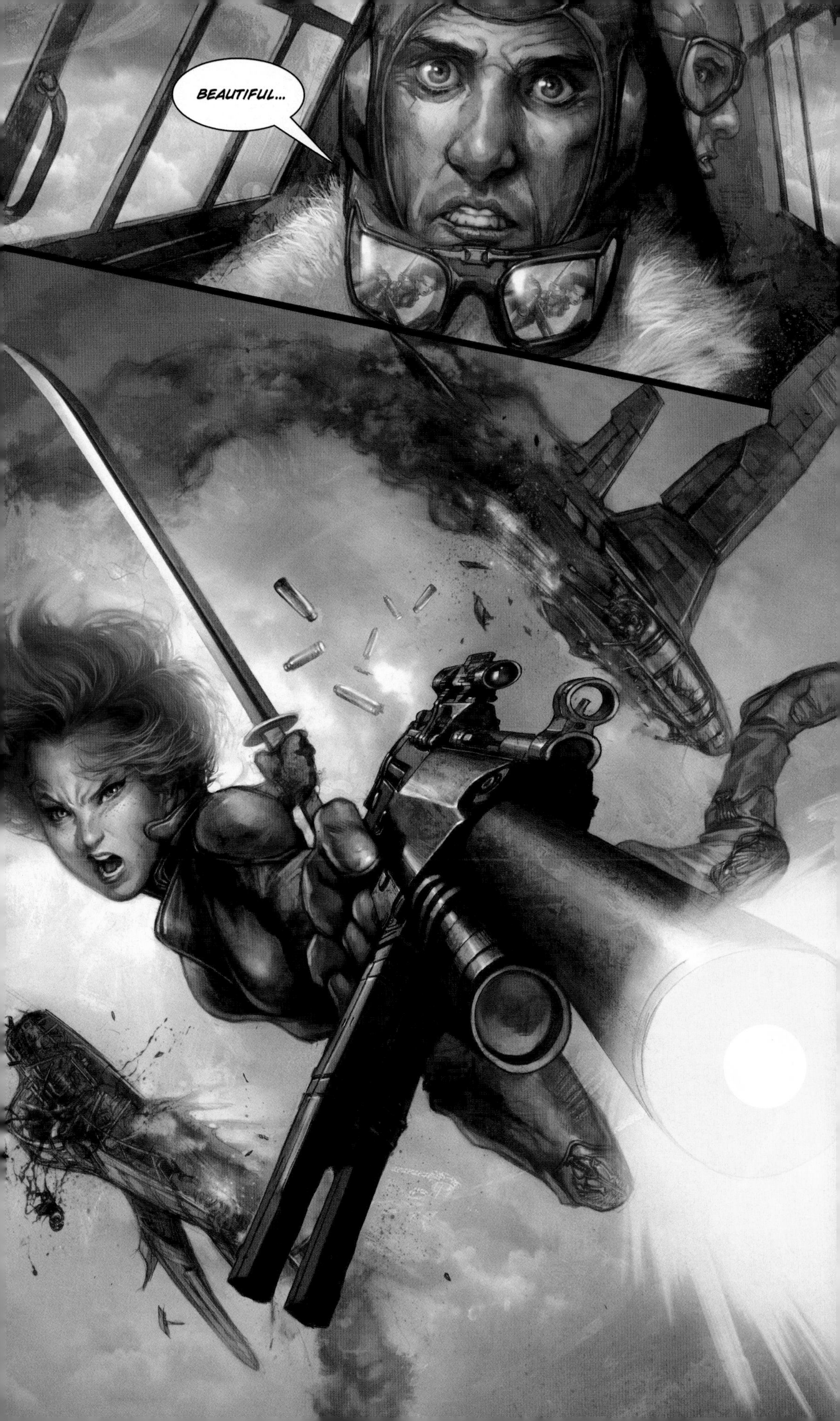
BEAUTIFUL...

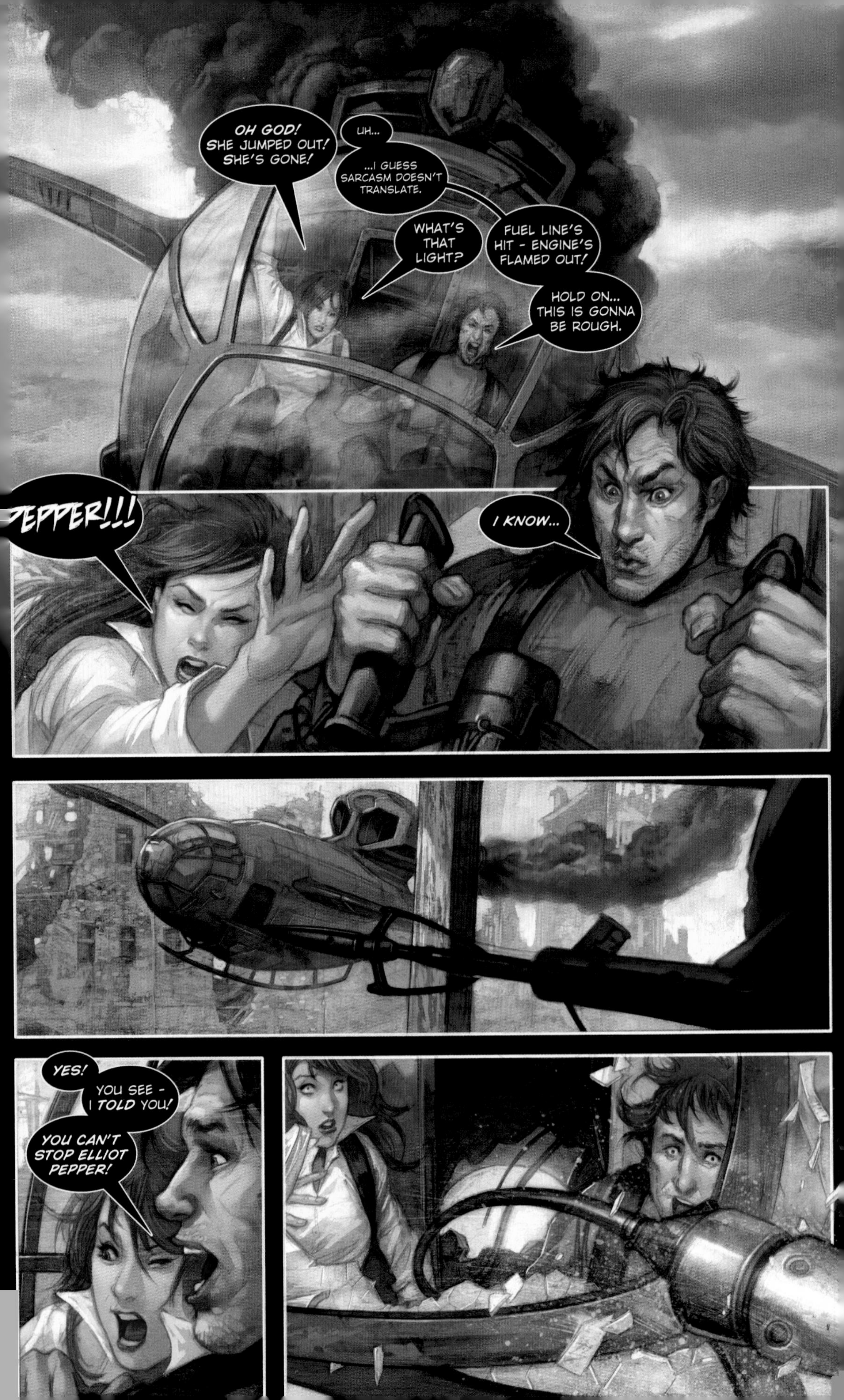
OH GOD! SHE JUMPED OUT! SHE'S GONE!
UH...
...I GUESS SARCASM DOESN'T TRANSLATE.
WHAT'S THAT LIGHT?
FUEL LINE'S HIT - ENGINE'S FLAMED OUT!
HOLD ON... THIS IS GONNA BE ROUGH.
PEPPER!!!
I KNOW...
YES!
YOU SEE - I TOLD YOU!
YOU CAN'T STOP ELLIOT PEPPER!

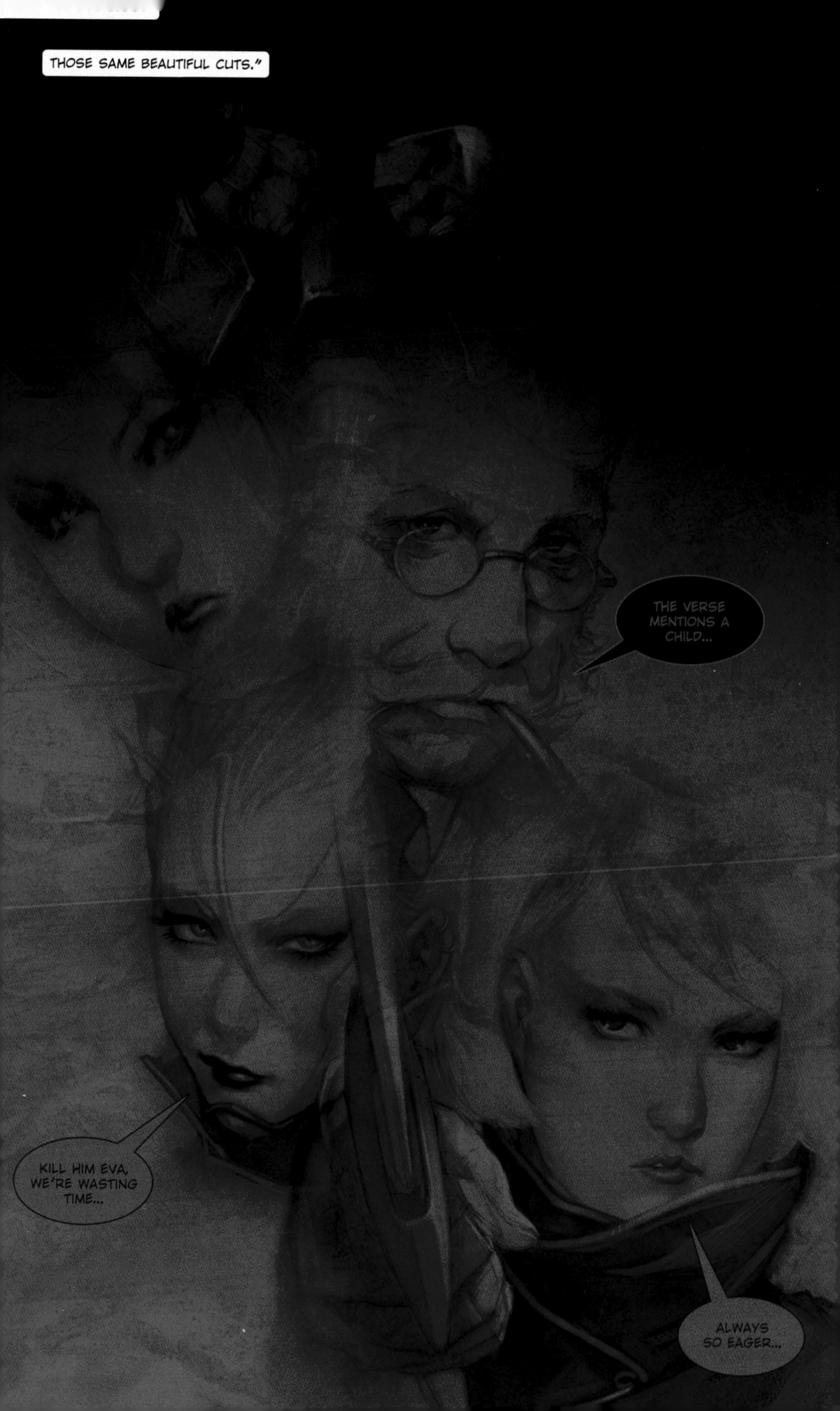
THOSE SAME BEAUTIFUL CUTS."
THE VERSE MENTIONS A CHILD...
KILL HIM EVA, WE'RE WASTING TIME...
ALWAYS SO EAGER...

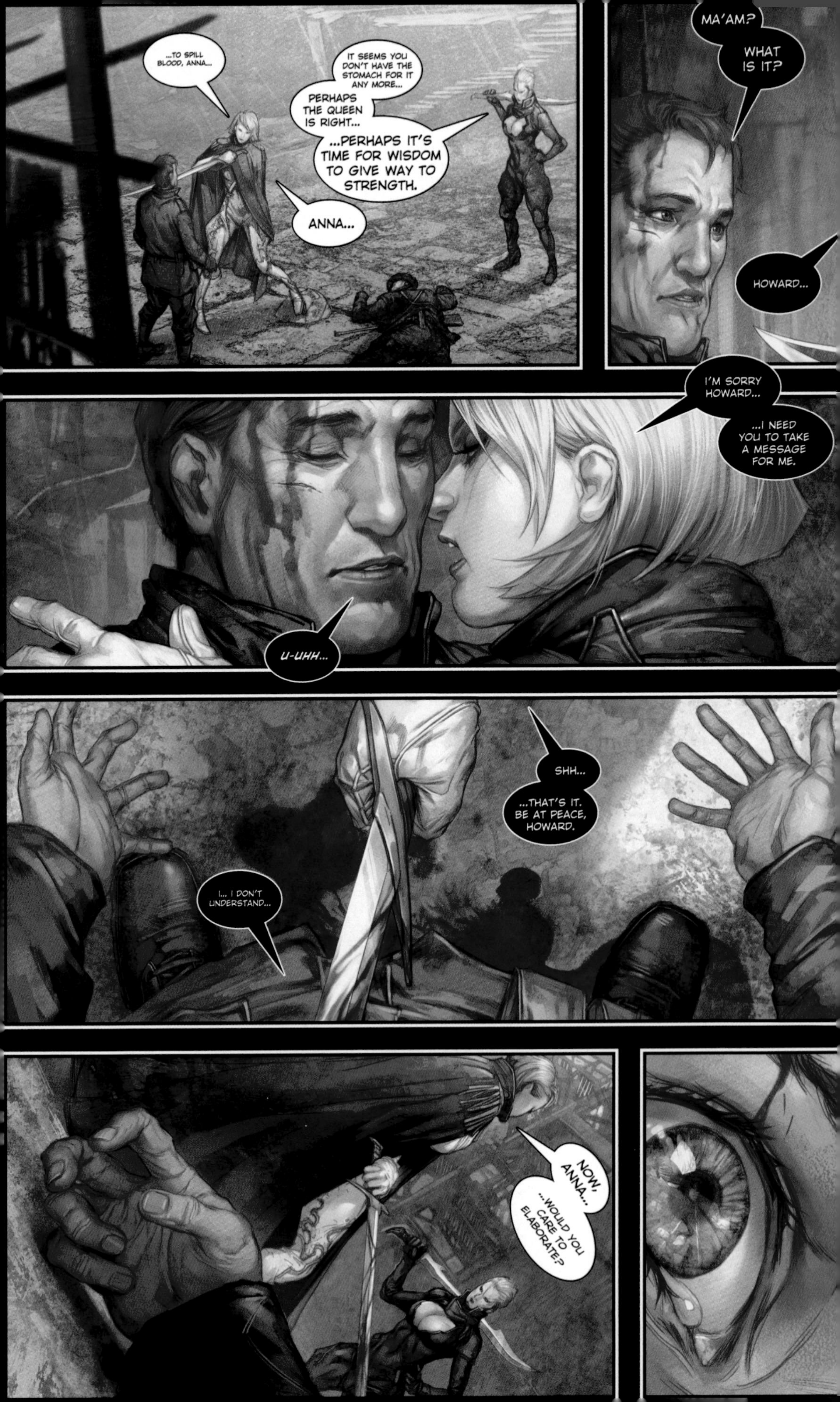

...TO SPILL BLOOD, ANNA...
IT SEEMS YOU DON'T HAVE THE STOMACH FOR IT ANY MORE...
PERHAPS THE QUEEN IS RIGHT...
...PERHAPS IT'S TIME FOR WISDOM TO GIVE WAY TO STRENGTH.
ANNA...
MA'AM?
WHAT IS IT?
HOWARD...
I'M SORRY HOWARD...
...I NEED YOU TO TAKE A MESSAGE FOR ME.
U-UHH...
SHH...
...THAT'S IT. BE AT PEACE, HOWARD.
I... I DON'T UNDERSTAND...
NOW, ANNA...
...WOULD YOU CARE TO ELABORATE?

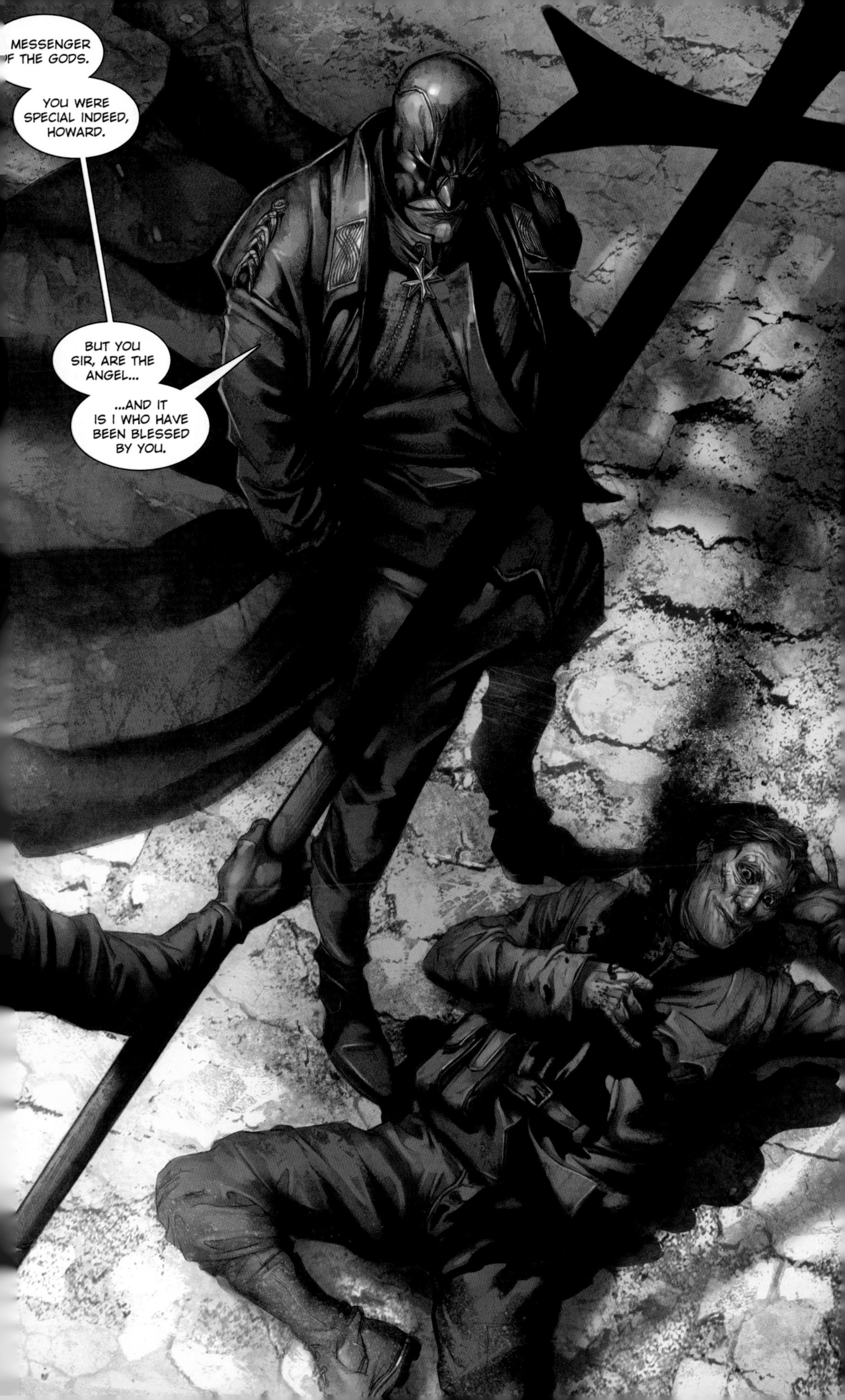

MESSENGER OF THE GODS.
YOU WERE SPECIAL INDEED, HOWARD.
BUT YOU SIR, ARE THE ANGEL...
...AND IT IS I WHO HAVE BEEN BLESSED BY YOU.

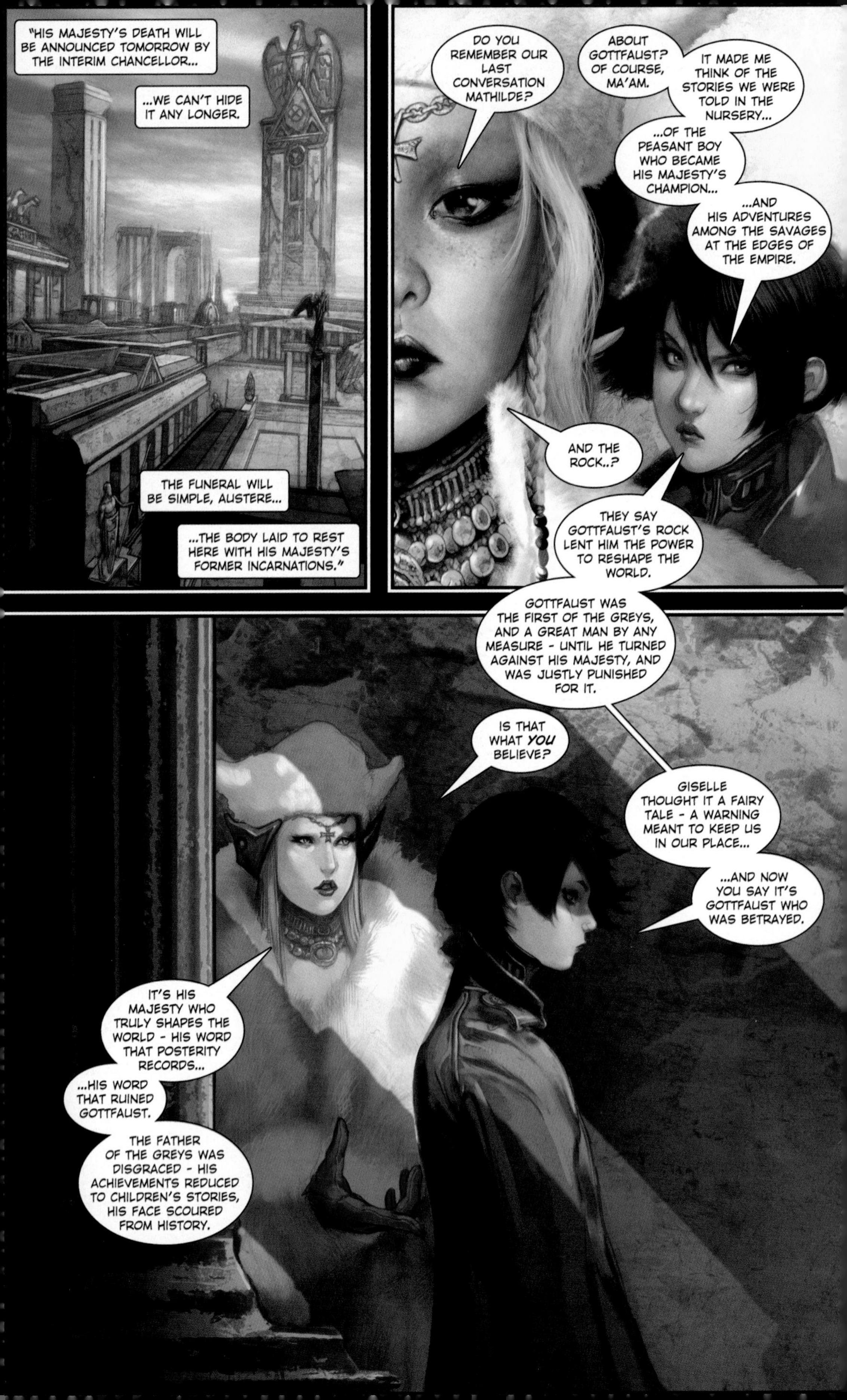
"HIS MAJESTY'S DEATH WILL BE ANNOUNCED TOMORROW BY THE INTERIM CHANCELLOR...
...WE CAN'T HIDE IT ANY LONGER.
THE FUNERAL WILL BE SIMPLE, AUSTERE...
...THE BODY LAID TO REST HERE WITH HIS MAJESTY'S FORMER INCARNATIONS."
DO YOU REMEMBER OUR LAST CONVERSATION MATHILDE?
ABOUT GOTTFAUST? OF COURSE, MA'AM.
IT MADE ME THINK OF THE STORIES WE WERE TOLD IN THE NURSERY...
...OF THE PEASANT BOY WHO BECAME HIS MAJESTY'S CHAMPION...
...AND HIS ADVENTURES AMONG THE SAVAGES AT THE EDGES OF THE EMPIRE.
AND THE ROCK..?
THEY SAY GOTTFAUST'S ROCK LENT HIM THE POWER TO RESHAPE THE WORLD.
GOTTFAUST WAS THE FIRST OF THE GREYS, AND A GREAT MAN BY ANY MEASURE - UNTIL HE TURNED AGAINST HIS MAJESTY, AND WAS JUSTLY PUNISHED FOR IT.
IS THAT WHAT *YOU* BELIEVE?
GISELLE THOUGHT IT A FAIRY TALE - A WARNING MEANT TO KEEP US IN OUR PLACE...
...AND NOW YOU SAY IT'S GOTTFAUST WHO WAS BETRAYED.
IT'S HIS MAJESTY WHO TRULY SHAPES THE WORLD - HIS WORD THAT POSTERITY RECORDS...
...HIS WORD THAT RUINED GOTTFAUST.
THE FATHER OF THE GREYS WAS DISGRACED - HIS ACHIEVEMENTS REDUCED TO CHILDREN'S STORIES, HIS FACE SCOURED FROM HISTORY.

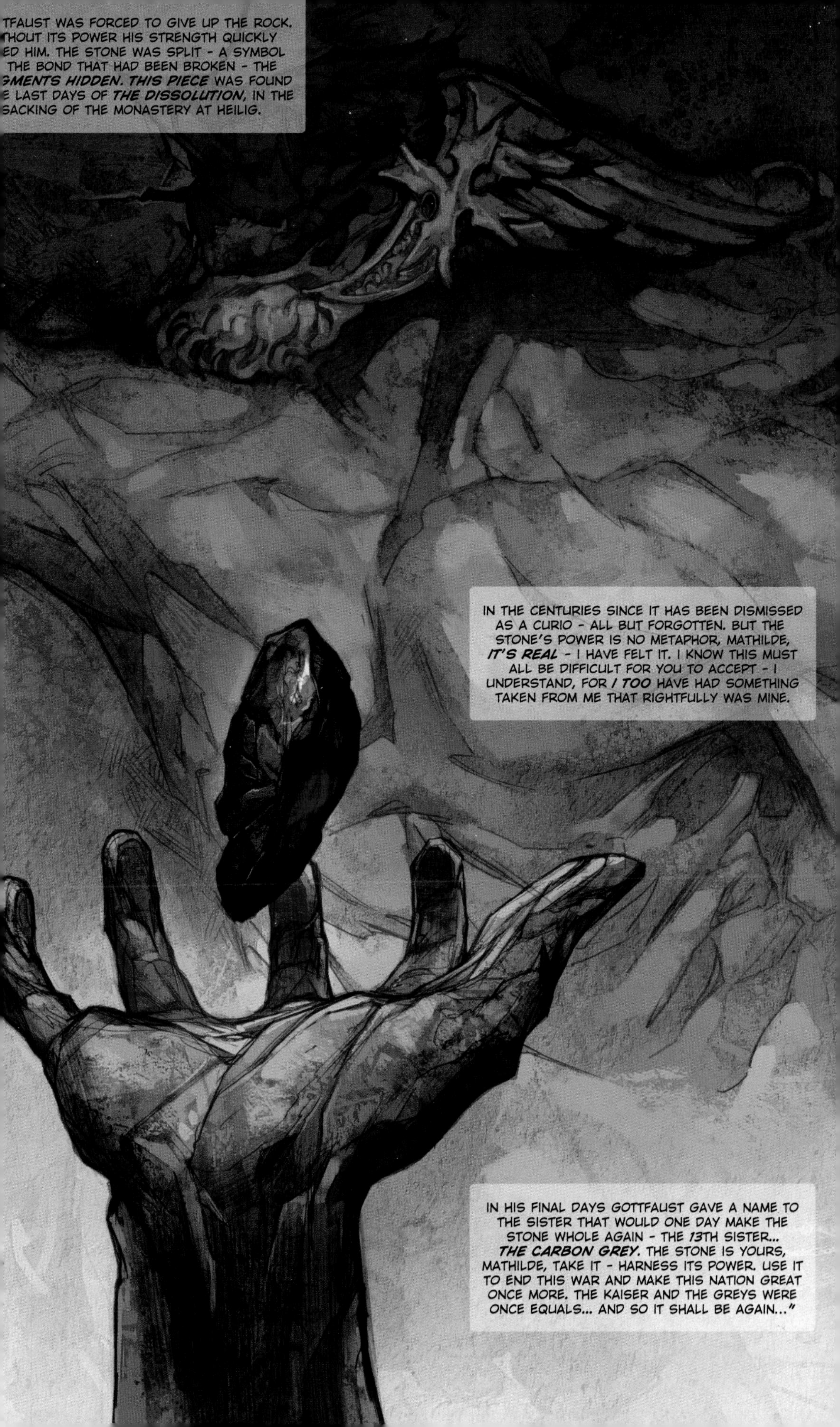
TFAUST WAS FORCED TO GIVE UP THE ROCK. THOUT ITS POWER HIS STRENGTH QUICKLY ED HIM. THE STONE WAS SPLIT - A SYMBOL THE BOND THAT HAD BEEN BROKEN - THE GMENTS HIDDEN. THIS PIECE WAS FOUND E LAST DAYS OF THE DISSOLUTION, IN THE SACKING OF THE MONASTERY AT HEILIG.
IN THE CENTURIES SINCE IT HAS BEEN DISMISSED AS A CURIO - ALL BUT FORGOTTEN. BUT THE STONE'S POWER IS NO METAPHOR, MATHILDE, IT'S REAL - I HAVE FELT IT. I KNOW THIS MUST ALL BE DIFFICULT FOR YOU TO ACCEPT - I UNDERSTAND, FOR I TOO HAVE HAD SOMETHING TAKEN FROM ME THAT RIGHTFULLY WAS MINE.
IN HIS FINAL DAYS GOTTFAUST GAVE A NAME TO THE SISTER THAT WOULD ONE DAY MAKE THE STONE WHOLE AGAIN - THE 13TH SISTER... THE CARBON GREY. THE STONE IS YOURS, MATHILDE, TAKE IT - HARNESS ITS POWER. USE IT TO END THIS WAR AND MAKE THIS NATION GREAT ONCE MORE. THE KAISER AND THE GREYS WERE ONCE EQUALS... AND SO IT SHALL BE AGAIN..."

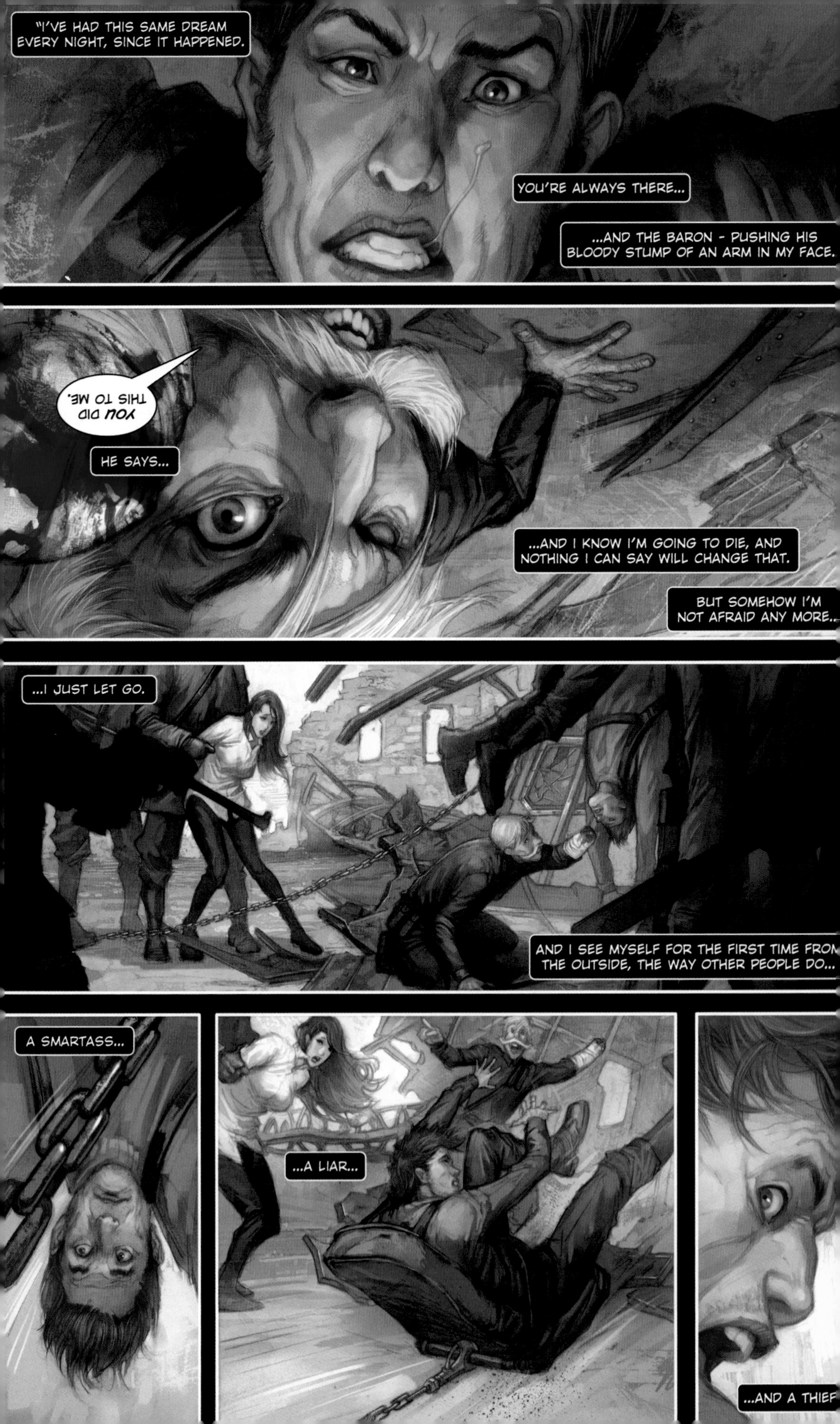
"I'VE HAD THIS SAME DREAM EVERY NIGHT, SINCE IT HAPPENED.
YOU'RE ALWAYS THERE...
...AND THE BARON - PUSHING HIS BLOODY STUMP OF AN ARM IN MY FACE.
YOU DID THIS TO ME.
HE SAYS...
...AND I KNOW I'M GOING TO DIE, AND NOTHING I CAN SAY WILL CHANGE THAT.
BUT SOMEHOW I'M NOT AFRAID ANY MORE...
...I JUST LET GO.
AND I SEE MYSELF FOR THE FIRST TIME FROM THE OUTSIDE, THE WAY OTHER PEOPLE DO...
A SMARTASS...
...A LIAR...
...AND A THIEF

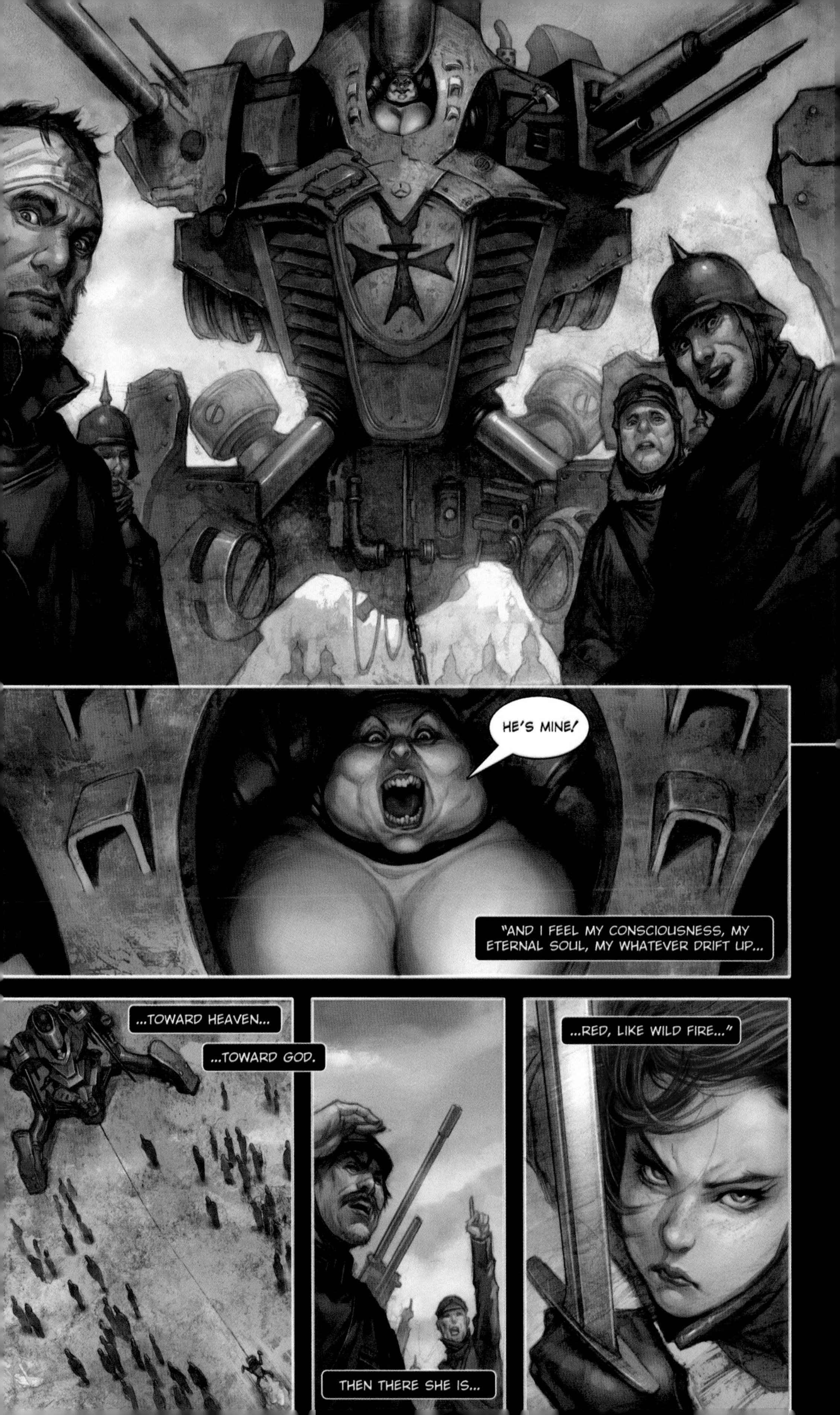
HE'S MINE!
"AND I FEEL MY CONSCIOUSNESS, MY ETERNAL SOUL, MY WHATEVER DRIFT UP...
...TOWARD HEAVEN...
...TOWARD GOD.
THEN THERE SHE IS...
...RED, LIKE WILD FIRE..."

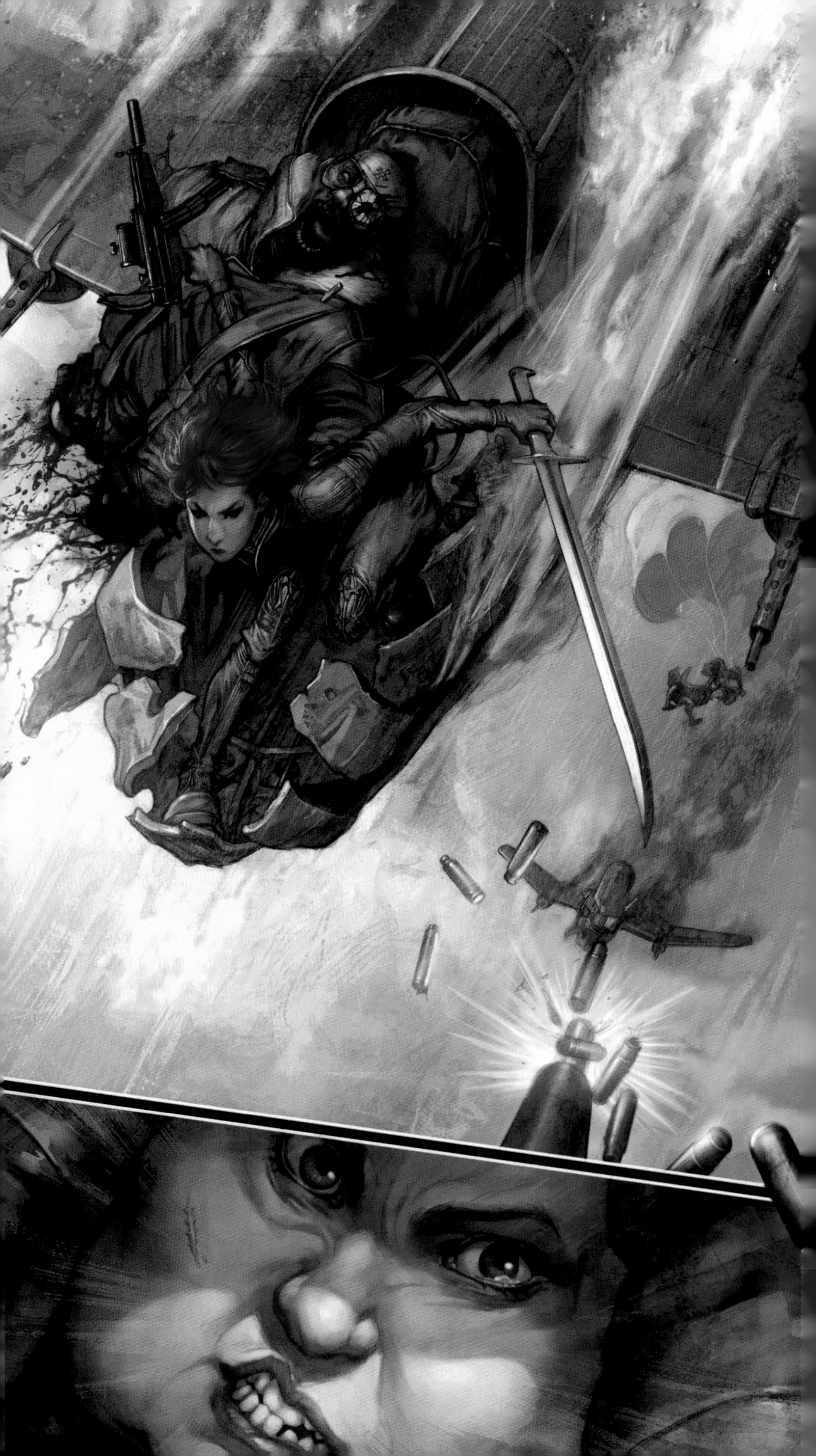

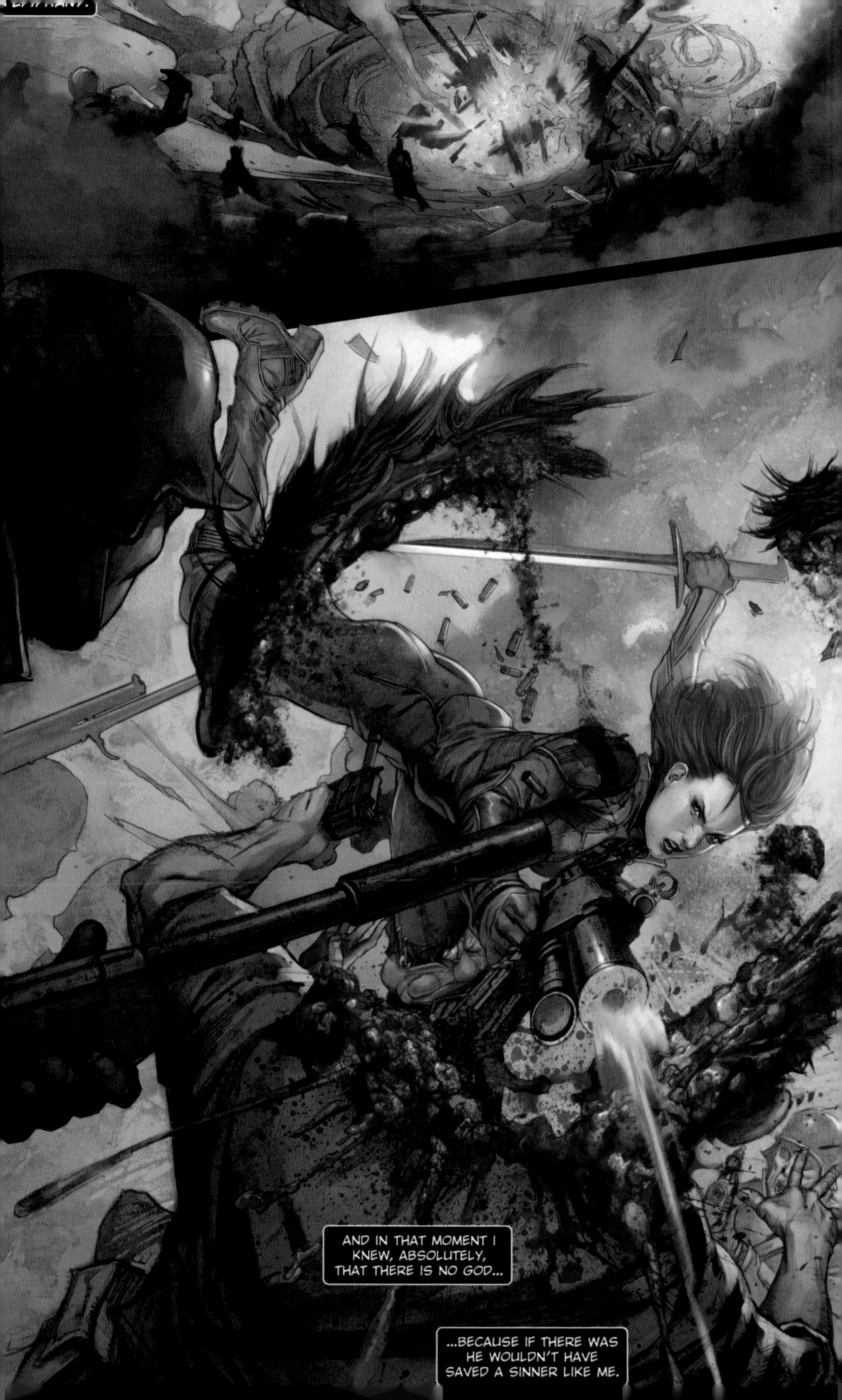
AND IN THAT MOMENT I KNEW, ABSOLUTELY, THAT THERE IS NO GOD...
...BECAUSE IF THERE WAS HE WOULDN'T HAVE SAVED A SINNER LIKE ME.

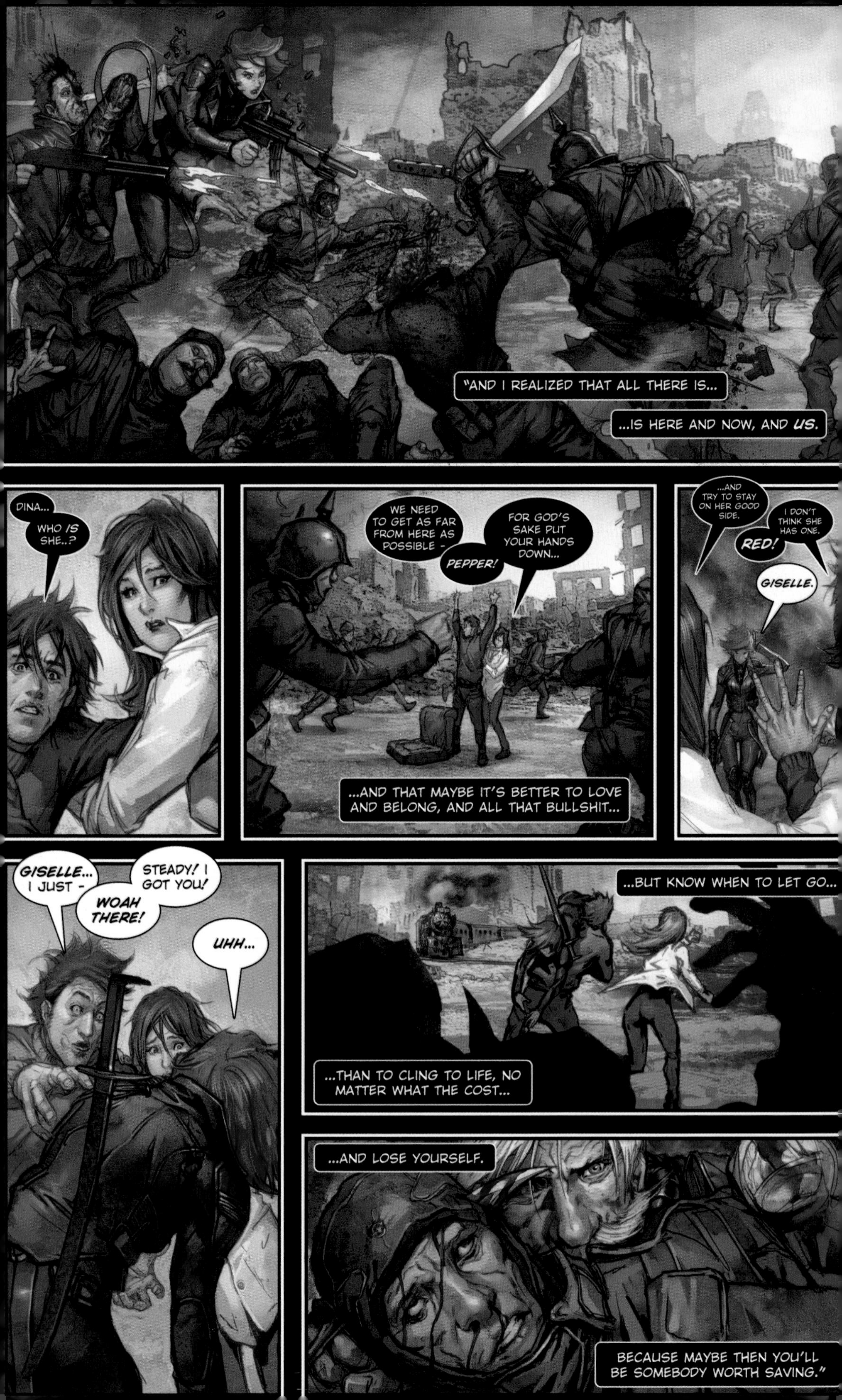
"AND I REALIZED THAT ALL THERE IS...
...IS HERE AND NOW, AND US.
DINA...
WHO IS SHE..?
WE NEED TO GET AS FAR FROM HERE AS POSSIBLE -
PEPPER!
FOR GOD'S SAKE PUT YOUR HANDS DOWN...
...AND THAT MAYBE IT'S BETTER TO LOVE AND BELONG, AND ALL THAT BULLSHIT...
...AND TRY TO STAY ON HER GOOD SIDE.
RED!
I DON'T THINK SHE HAS ONE.
GISELLE.
GISELLE... I JUST -
WOAH THERE!
STEADY! I GOT YOU!
UHH...
...BUT KNOW WHEN TO LET GO...
...THAN TO CLING TO LIFE, NO MATTER WHAT THE COST...
...AND LOSE YOURSELF.
BECAUSE MAYBE THEN YOU'LL BE SOMEBODY WORTH SAVING."

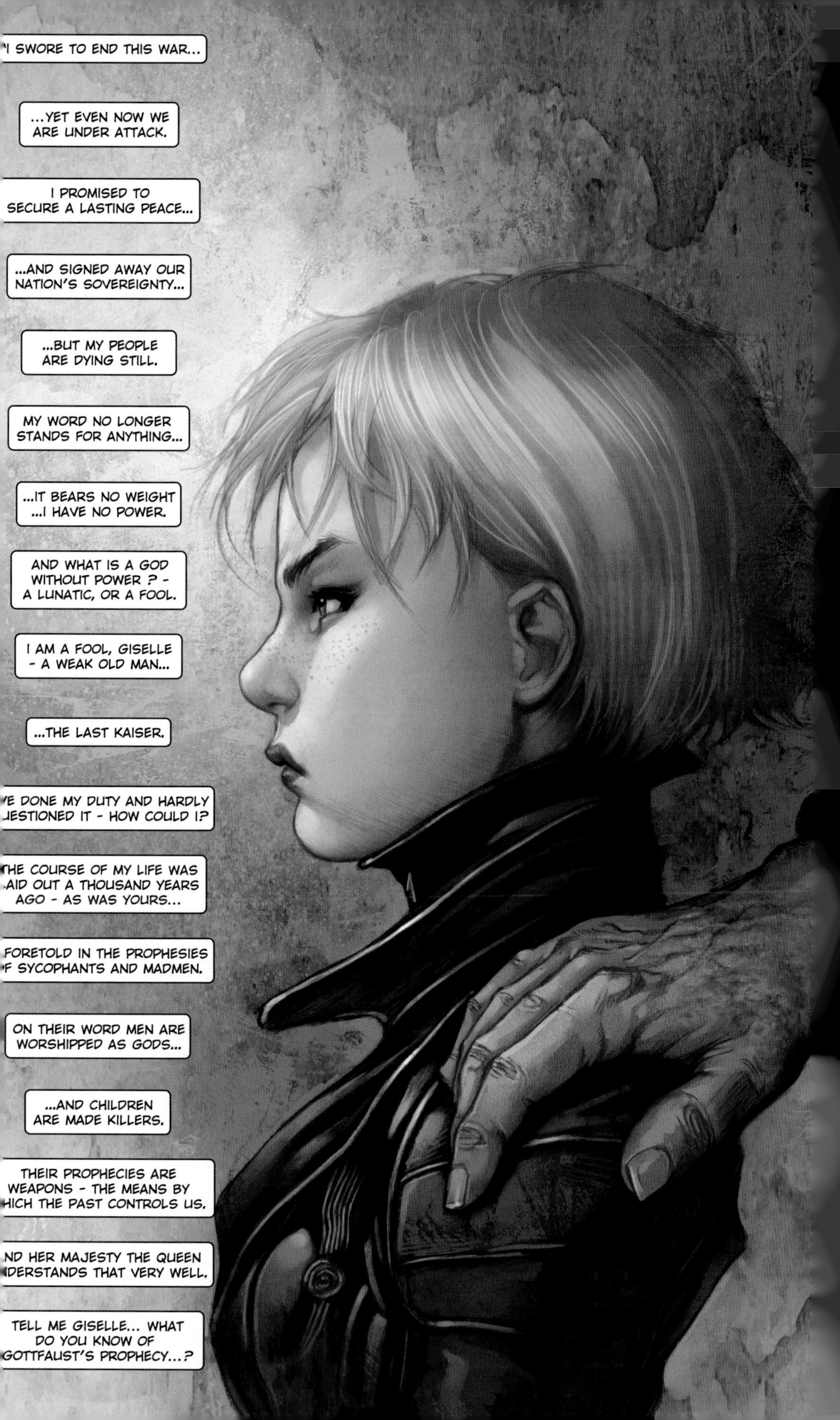
'I SWORE TO END THIS WAR...
...YET EVEN NOW WE ARE UNDER ATTACK.
I PROMISED TO SECURE A LASTING PEACE...
...AND SIGNED AWAY OUR NATION'S SOVEREIGNTY...
...BUT MY PEOPLE ARE DYING STILL.
MY WORD NO LONGER STANDS FOR ANYTHING...
...IT BEARS NO WEIGHT ...I HAVE NO POWER.
AND WHAT IS A GOD WITHOUT POWER ? - A LUNATIC, OR A FOOL.
I AM A FOOL, GISELLE - A WEAK OLD MAN...
...THE LAST KAISER.
'E DONE MY DUTY AND HARDLY JESTIONED IT - HOW COULD I?
THE COURSE OF MY LIFE WAS AID OUT A THOUSAND YEARS AGO - AS WAS YOURS...
FORETOLD IN THE PROPHESIES F SYCOPHANTS AND MADMEN.
ON THEIR WORD MEN ARE WORSHIPPED AS GODS...
...AND CHILDREN ARE MADE KILLERS.
THEIR PROPHECIES ARE WEAPONS - THE MEANS BY HICH THE PAST CONTROLS US.
ND HER MAJESTY THE QUEEN IDERSTANDS THAT VERY WELL.
TELL ME GISELLE... WHAT DO YOU KNOW OF GOTTFAUST'S PROPHECY...?

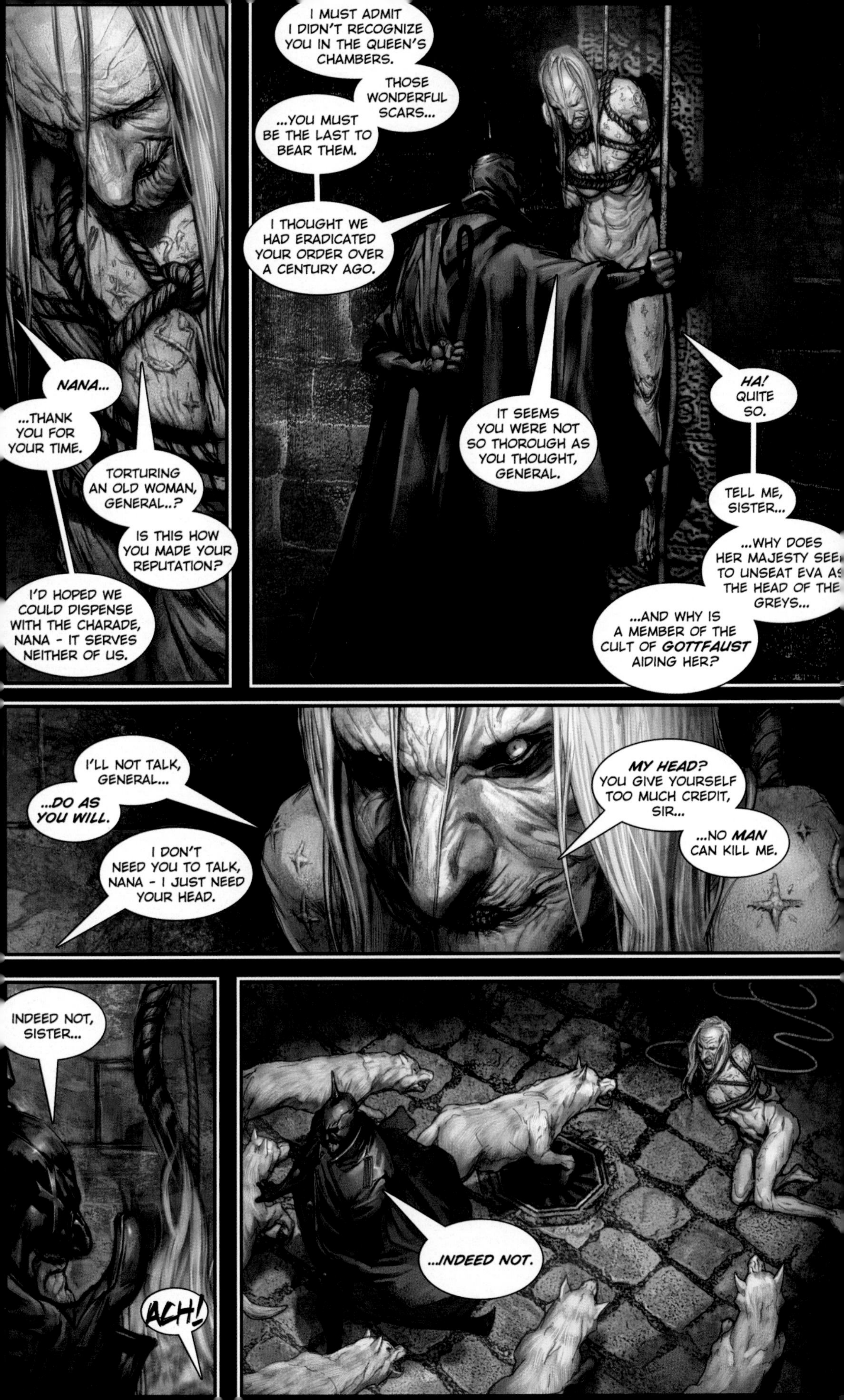
NANA...
...THANK YOU FOR YOUR TIME.
TORTURING AN OLD WOMAN, GENERAL..?
IS THIS HOW YOU MADE YOUR REPUTATION?
I'D HOPED WE COULD DISPENSE WITH THE CHARADE, NANA - IT SERVES NEITHER OF US.
I MUST ADMIT I DIDN'T RECOGNIZE YOU IN THE QUEEN'S CHAMBERS.
THOSE WONDERFUL SCARS...
...YOU MUST BE THE LAST TO BEAR THEM.
I THOUGHT WE HAD ERADICATED YOUR ORDER OVER A CENTURY AGO.
IT SEEMS YOU WERE NOT SO THOROUGH AS YOU THOUGHT, GENERAL.
HA! QUITE SO.
TELL ME, SISTER...
...WHY DOES HER MAJESTY SEE TO UNSEAT EVA AS THE HEAD OF THE GREYS...
...AND WHY IS A MEMBER OF THE CULT OF GOTTFAUST AIDING HER?
I'LL NOT TALK, GENERAL...
...DO AS YOU WILL.
I DON'T NEED YOU TO TALK, NANA - I JUST NEED YOUR HEAD.
MY HEAD? YOU GIVE YOURSELF TOO MUCH CREDIT, SIR...
...NO MAN CAN KILL ME.
INDEED NOT, SISTER...
ACH!
...INDEED NOT.

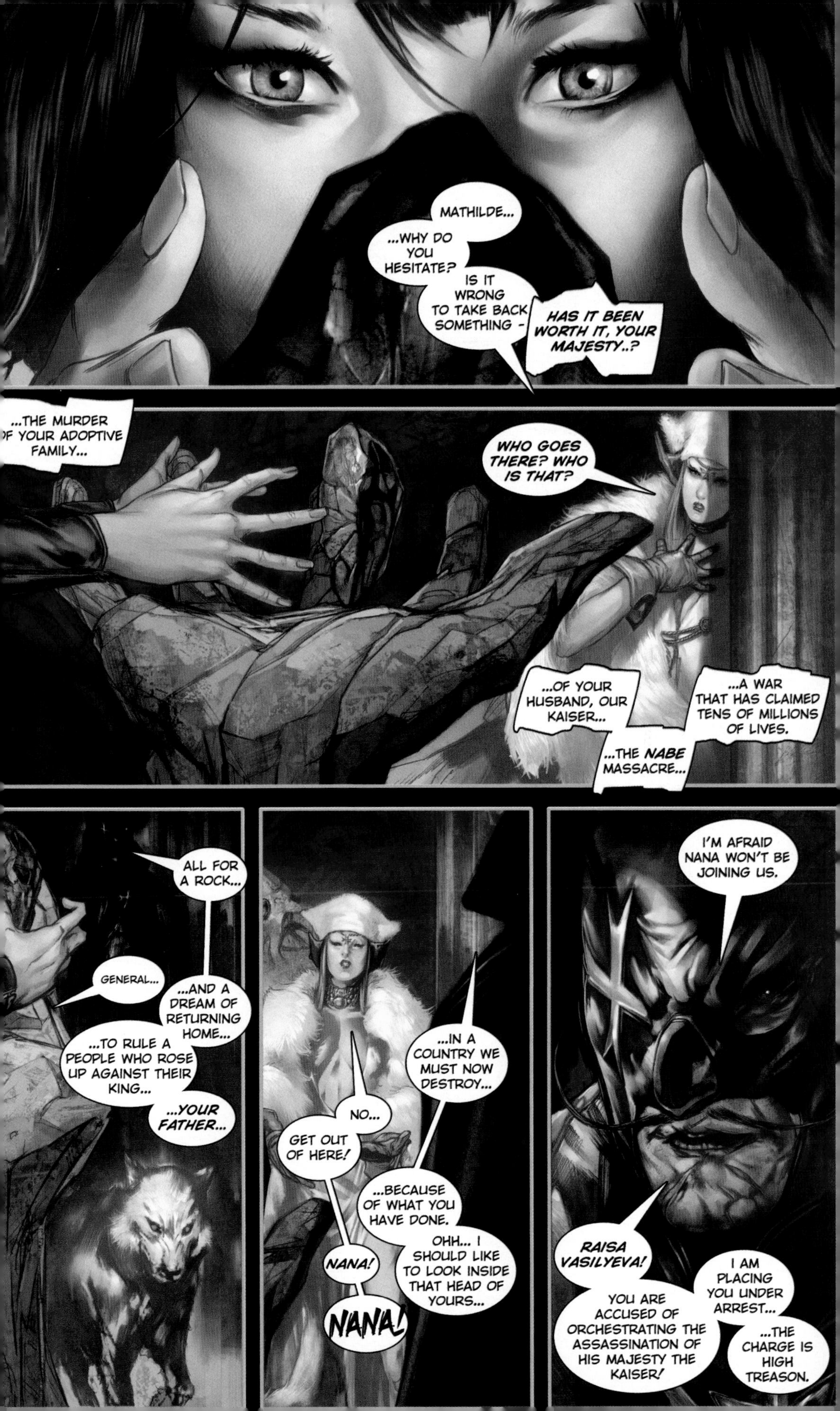
MATHILDE...
...WHY DO YOU HESITATE?
IS IT WRONG TO TAKE BACK SOMETHING -
HAS IT BEEN WORTH IT, YOUR MAJESTY..?
...THE MURDER OF YOUR ADOPTIVE FAMILY...
WHO GOES THERE? WHO IS THAT?
...OF YOUR HUSBAND, OUR KAISER...
...THE NABE MASSACRE...
...A WAR THAT HAS CLAIMED TENS OF MILLIONS OF LIVES.
ALL FOR A ROCK...
GENERAL...
...AND A DREAM OF RETURNING HOME...
...TO RULE A PEOPLE WHO ROSE UP AGAINST THEIR KING...
...YOUR FATHER...
...IN A COUNTRY WE MUST NOW DESTROY...
NO...
GET OUT OF HERE!
...BECAUSE OF WHAT YOU HAVE DONE.
OHH... I SHOULD LIKE TO LOOK INSIDE THAT HEAD OF YOURS...
NANA!
NANA!
I'M AFRAID NANA WON'T BE JOINING US.
RAISA VASILYEVA!
YOU ARE ACCUSED OF ORCHESTRATING THE ASSASSINATION OF HIS MAJESTY THE KAISER!
I AM PLACING YOU UNDER ARREST...
...THE CHARGE IS HIGH TREASON.

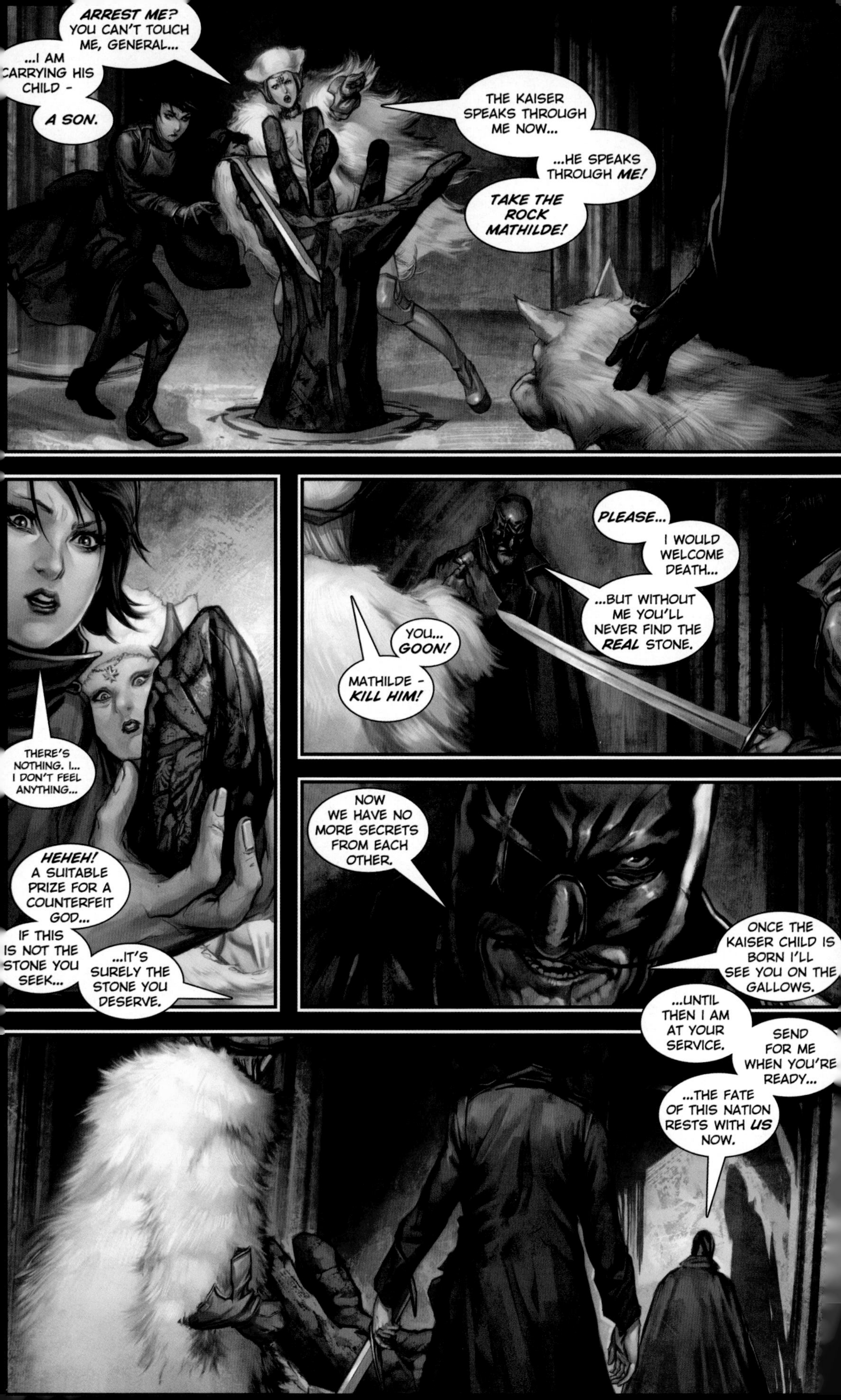

ARREST ME? YOU CAN'T TOUCH ME, GENERAL...
...I AM CARRYING HIS CHILD -
A SON.
THE KAISER SPEAKS THROUGH ME NOW...
...HE SPEAKS THROUGH ME!
TAKE THE ROCK MATHILDE!
THERE'S NOTHING. I... I DON'T FEEL ANYTHING...
HEHEH! A SUITABLE PRIZE FOR A COUNTERFEIT GOD...
IF THIS IS NOT THE STONE YOU SEEK...
...IT'S SURELY THE STONE YOU DESERVE.
PLEASE...
I WOULD WELCOME DEATH...
...BUT WITHOUT ME YOU'LL NEVER FIND THE REAL STONE.
YOU... GOON!
MATHILDE - KILL HIM!
NOW WE HAVE NO MORE SECRETS FROM EACH OTHER.
ONCE THE KAISER CHILD IS BORN I'LL SEE YOU ON THE GALLOWS.
...UNTIL THEN I AM AT YOUR SERVICE.
SEND FOR ME WHEN YOU'RE READY...
...THE FATE OF THIS NATION RESTS WITH US NOW.

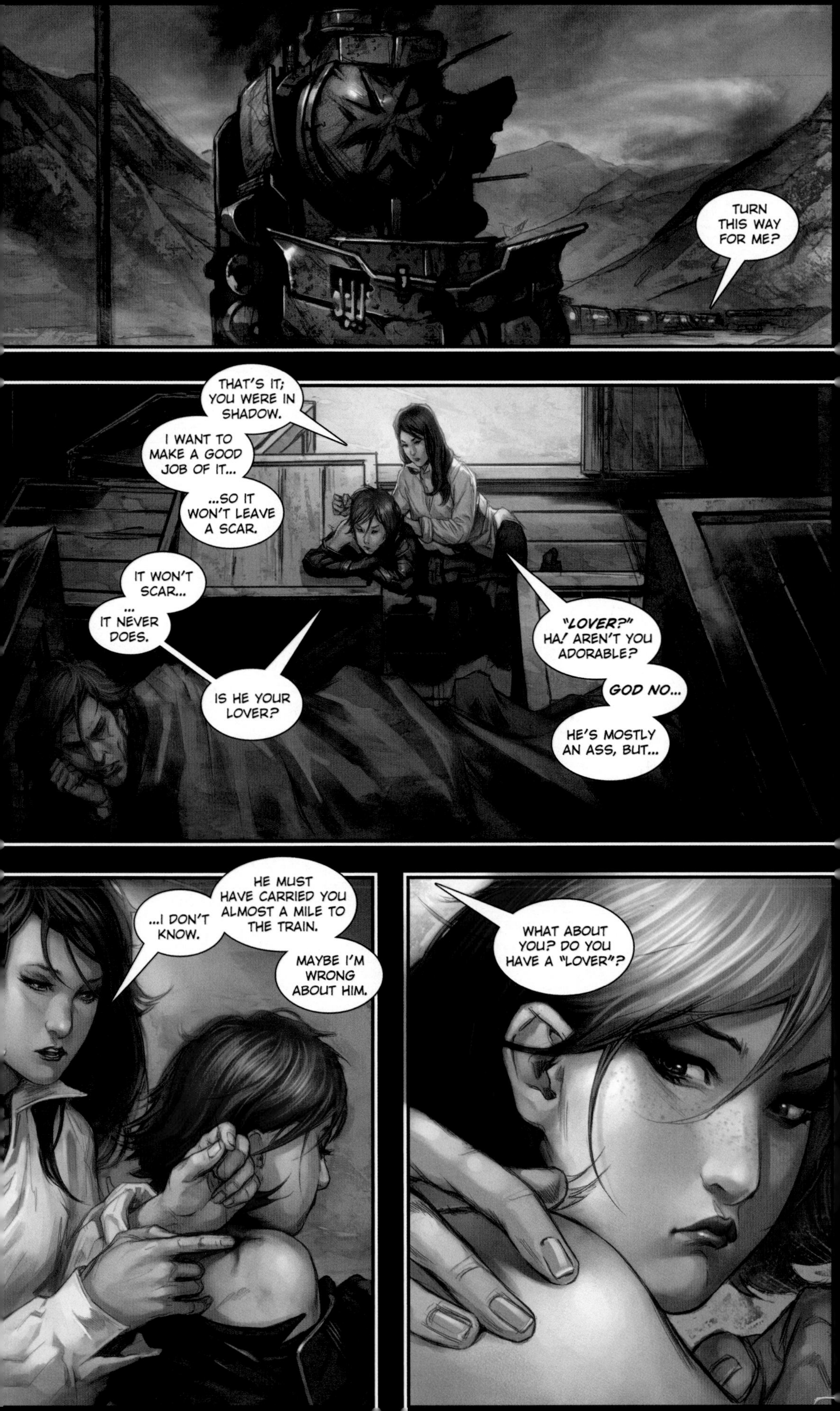
TURN THIS WAY FOR ME?
THAT'S IT; YOU WERE IN SHADOW.
I WANT TO MAKE A GOOD JOB OF IT...
...SO IT WON'T LEAVE A SCAR.
IT WON'T SCAR... ...IT NEVER DOES.
IS HE YOUR LOVER?
"LOVER?" HA! AREN'T YOU ADORABLE?
GOD NO...
HE'S MOSTLY AN ASS, BUT...
HE MUST HAVE CARRIED YOU ALMOST A MILE TO THE TRAIN.
MAYBE I'M WRONG ABOUT HIM.
...I DON'T KNOW.
WHAT ABOUT YOU? DO YOU HAVE A "LOVER"?

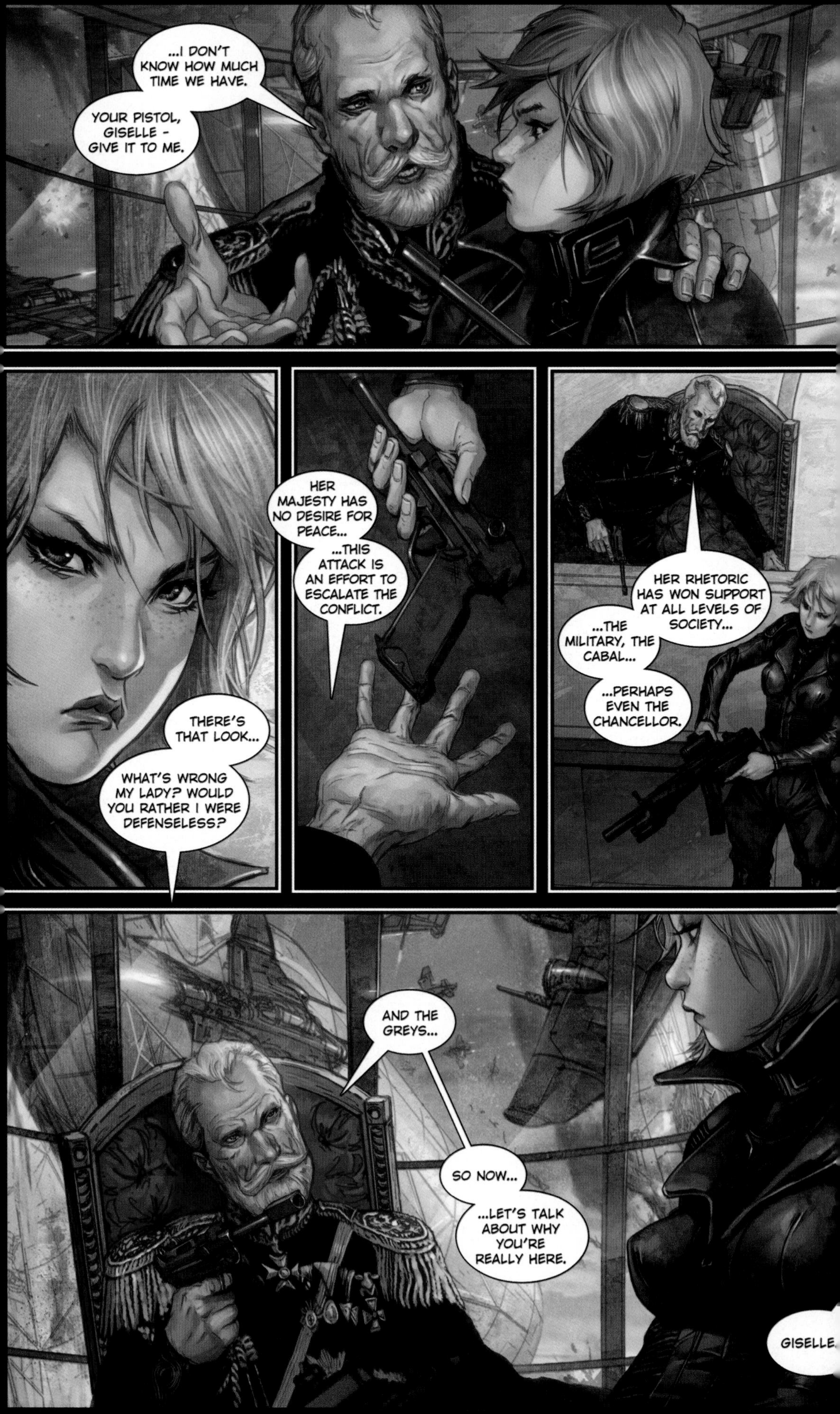
...I DON'T KNOW HOW MUCH TIME WE HAVE.
YOUR PISTOL, GISELLE - GIVE IT TO ME.
THERE'S THAT LOOK...
WHAT'S WRONG MY LADY? WOULD YOU RATHER I WERE DEFENSELESS?
HER MAJESTY HAS NO DESIRE FOR PEACE...
...THIS ATTACK IS AN EFFORT TO ESCALATE THE CONFLICT.
HER RHETORIC HAS WON SUPPORT AT ALL LEVELS OF SOCIETY...
...THE MILITARY, THE CABAL...
...PERHAPS EVEN THE CHANCELLOR.
AND THE GREYS...
SO NOW...
...LET'S TALK ABOUT WHY YOU'RE REALLY HERE.
GISELLE

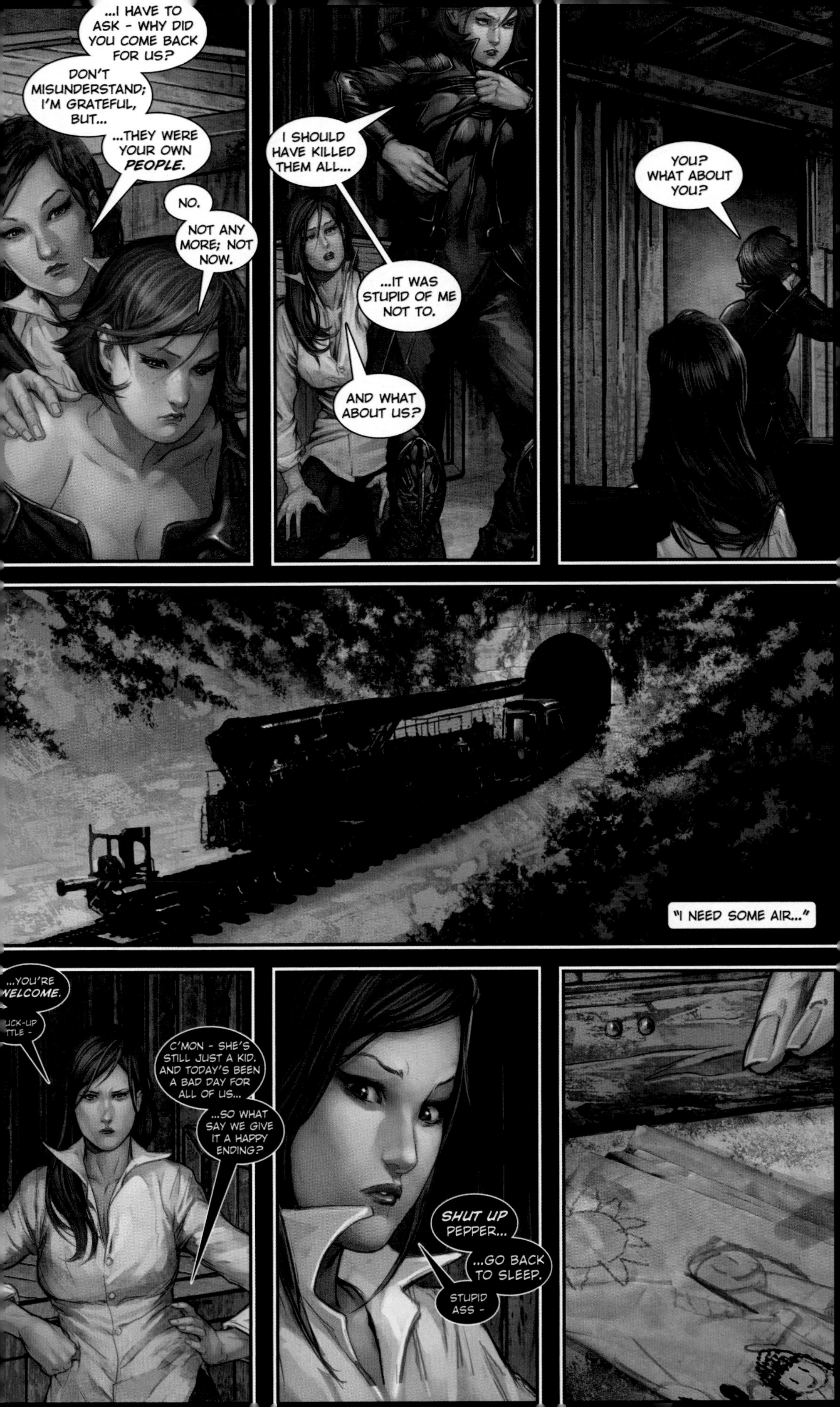
...I HAVE TO ASK - WHY DID YOU COME BACK FOR US?
DON'T MISUNDERSTAND; I'M GRATEFUL, BUT...
...THEY WERE YOUR OWN *PEOPLE*.
NO.
NOT ANY MORE; NOT NOW.
I SHOULD HAVE KILLED THEM ALL...
...IT WAS STUPID OF ME NOT TO.
AND WHAT ABOUT US?
YOU? WHAT ABOUT YOU?
"I NEED SOME AIR..."
...YOU'RE *WELCOME*.
C'MON - SHE'S STILL JUST A KID. AND TODAY'S BEEN A BAD DAY FOR ALL OF US...
...SO WHAT SAY WE GIVE IT A HAPPY ENDING?
SHUT UP PEPPER...
...GO BACK TO SLEEP.
STUPID ASS -

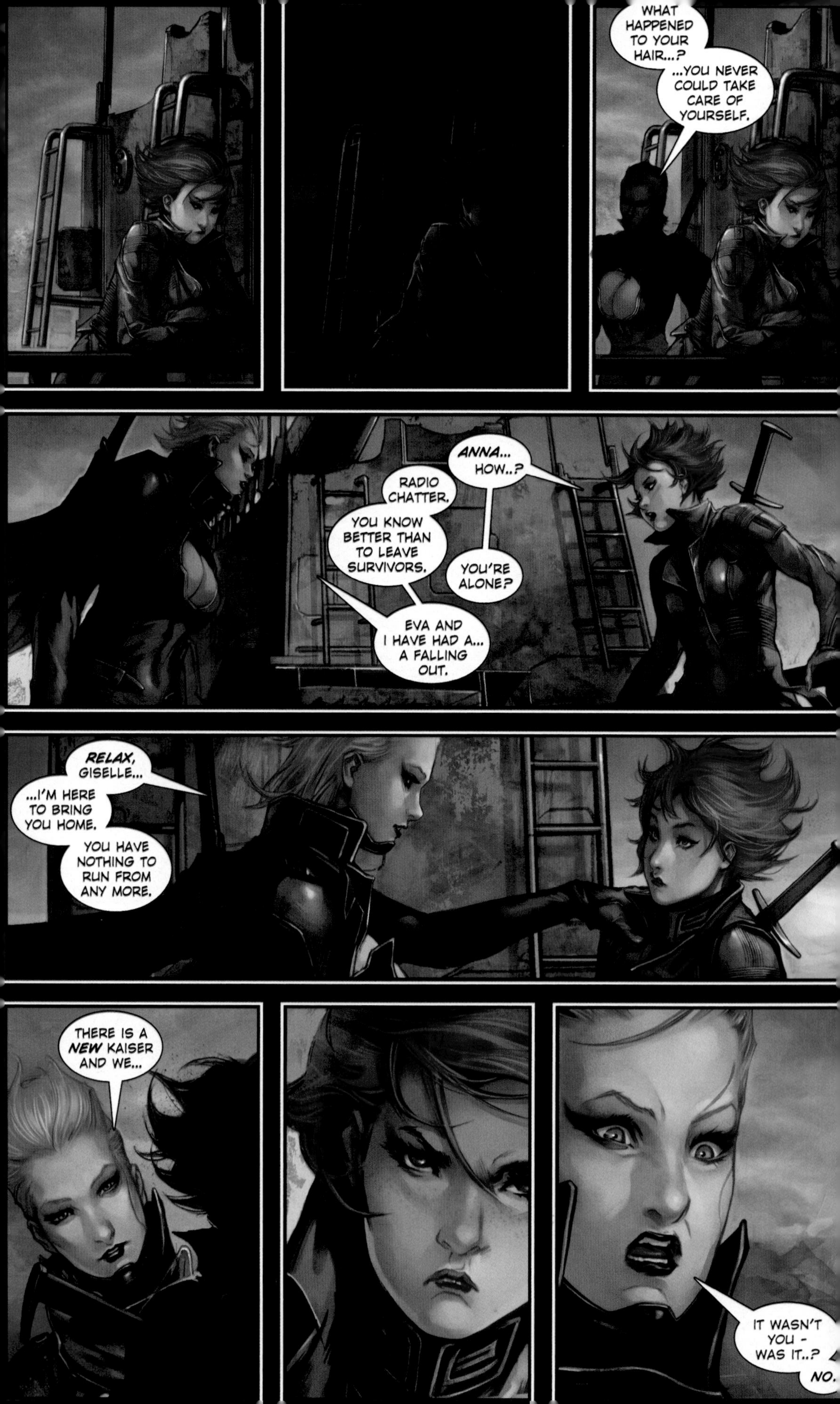

WHAT HAPPENED TO YOUR HAIR...?
...YOU NEVER COULD TAKE CARE OF YOURSELF.
RADIO CHATTER.
YOU KNOW BETTER THAN TO LEAVE SURVIVORS.
ANNA... HOW..?
YOU'RE ALONE?
EVA AND I HAVE HAD A... A FALLING OUT.
RELAX, GISELLE...
...I'M HERE TO BRING YOU HOME.
YOU HAVE NOTHING TO RUN FROM ANY MORE.
THERE IS A NEW KAISER AND WE...
IT WASN'T YOU - WAS IT..?
NO.

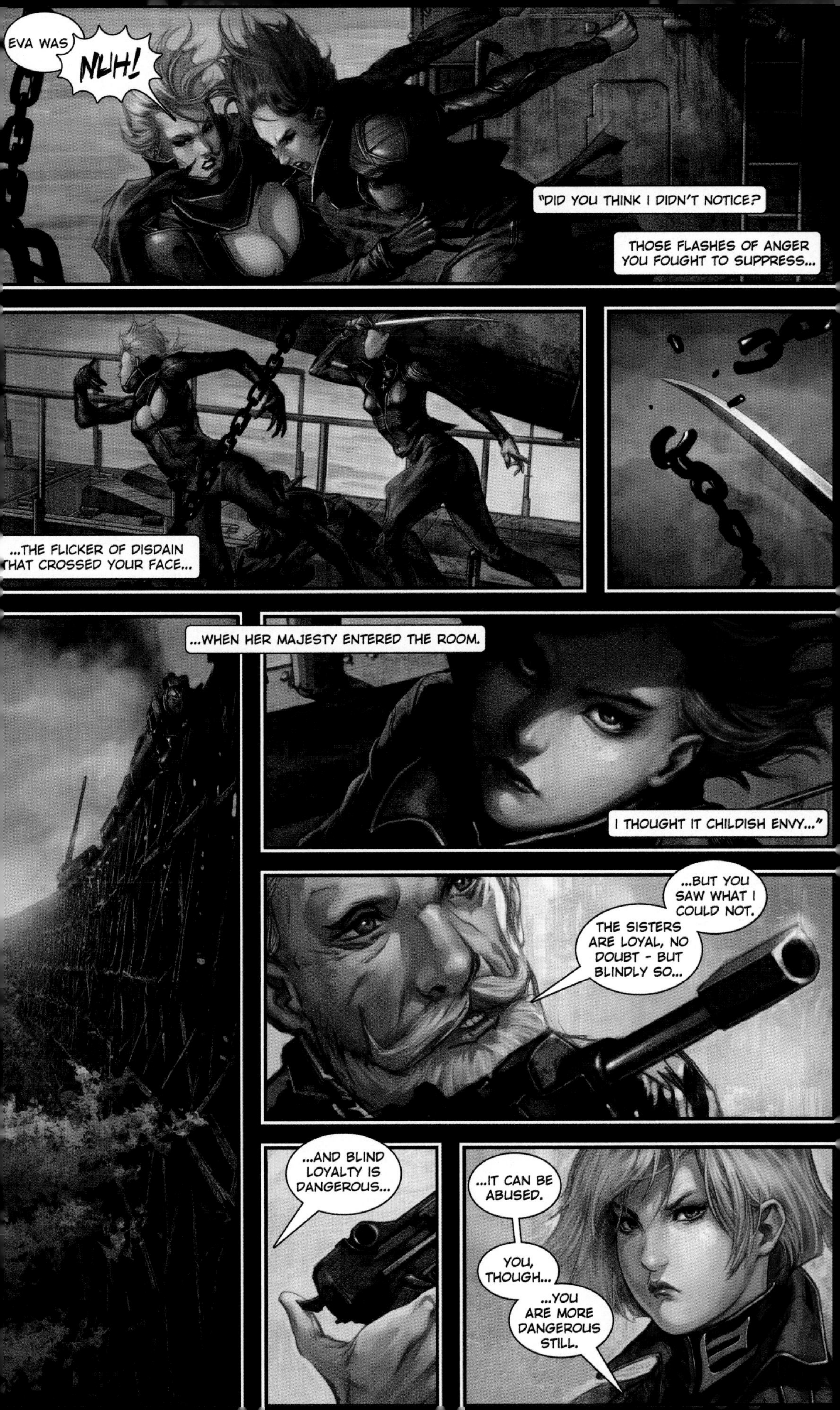
EVA WAS
NUH!
"DID YOU THINK I DIDN'T NOTICE?
THOSE FLASHES OF ANGER YOU FOUGHT TO SUPPRESS...
...THE FLICKER OF DISDAIN THAT CROSSED YOUR FACE...
...WHEN HER MAJESTY ENTERED THE ROOM.
I THOUGHT IT CHILDISH ENVY..."
...BUT YOU SAW WHAT I COULD NOT.
THE SISTERS ARE LOYAL, NO DOUBT - BUT BLINDLY SO...
...AND BLIND LOYALTY IS DANGEROUS...
...IT CAN BE ABUSED.
YOU, THOUGH...
...YOU ARE MORE DANGEROUS STILL.

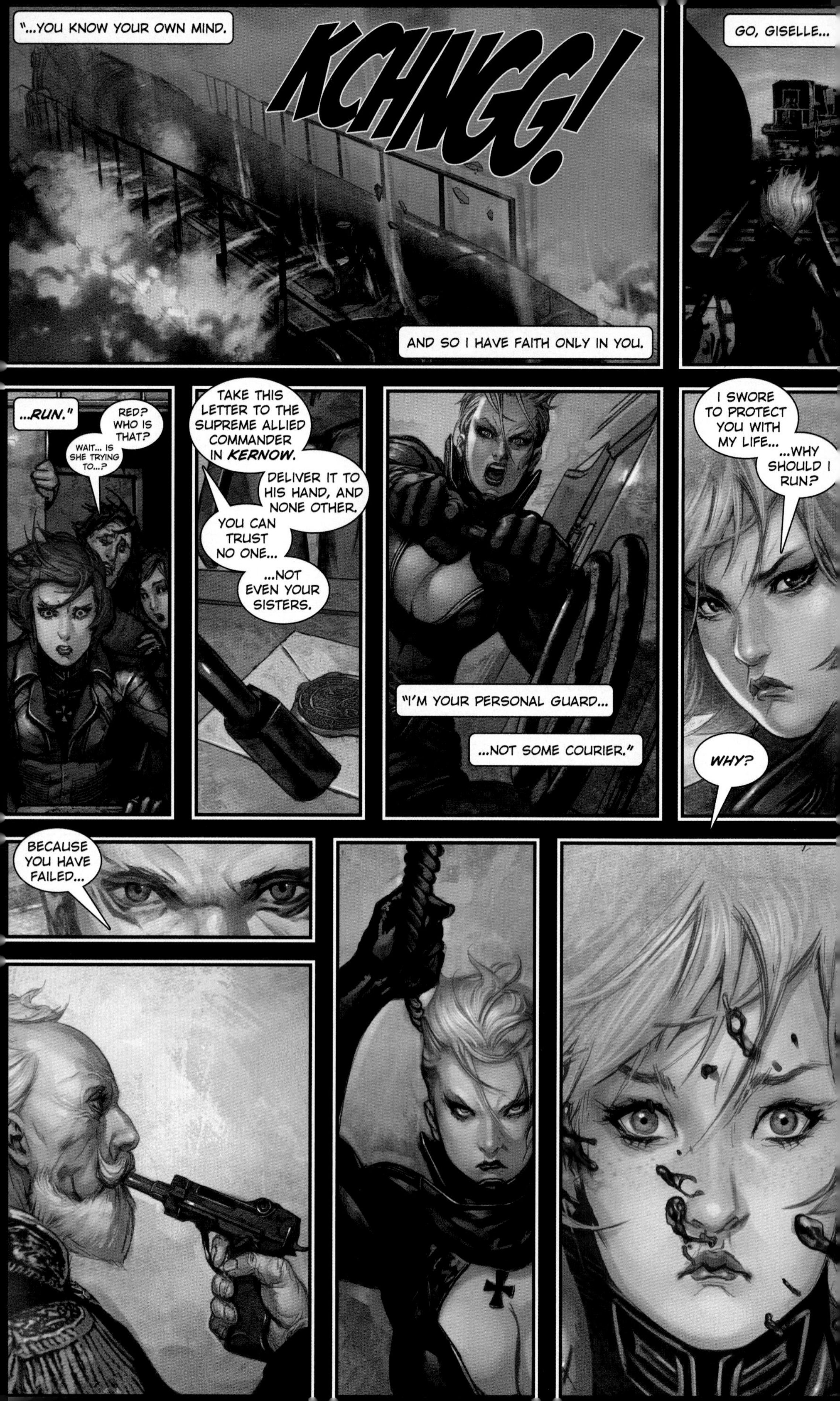
"...YOU KNOW YOUR OWN MIND.
KCHNGG!
AND SO I HAVE FAITH ONLY IN YOU.
GO, GISELLE...
...RUN."
RED? WHO IS THAT?
WAIT... IS SHE TRYING TO...?
TAKE THIS LETTER TO THE SUPREME ALLIED COMMANDER IN KERNOW.
DELIVER IT TO HIS HAND, AND NONE OTHER.
YOU CAN TRUST NO ONE...
...NOT EVEN YOUR SISTERS.
"I'M YOUR PERSONAL GUARD...
...NOT SOME COURIER."
I SWORE TO PROTECT YOU WITH MY LIFE...
...WHY SHOULD I RUN?
WHY?
BECAUSE YOU HAVE FAILED...

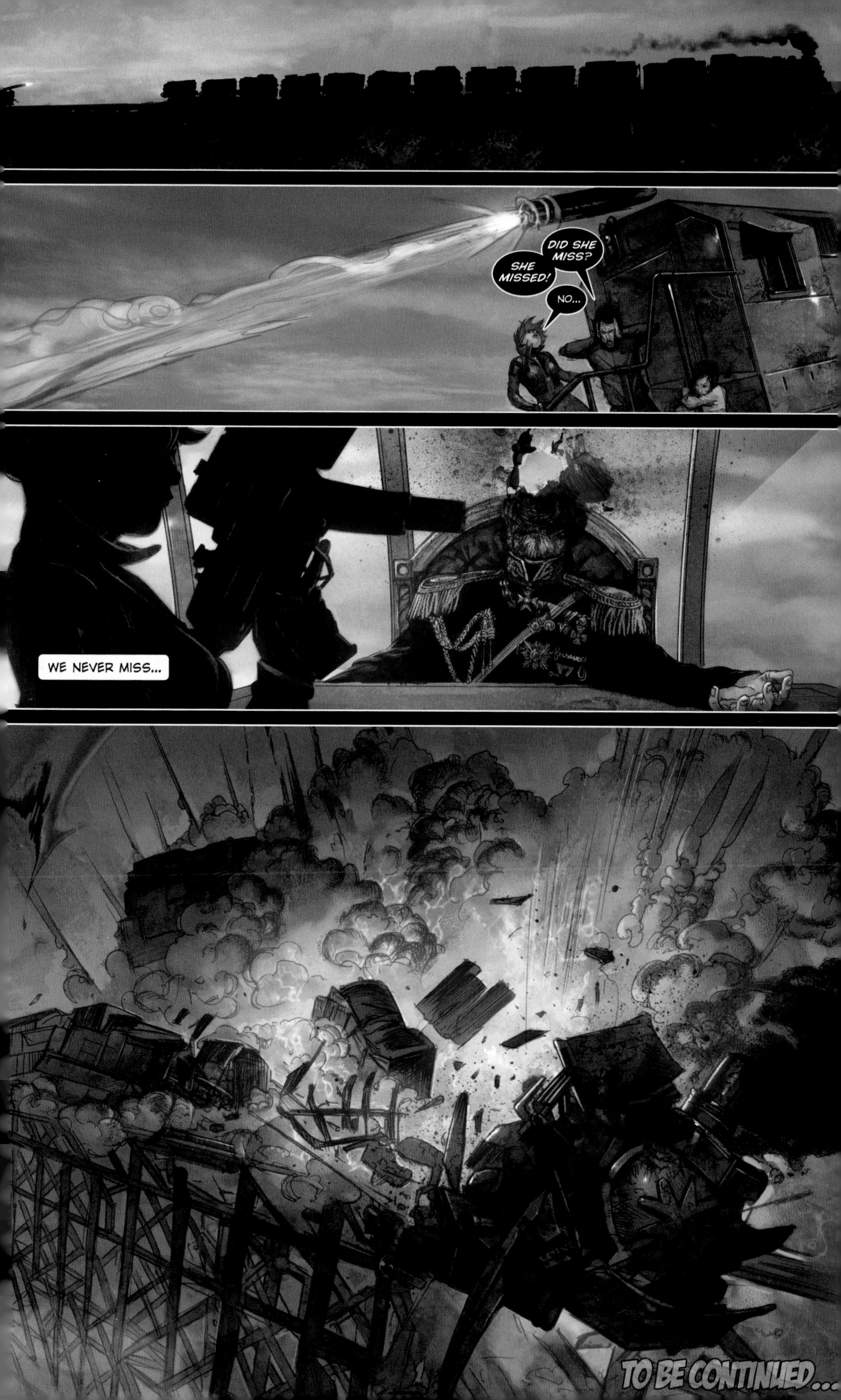
DID SHE MISS?
SHE MISSED!
NO...
WE NEVER MISS...
TO BE CONTINUED...

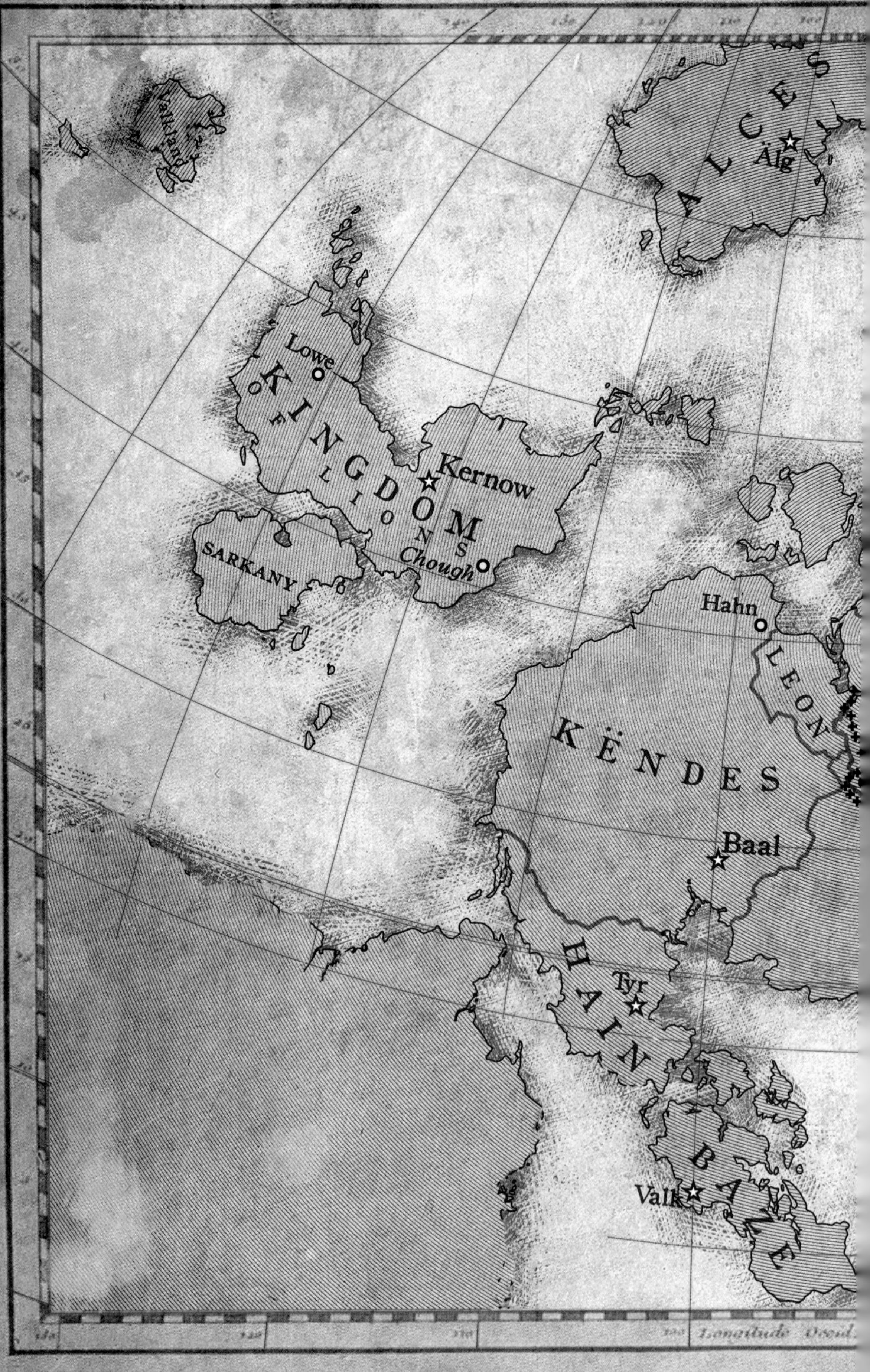

Valkland
ALCES
Älg
Lowe
KINGDOM
OF LIONS
Kernow
SARKANY
Chough
Hahn
LEON
KËNDES
Baal
HAIN
Tyr
BANE
Valk
Longitude Occid.

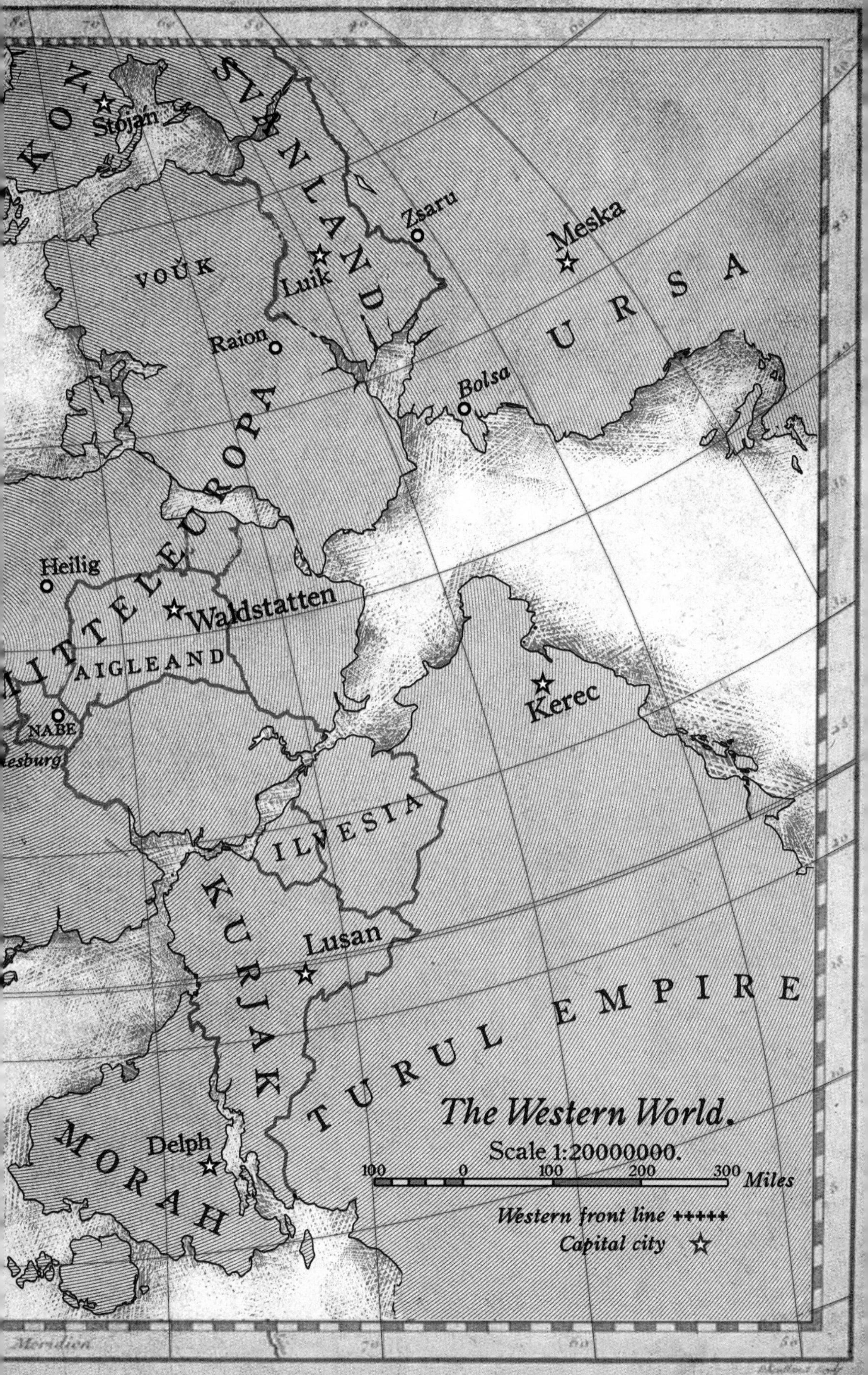

KONZ
Stojan
SVANLAND
Zsaru
Meska
Luik
VOÜK
URSA
Raion
Bolsa
MITTELEUROPA
Heilig
Waldstatten
AIGLEAND
NABE
esburg
Kerec
ILVESIA
KURJAK
Lusan
TURUL EMPIRE
MORAH
Delph
The Western World.
Scale 1:20000000.
100 0 100 200 300 Miles
Western front line +++++
Capital city ☆
Meridien

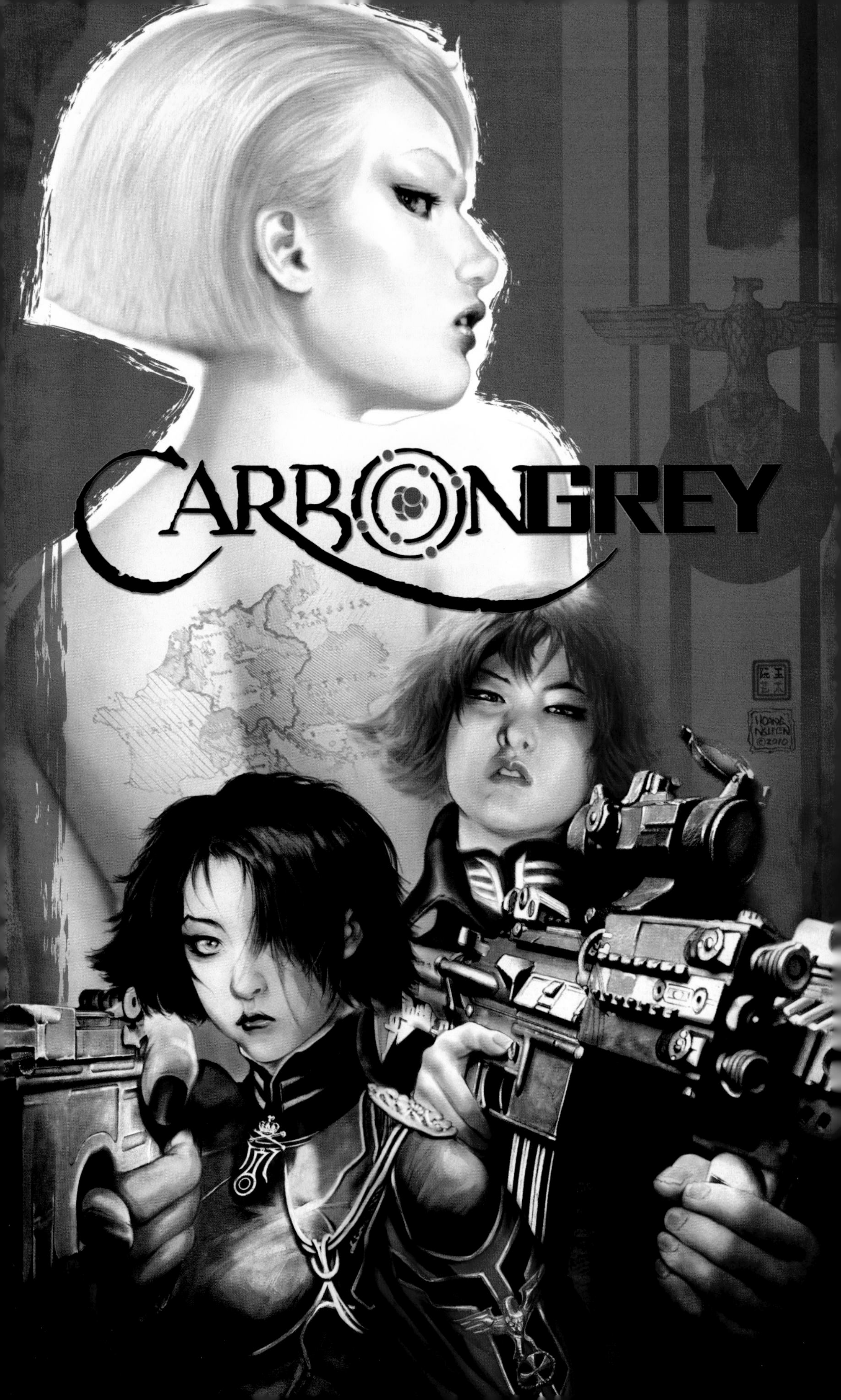
CARBON GREY
HOANG NGUYEN ©2010

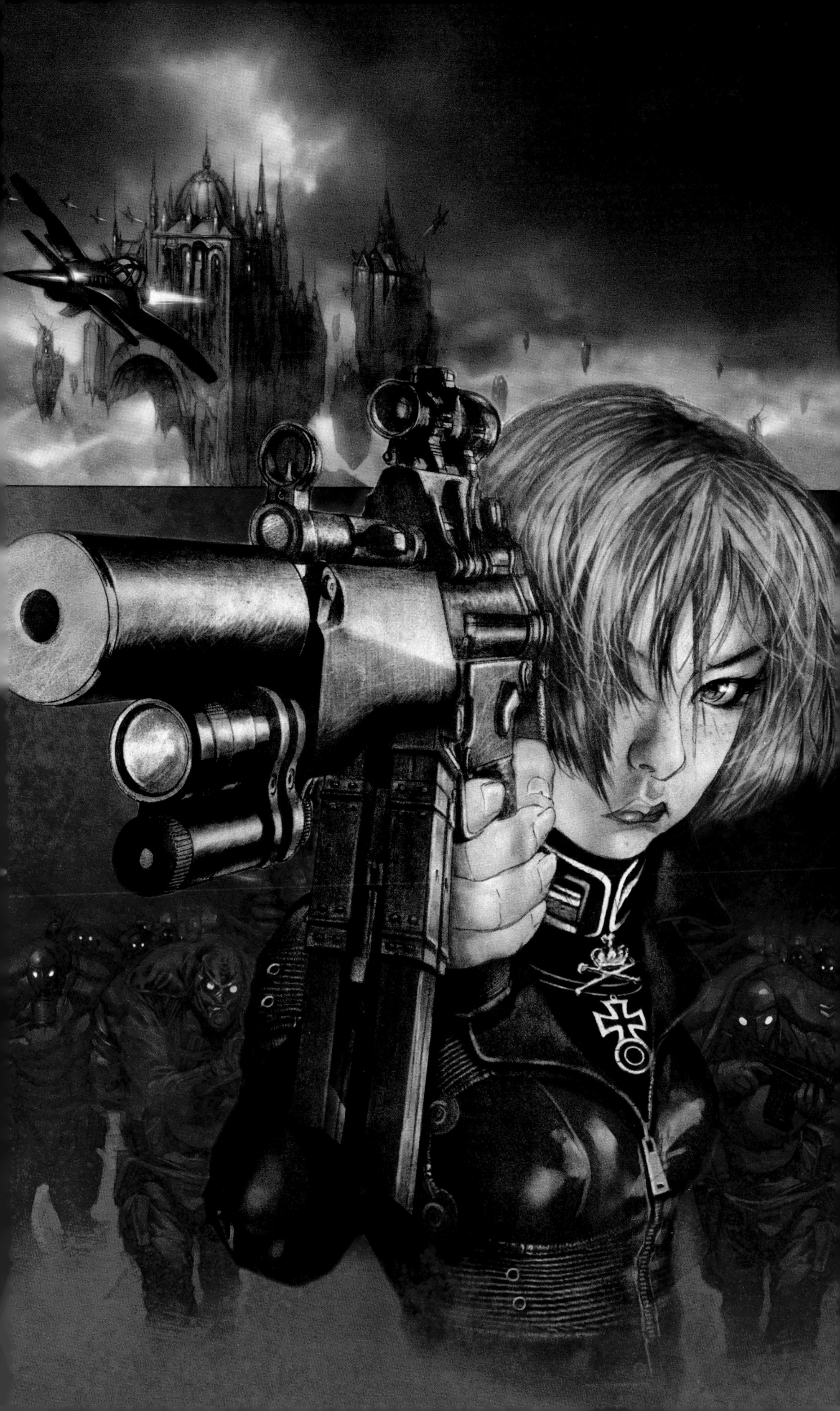

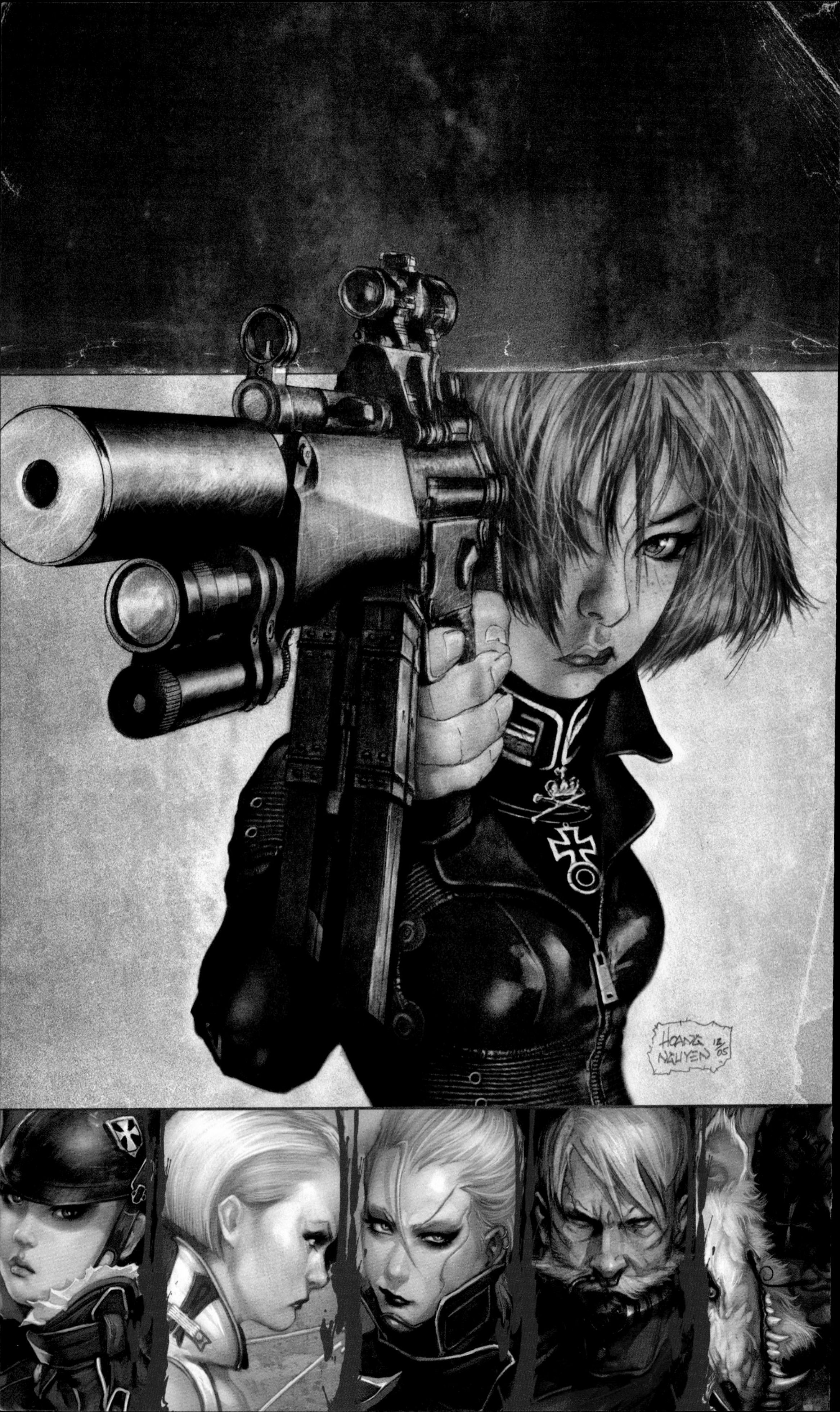
HOANG NGUYEN 12/05

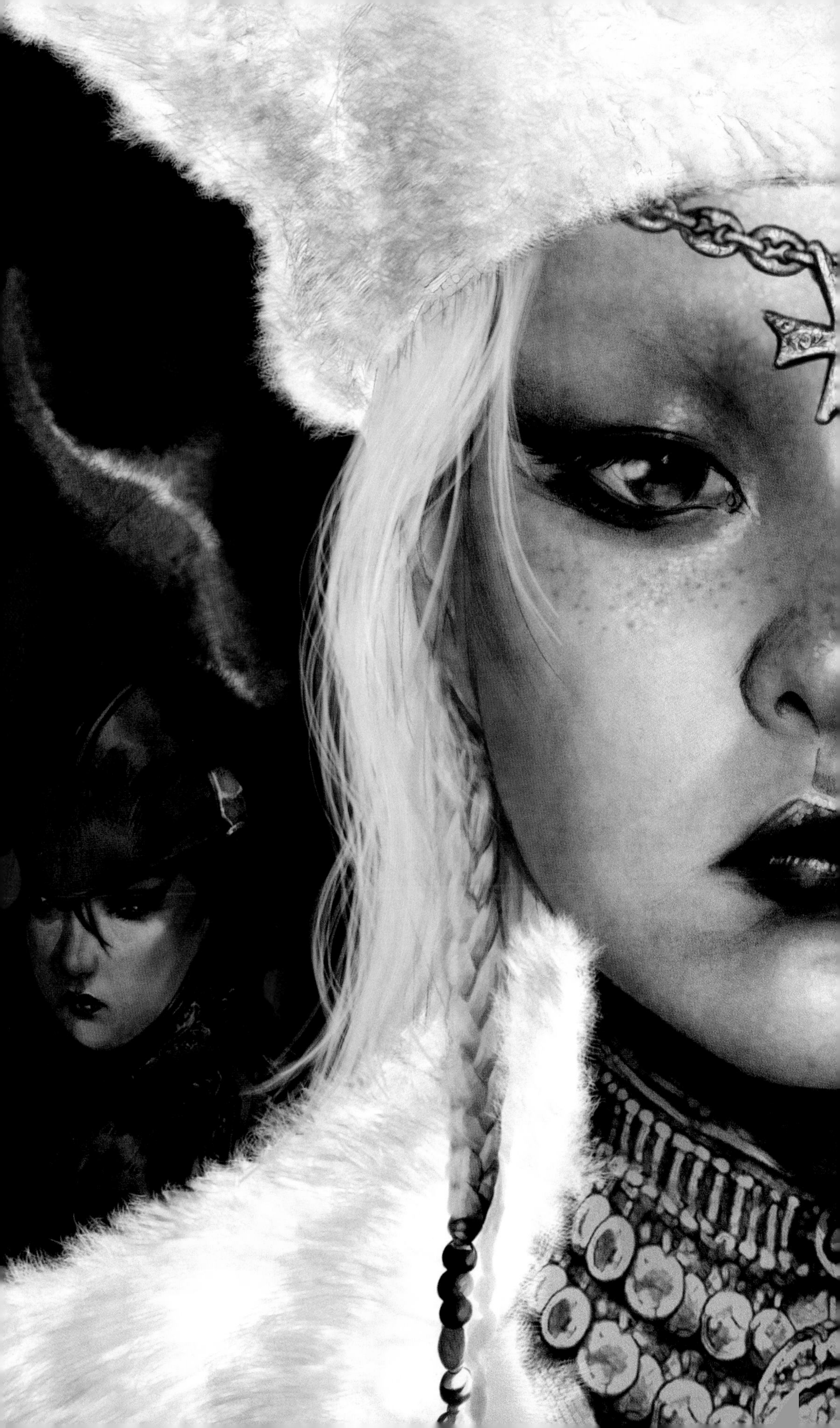

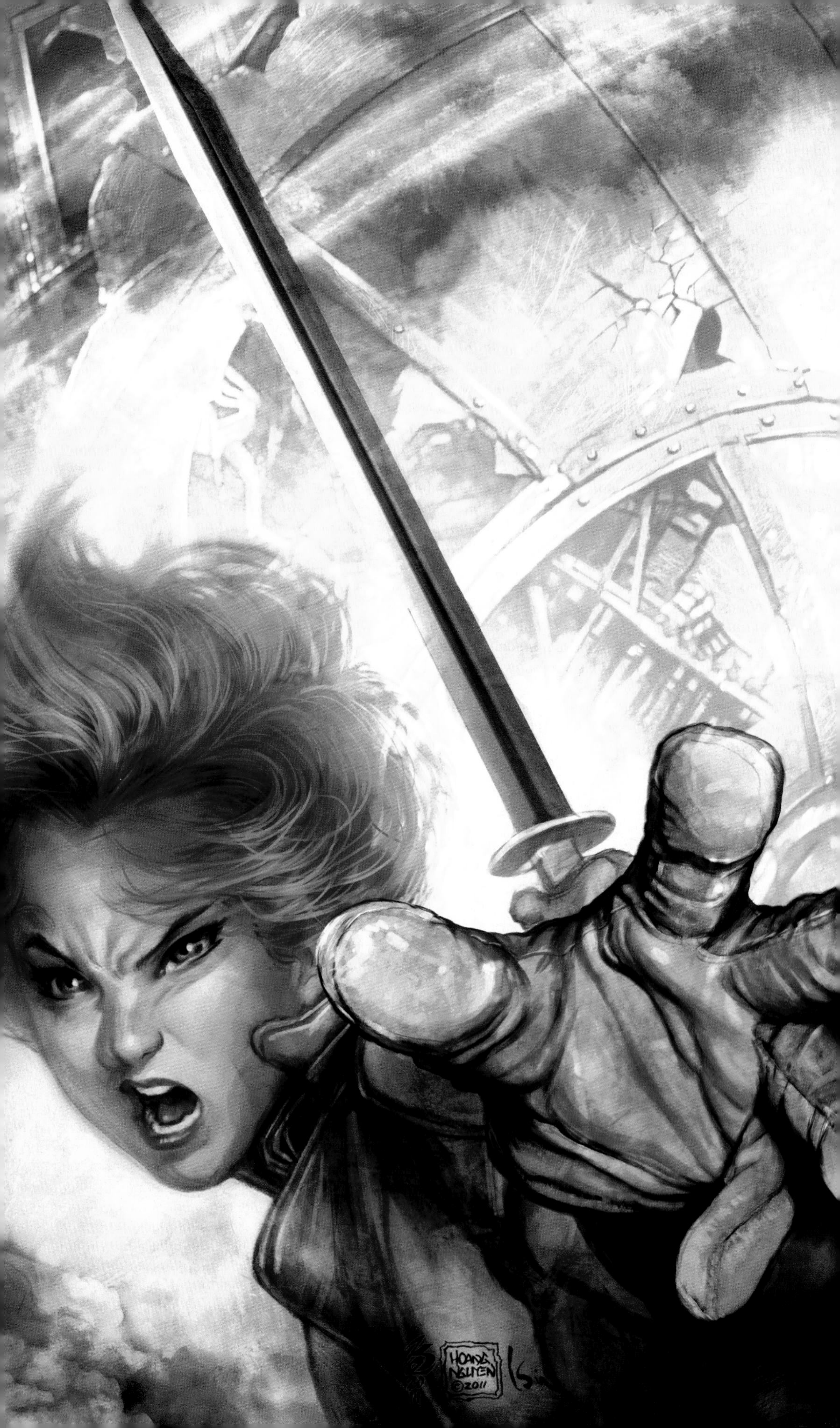
HOANG NGUYEN ©2011

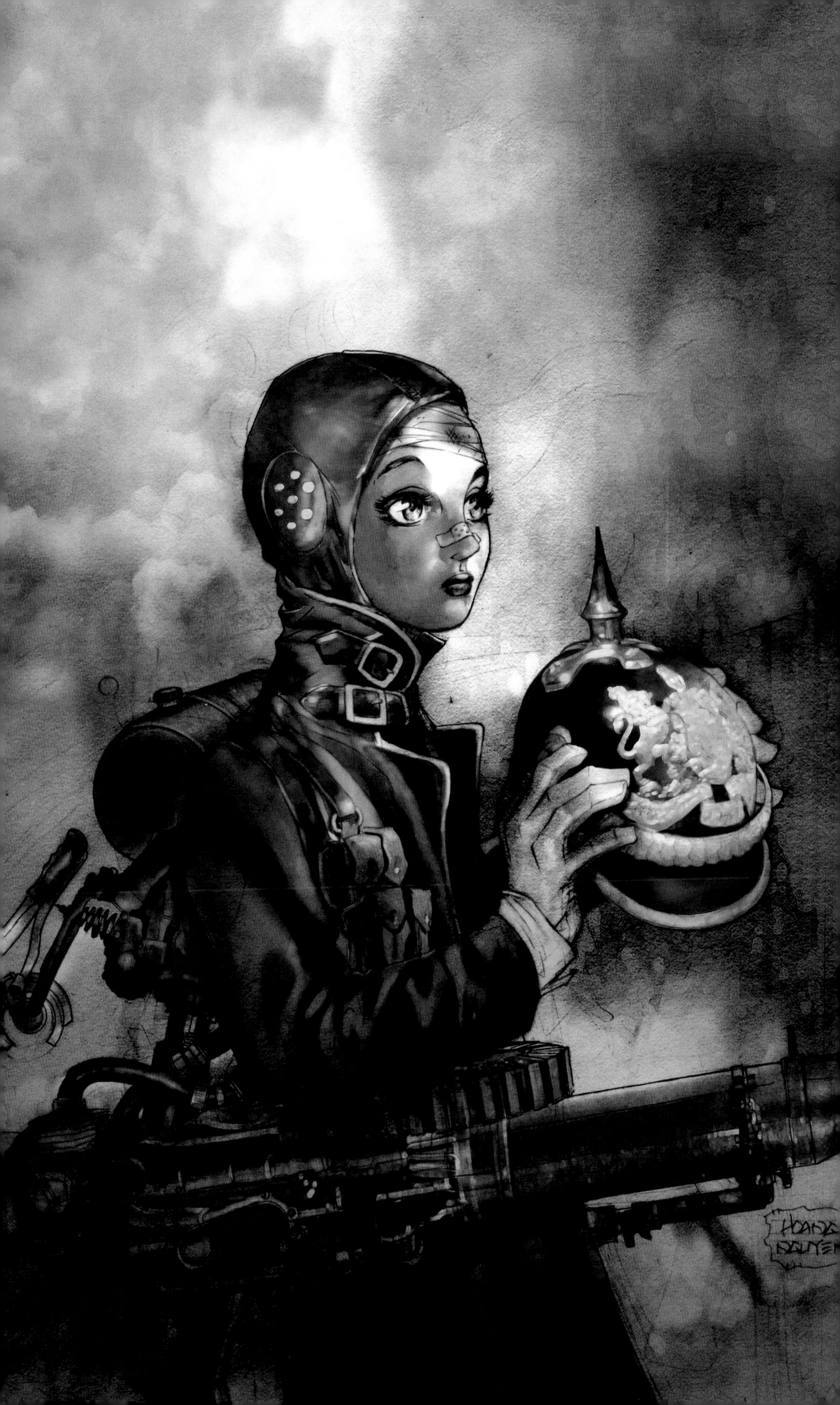

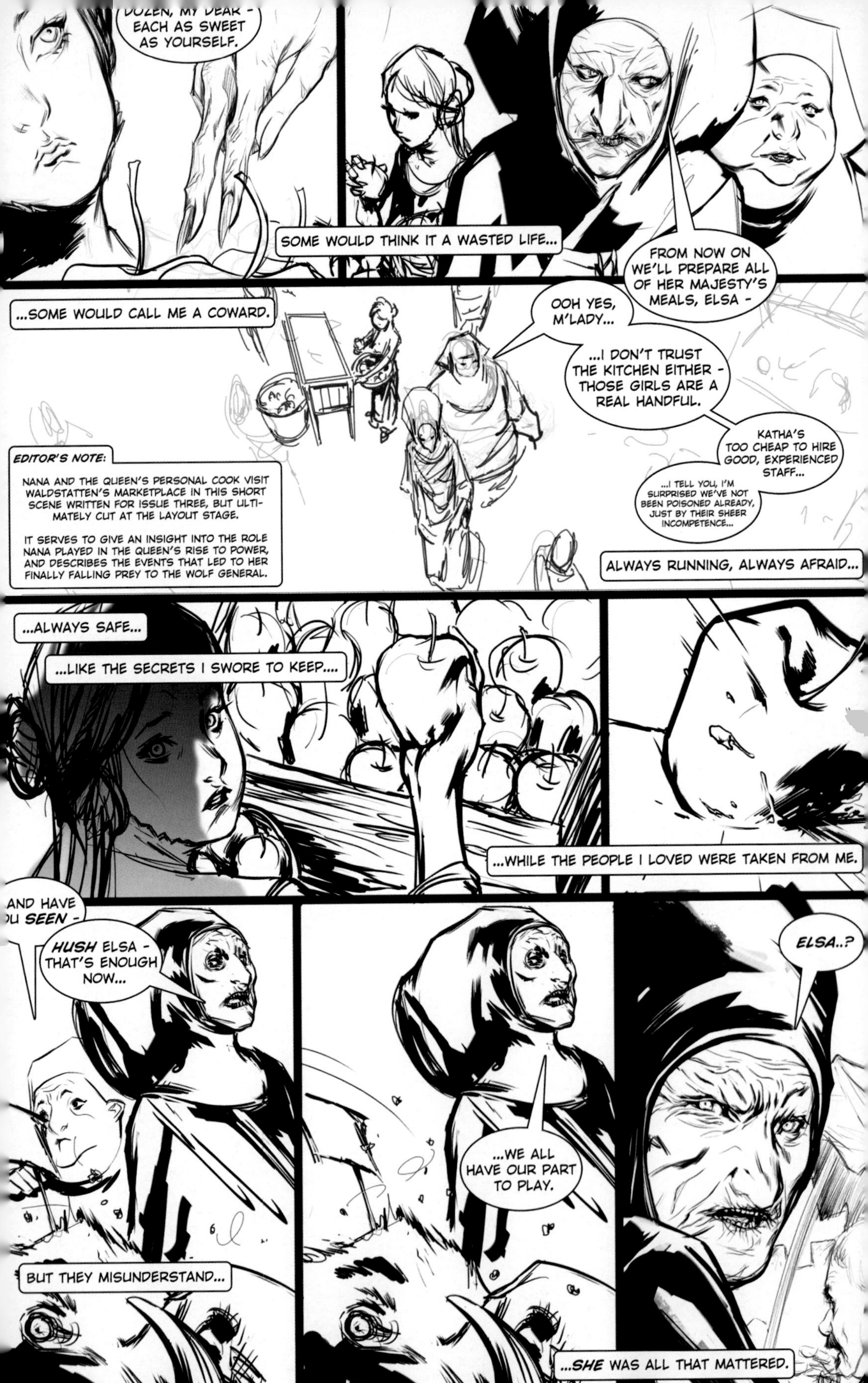
DOZEN, MY DEAR - EACH AS SWEET AS YOURSELF.
SOME WOULD THINK IT A WASTED LIFE...
FROM NOW ON WE'LL PREPARE ALL OF HER MAJESTY'S MEALS, ELSA -
...SOME WOULD CALL ME A COWARD.
OOH YES, M'LADY...
...I DON'T TRUST THE KITCHEN EITHER - THOSE GIRLS ARE A REAL HANDFUL.
KATHA'S TOO CHEAP TO HIRE GOOD, EXPERIENCED STAFF...
...I TELL YOU, I'M SURPRISED WE'VE NOT BEEN POISONED ALREADY, JUST BY THEIR SHEER INCOMPETENCE...
EDITOR'S NOTE:
NANA AND THE QUEEN'S PERSONAL COOK VISIT WALDSTATTEN'S MARKETPLACE IN THIS SHORT SCENE WRITTEN FOR ISSUE THREE, BUT ULTIMATELY CUT AT THE LAYOUT STAGE.
IT SERVES TO GIVE AN INSIGHT INTO THE ROLE NANA PLAYED IN THE QUEEN'S RISE TO POWER, AND DESCRIBES THE EVENTS THAT LED TO HER FINALLY FALLING PREY TO THE WOLF GENERAL.
ALWAYS RUNNING, ALWAYS AFRAID...
...ALWAYS SAFE...
...LIKE THE SECRETS I SWORE TO KEEP....
...WHILE THE PEOPLE I LOVED WERE TAKEN FROM ME.
AND HAVE U SEEN -
HUSH ELSA - THAT'S ENOUGH NOW...
BUT THEY MISUNDERSTAND...
...WE ALL HAVE OUR PART TO PLAY.
ELSA..?
...SHE WAS ALL THAT MATTERED.
SHE IS MY LIFE.

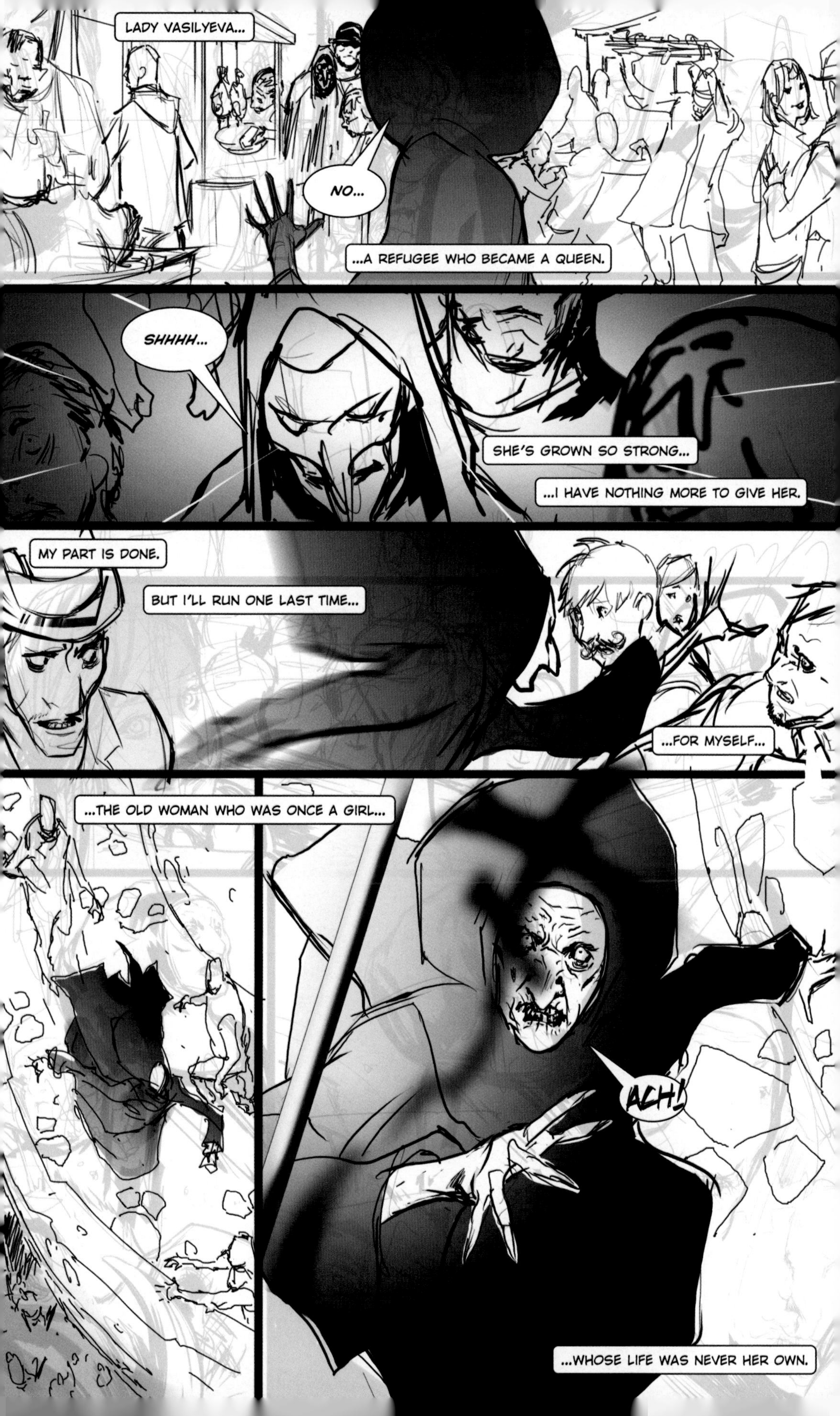
LADY VASILYEVA...
NO...
...A REFUGEE WHO BECAME A QUEEN.
SHHHH...
SHE'S GROWN SO STRONG...
...I HAVE NOTHING MORE TO GIVE HER.
MY PART IS DONE.
BUT I'LL RUN ONE LAST TIME...
...FOR MYSELF...
...THE OLD WOMAN WHO WAS ONCE A GIRL...
ACH!
...WHOSE LIFE WAS NEVER HER OWN.

The Adventures of Giselle and Mathilde by Mathilde and Giselle

In Mitteleuropa a great war was fought between the Axis and the Allied Powers.

The Kaiser was the ruler of the Axis nations. People thought he was a god.

He was protected by the Greys. They were sisters, brave and strong.

The sisters Grey had promised to keep the kaiser safe, like their ancestor Gottfaust had done.

In each generation there were three Grey sisters, for hundreds and hundreds of years.

Then one day there were four - Eva, Anna and the twins - Giselle and Mathilde

The 13th sister was prophesized by Gottfaust. "she will change everything" he said.

One of the twins was the 13th Grey sister - But which one?

Somebody whispered in Mathilde's ear "you are the 13th sister."

Giselle was meant to keep the Kaiser safe - but she did the opposite. His head got blown off.
Giselle fell, and her blonde hair turned red.

An allied soldier called Howard was saved by Giselle, and wrote a poem about her.

The Chancellor spoke to Eva, the eldest Grey. "Giselle killed the Kaiser" he said. Eva chopped him up.

A handsome man stole another man's wallet and pretended to be him.
A beautiful lady tried to steal the wallet from him. Neither of them was who they said they were. The Red Baron caught them fighting and was angry.

The Wolf General investigated the chancellor's death.
He could read the chancellor's mind and saw Eva had done it.
He heard what the chancellor said about Giselle. He set off to arrest the sisters Grey...

hen she was a little girl Mathilde drew a picture of her
amily. Her teacher was very angry and told her twin
ster Giselle to tear it up, but Giselle kept it instead.

Howard was called to the Allied base. The major and the
general had read his poem about Giselle and wanted to know
what it was about. A man with a bomb blew them all up.

Only Howard didn't die. He was sure an angel was watching over
him. He went to find her.

va, Anna and Mathilde had a meeting. Mathilde was angry.
hy did you hurt the Chancellor Eva? Now we are going to
t arrested." Eva was more worried about Giselle.
hey think she killed the Kaiser." Eva and Anna went
o look for her. Mathilde stay behind to look
after the Queen.

Dina and Pepper escaped out of the window.
The Red Baron jumped after them and his hand came off.

Giselle went to see her teacher. He asked her what had
appened to the Kaiser and she told him a lie. He got mad
nd hurt Giselle really bad. She chopped him in half.

nna and Eva traveled west. They traveled in disguise, to
de from the police. At a gate Eva talked to an old
oliceman. "Please let us go" she asked. Before he could
answer Anna chopped his head off. It was gross.

Dina paid Pepper to take her in
his airplane, but the airplane was
too heavy to fly. They found
Giselle was somehow hiding in the back.

Howard met Eva and Anna.
He thought they were angels like
Giselle. Anna said something that
made Eva worried. She asked Howard

o deliver an important message for her.

the Wolf General came to arrest the sister.
He went into the Queen's bedroom and saw
her getting dressed! She told him that she
needed to talk to him about something very
important...

The Adventures of Giselle and Mathilde by Mathilde and Giselle

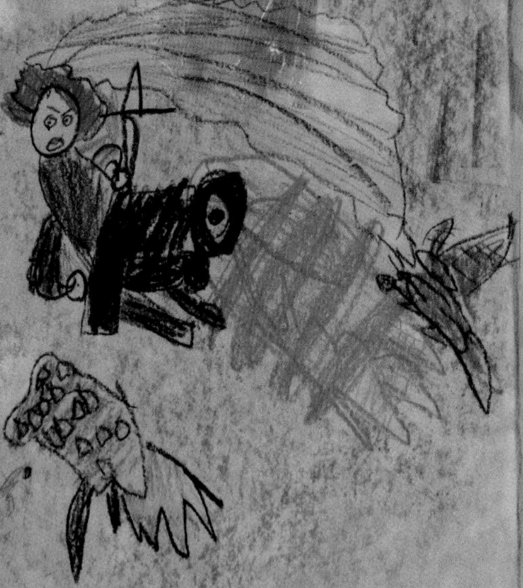

Pepper and Dina and Giselle flew west. Pepper was mad that Giselle was in his airplane. He told her to get out. Suddenly three airplanes attacked them - it was the Baron!

Giselle grabbed a gun and jumped out. She chopped a plane in half. Then Pepper's plane got skewered on a spike and crashed.

The Wolf General found Howard's body and read his mind and saw Eva's message - the Queen was plotting to make Anna the head of the Greys!

The queen showed Mathilde Gottfaust's stone, which had gotten split in half "It has magical powers" she said and only you can use it - "you are the carbon Grey!"

Secretly the queen wanted it for herself.

There was a big lady and a lot of soldiers and the Baron laughed at Pepper. Pepper thought he was going to die, and realized he'd been a jerk all his life. Giselle saved him and Dina by chopping everybody up, but then she got shot in the arm and fell over. Pepper picked her up and they ran for a train. The Baron hid from Giselle behind a man he had stabbed in the head

Back at his secret base the Wolf General had tied up Nana, the Queen's nurse. "What is the Queen up to?" He asked, but she wouldn't talk so he fed her to his wolves and read her mind and found out anyway.

On the train Dina fixed up Giselle's arm. Pepper was asleep. Giselle remembered the last time she saw the Kaiser. He told her that the Queen was now in control of everything and was planning to kill him. Thinking about it made her sad. Giselle went outside to get some air. Dina saw that Giselle had dropped the picture drawn by Mathilde.

Meanwhile Mathilde was about to take the stone when the Wolf General arrived. "The war is all your fault and you killed the Kaiser," he said to the Queen, "just so you can steal the stone. You're under arrest!" "I'm going to have a baby!" she said, "now I'm the Kaiser!" Then she told Mathilde to take the stone, but when Mathilde did nothing happened - the stone was a fake! The Wolf General laughed at her and the Queen got mad. "Kill him!" she told Mathilde. The General laughed again, "Haha, you can't kill me if you want to find the stone". They made a deal to work together.

There was a big gun on the train and Giselle was there thinking about things when Anna suddenly showed up. "come home Giselle, I'm proud of you for killing the Kaiser - you did great." Giselle was scared. She made a diversion and unhooked the gun from the train. She remembered what the Kaiser had said to her before he died. "I want you to deliver a letter to the Allied commander". "No way, I'm your body guard, not the postman. I promised to protect you". "You failed" said the Kaiser, and blew his head off. Now Giselle had to run.

Back on the train Anna was really mad. She fired the big gun at the train and blew the whole thing up.

What happened to Giselle, Pepper and Dina? Did they all died? Find out in the next issue of the Adventure of Giselle and Mathilde...

by: Mathilde